Conversations
With My Sister

A Fool's Journey Through the Tarot

Conversations With My Sister

A FOOL'S JOURNEY THROUGH THE TAROT

By Annie Carmitchell

Sweetspire Press

Copyedited, typeset, and printed in the United States of America

First printing: 2019

ISBN: 978-1-7329826-2-8
eISBN: 978-1-7329826-3-5

Published by Sweetspire Press
P.O. Box 912
Fulton, Missouri 65251
www.sweetspirepress.com

Sweetspire Press is an imprint of Carter Publishing Studio, Inc.
www.carterpublishingstudio.com

Cover illustration © 2019 by Regina Troyer
Card design by Regina Troyer
Art direction, interior design, and editing by Laura Carter
Copy editing by Pat George

Special thanks to Heidi Whiskeyman Carles for her encouragement
and to Heather Erickson for her editorial assistance.

Cover and interior photographs are from the author's archives unless otherwise noted.
Card 7 Annie/Bill photo by Jane Fetner, The Photography Whisperer
Card 12 drawing and Ace of Wands photo by Bobbi Carmitchell
Ace of Cups photo by Laura Roberts
Knight and Page of Pentacles photo by Amy Skillman
Some montage elements from Adobe Stock (stock.adobe.com)

10 9 8 7 6 5 4 3 2 1

For Bubbles and Bob.

TABLE OF CONTENTS

FOREWORD

ONCE UPON A TIME there were two sisters who loved to laugh together, sing together, and lay under the stars together in their Pennsylvania yard, cows gently lowing in the field beside them. (Well, at least one of them loved that, while the other preferred the safety of her nice warm bedroom, cows on the other side of the wall, thank you very much.) Along with their parents, Bubbles and Bud, they would all laugh and sing and then laugh some more. Life was good.

As usually happens, the girls eventually grew up and left their family home, but they still sang and played together, talking on the phone almost every night. Friends might come and friends might go, but Annie and Bobbi were always there for each other, as constant as the sun, the moon, and the stars.

One day Annie, the elder sister, stumbled upon a deck of 78 extraordinary cards. Utterly fascinated, she plumbed their metaphysical depths to discover how to apply the cards' lessons to her own life. She began with the first 22 cards of that tarot deck, which she learned were called "The Major Arcana." Some cards were beautiful (Temperance, the World), others puzzling (the Hierophant) or exciting (the Lovers). Quite a few were frightening (Death, the Devil, the Tower), and those like the Strength card were even inspiring. The Fool, with his carefree demeanor as he stood on the precipice of his next adventure, reminded her of her beloved sister Bobbi, and she loved him most of all.

The four suits that comprised the Minor Arcana—Wands, Cups, Swords, and Pentacles—were full of their own wisdom, and Annie was determined to absorb all of it. Soon she found that she'd filled a shelf with different tarot decks and books, all with their own unique takes on the cards from which she'd come to enjoy seeking guidance and a fresh perspective. She filed those tarot books next to books by David Sedaris and P. G. Wodehouse, *Ethics for the New Millennium* by the Dali Lama, *Paths to God: Living the Bhagavad Gita* by Ram Dass, *The God*

Delusion by Richard Dawkins, *My Life and Hard Times* by James Thurber, *When Bad Things Happen to Good People* by Harold S. Kushner, and the New Revised Standard Bible.

"Why," she thought to herself as she examined each card and read each book, "there's no doubt that the Empress is my mother and the Emperor my father, and I sure as heck can relate to the Hanged Man . . . in fact, *all* these cards remind me of stories from my own life. Where's my cell phone? I've gotta call Bobbi!"

And with that, this book was born.

Laura Carter
Editor and Publisher, Sweetspire Press, January 2019

CAST OF CHARACTERS

HUMANS

Annie — Sister of Bobbi. Partner of Bill. Lives in Washington Boro, Pennsylvania, a town known only to its inhabitants. Lover of most creatures great and small, except stink bugs and snakes.

Bobbi — Sister of Annie. Known as Boogsla Carmrod to most of her friends. Lives in Pequea,* Pennsylvania, a town whose name no outsider can pronounce. Singer/songwriter and artist, maker of all things stained glass, and builder of everything from bookcases to cat condos. Petty thief. Star Trek enthusiast.

Charlotte — Matriarch of the clan. Known to her family and friends as Bubbles or Bubs. From Lancaster, Pennsylvania. Master piano player who knew everything about music theory but didn't know what it was called. Harmonizer extraordinaire. Highly skilled in the varied uses of fly swatters.

Bob — Patriarch of the clan. Husband to Bubs. Known to his siblings as Bud. From the Coal Regions of Pennsylvania. Industrial engineer by trade, extraordinary singer by hobby. Woodworker and family humorist. Originator of The Pointer. No slave to fashion.

Bill — Partner of Annie. Distance runner. Retired IT guy from Philadelphia with degrees in business and accounting and some kind of computer stuff. Agnostic or atheist, depending on the day. Embraces Buddhism and Taoism. Fears the female mind.

PETS

Maggie and Emma — Boxer-lab siblings. Owners of Bill and Annie.

Yon, Farra, William, Arthur, Guinevere — Parakeets who never warmed to their owners, Bill and Annie. Known lovingly as the ULBs (Ungrateful Little Bastards). Freedom seekers. Frequent Flyers.

Peep — Baby chicken who came to a tragic end.

---

*(PECK -way)

The Major Arcana

The first 22 cards in a tarot deck are known as the Major Arcana. These numbered cards represent our life's journey, and they follow the adventures of a young man named the Fool who meets various archetypes that will instruct him in the challenges and joys inherent along his path. These cards represent important life events that reveal universal truths common to us all.

~

"Tell me but truly, but then speak the truth,
Do you not love my sister?"
— WILLIAM SHAKESPEARE, *KING LEAR*

"Stupid Justice with her stupid double-edged sword."
— ANNIE CARMITCHELL

"Cut the schtick and just play the music."
— UNKNOWN

Taking the Leap

"HEY, YOU BUSY?" I asked my sister when she answered the phone.

"Not really. Just eating ice cream and watching a Star Trek DVD."

"Can you pause it for a second? I wanted to bounce something off you."

I was finally ready to talk with Bobbi about that book that she'd been telling me I should write. She'd always enjoyed my humorous essays and thought that other people might appreciate reading my work as well. I had toyed with the idea for a number of years, but I never knew what kind of framework would be required to tie together all of the stories that I wanted to share. I had a flash of inspiration now, and I wanted to share it with her.

"I think I figured out how to format some of my essays into a book."

"Seriously?"

"Yeah. I'm gonna look at tarot cards in a humorous way and show how they relate to the Carmitchell Sisters."

"Oh, I think that would be hysterical."

"I hope so. But here's the deal: I'd like to interview you after I write about each card. I'll describe it to you, and we can talk about its meaning and how it applies to our lives. And I thought we could include family stories, too, that involve Mom and Dad and our extended family."

"You know," she said, "I have that Motherpeace tarot deck at my place. Had it since the 80's."

"Do you use it?"

"No. Not really. Maybe once in a while." She paused. "Nope. Never used it. But all lesbians back then had to have that deck. It was like a requirement or something. I just thought the artwork was amazing. But you actually use your cards."

3

"I do."

"So I kind of know what they're about. Fortune telling, right?"

"Some people use them that way. I don't. I use them as guidance, as a way to connect to the universe. Or God. Whatever you call it."

"That sounds cool. I'm in."

Her response was a bit abrupt. "That's it? You don't want to know any more about the book?"

"No, I'm good. This'll be fun. But my ice cream's melting."

I didn't have a chance to explain further that tarot is as much a spiritual practice for me as prayer or meditation, since both of these are included in my contemplation of the cards that I draw. But I could tell that she was losing interest because Spock was waiting.

After we hung up, I felt relieved. I couldn't write this book without Bobbi's input. Most of the time, she's the reason I'm funny since most of my shenanigans involve her. I also felt a bit of trepidation. This was going to be a big leap for me into the world of publishing with which I was totally unfamiliar. So I could completely relate to the young man pictured in the first card of the tarot deck.

The Fool stands precariously on the edge of a cliff, ready to step off into the unknown, his childlike wonder preventing fear from getting in his way. He carries his belongings in a bundle on a stick, hobo-style, and is accompanied by a dog, his loving companion who will stay with him through his leaps of faith (except over that cliff because no dog is that stupid). The young man is depicted in torn pants in some decks, indicating his carefree attitude. He represents the start of a new undertaking, and he was encouraging me to embrace my potential and to take a chance on this book without hesitation. Like him, I was going to embark on quite a journey.

As the book took form, Bobbi and I spent hours on the phone talking about tarot. We also reminisced about our lives together and shared each other's philosophies on a myriad of subjects. The whole undertaking made me examine myself—my fears, my beliefs, even my hair—a little more closely.

As our journey progressed, we found ourselves identifying easily with the cards. Like the Fool, for example, we always had our dogs beside us as we chatted. And we felt that our conversations were balanced and playful, two characteristics of the young man on the cliff.

"But who's more like the Fool, you or me?" I asked Bobbi. "I think both of us resemble him because we're always up for something new."

"Sure," she said. "But if you're talking about adventures, any of yours would have to take place close to home. I mean, you have zero sense of direction."

My sister's remark would be considered harsh if it weren't so true. If I were standing on the Fool's precipice, trying to figure out whether to go right or left, I would trust my instincts, which are always dead wrong, and would end up at the bottom of the ravine. I am so directionally impaired that I become disoriented walking out of a mall and into the vast expanses of its parking lot, compelled to summon the help of mall security in order to find my car—a humbling and numbing experience for one as independent as I imagine myself to be.

"It's like when you got your license and could drive yourself to piano lessons. Mom took you once a week for three years, and she'd take you the same way every time, just down our road, across the highway, and left at the ballpark. Then it was your turn to make the trip on your own, and Mom said, 'Just don't forget to turn left at the ballpark.' And you said, 'There's a ballpark there?'"

"I can't believe you remember that."

"And I remember thinking that I couldn't believe you were that stupid."

I had to agree with my sister on this point. I shall willingly admit that I'm the Fool on the cliff, looking around at everything except the road signs in front of me. But Bobbi's the Fool in the pants . . . if she's actually wearing them. She sometimes gets so caught up in what she's doing that she forgets to get completely dressed. This issue of missing clothing usually pops into her head as she is entering a convenience store after working all day in her art studio, dressed in pajamas, and then buzzing out to get some iced tea. And when she does remember to wear her pants, they're often torn and tattered like the Fool's are sometimes depicted.

"Good God, you exaggerate," Bobbi said. "One time. I leave the house without pants one time, and it haunts me for the rest of my life."

"What were you thinking?" I asked.

"I'll tell you exactly what happened. I was getting ready to go to work one morning and talking to Tam on the phone about a gig. She didn't have a lot of time, so I wanted to stay on the phone with her as long as I could. I put on my work shirt and got my stuff together. Then I hopped in the car and took off."

"And you were still on the phone?"

"Yeah, for a little bit. Then we hung up. Then when I was at the stop light in Millersville, I thought, 'Wow. It got really cold all of a sudden.' I thought I had a hole in my pants or something."

Of course, the "something" of which Bobbi spoke was the total lack of pants themselves, so she had to turn around and drive back to the house.

"And that's when the panic really set in," she said. "All the way home, I'm thinking, 'How am I going to get into the house without anyone seeing me?'"

She didn't realize that she may have already put on quite a show getting into her car in the first place; however, I didn't want to interrupt her story. It reflected what must have been the same urgency she experienced on her return trip.

"So what did you do?"

"The only thing I could do. I pulled into my driveway, but instead of stopping at the end of it, I kept going across the front yard and up the hill. I stopped right by the door, yanked on my parking brake, and ran into the house."

There would be many lessons to be learned as Bobbi and I made our way through the tarot. And one of the most important was what the Fool had to tell us: Embrace the exuberance of starting something new, like writing a book. Take that leap of faith. Just be sure that you know where the ballpark is and that you're fully dressed.

If you want to follow along with our adventures but don't have cards of your own, you can view tarot cards online for free (try Wikipedia) or purchase a deck of your own from countless online retailers and brick-and-mortar stores. Many types of tarot card decks can be found with a simple search, including the still-popular Rider-Waite deck that was originally published in 1910.

Beware the Trickster

AS THE FOOL BEGINS HIS LIFE'S JOURNEY, full of hope and dreams, the first person he meets is the Magician, who has at his disposal four important items that the Fool carried hidden in his sack: a cup, a sword, a wand, and a pentacle. These correspond with the Minor Arcana of the tarot deck and are handy tools for the traveler to use in making dreams come true. He is also known as the Trickster, so with him at your side, anything's possible, even pulling pranks on an unsuspecting sister.

It was 1991. I was living with Bobbi during my separation from my husband, and while divorce can sometimes spell heartbreak and financial ruin for some, it provided joy and tomfoolery for the Carmitchell girls. Every night was a pajama party in the living room, as one of us (read: Bobbi) slept on the air mattress on the floor, while the other stayed on the couch. Comcast didn't make it out to Anchor Road, but *Star Trek* VHS tapes were plentiful, as were Turkey Hill ice cream, laughing fits, and dreams of better relationships to come.

One morning, as I was getting in my car to drive to work, Bobbi came flying down the driveway yelling, "Stop! Anne! Wait!" It seems that, as a joke—because who would do this for any other reason?—Bobbi had attached an adhesive maxi-pad to the back of my Honda. She thought that I would see it before taking off, have a good laugh about it, and remove it, which is exactly what happened. When Bobbie verified that I had, indeed, spotted and removed the maxi-pad, she started back to the house. Behind her back (literally) I quickly transferred the pad to the back of her Hyundai. And I wasn't home to warn her when she left the house that night to play a gig in downtown Lancaster.

Imagine, if you will, following a Hyundai on King Street with a pad stuck to the back of it, right above the license plate, proudly attached like some twisted, feminist bumper sticker for all to admire. Looking back, after Bobbi had discovered the trick, she understood the thumbs up that she got from some female drivers as they passed, the "Hell YEAH!"s that were shouted in triumph. She also understood the quizzical sidelong glances of male motorists, and, most sadly, the frightened countenances of those men who drove behind her, and stayed a fair distance behind her, convinced that the Gloria Steinem in front of them was about to have a menstrual meltdown at any moment.

When she pulled into the back parking lot to unload her gear, she noticed two young cooks from the restaurant, outside taking a smoke break, staring at her. For quite a long time. Their eyes followed her and her car as it backed up to the ramp, their faces expressionless and vacant. Getting out of her vehicle and being quite hot under the collar by now, Bobbi was ready to accuse them of everything from rudeness to lesbian voyeurism, until she walked around to her hatchback to open it. There she saw, attached securely against the Hyundai, the pad. She smiled knowingly. The gauntlet had been thrown. "Well played, my sister," she murmured to herself.

Not to be outdone, Bobbi placed another feminine hygiene product, this one complete with wings, on my vehicle shortly thereafter. This time, though, there was no sisterly concern, no warning of embarrassment as drivers followed me the next day through Millersville and out to Route 30. I was unaware of the Trickster's stunt until I pulled into a store parking lot to meet members of my carpool. One of my colleagues, Mike, a phys ed and health teacher, approached my car slowly from the back. "Anne," he said, through my open window. "You, ah, you have something stuck to the back of your car. . . . I think it's one of those panty shields."

I got out of the car and walked back to take a look.

"THAT, Mike," I told him, "is no panty shield. That is an overnighter, the queen mother of all sanitary napkins."

So rejoice in the Magician, as he can show you your full potential. But beware of the fact that he can also help your sister, who is post-menopausal and has a closet full of leftover pads.

Meditation for Constipation

THE MAGICIAN HAS SHOWN THE FOOL that nothing is impossible, that he can do anything that he chooses. However, he also must learn how to just *be*. Enter the High Priestess, the Queen of Meditation, who reminds us that we are human beings, not just human-doings, and that sometimes we need to take a break from the world of outwardly creating and retreat into the world of inner manifestation. In other words, stop running around like a hamster on crack and just chill for a while.

This card is a beaut. It features a stunning goddess sitting between two pillars, one labeled B and other J. The High Priestess reminds us that when we meditate, we should NOT be making a mental list of what to buy at BJ's Wholesale Club when we shop next week. This defeats the purpose of meditating. Unless, of course, you're using this quiet time to make a mental note to buy a meditation cushion, which is not what you should be doing when you're meditating, so just stop it and start meditating already. And don't make, "I have to go to BJ's" part of your mantra. (See how difficult meditation can be? I can't even write about it coherently.)

This card also may signal that you've been still, you've heard your inner voice, but darn it, you're not going to listen. We've all been there. We know what it's like to talk to God and say, for example, "Hey, God, I'd really like to be healthy." And God says, "Then get thee to a gym," and we say, "Wait. You didn't let me finish. I was going to add, 'Without going to the gym.' I really wish that you'd stop interrupting me. . . ." Or when Buddhists are doing a loving-kindness chant, trying to disperse unconditional love to all sentient beings, they may find themselves interrupting the meditation with, "Except for my neighbors who really don't deserve my love, as they continue to allow their dog to do number two in my yard."

The only number two with which we should be concerned is the High Priestess. Consider what she has to say. Stop arguing with yourself. You'll know the right answer if you just shut your pie-hole and listen for once. The Carmitchell Sisters understand this concept, but they approach it in different ways.

I have always been interested in several types of meditation, dabbling in Zen, Vipassana, Mindfulness, and Loving-Kindness. I have practiced with classical music, guided meditation CDs, and have even done past-life regressions. I've met with a Presbyterian minister and studied contemplative prayer in the Christian tradition and I have bought so many books on all of these subjects that Bobbi had to build me an extra bookcase. Walk into my house and count the number of Buddhas sitting around incense burners. Then notice the Zen wall hangings adorning my walls. You'd think that you'd entered the temple of an enlightened goddess, but that thought is enough to make the Buddha laugh and laugh. I don't consider myself any more enlightened than the next gal. I couldn't even make that comparison because I don't know how much other people meditate, or pray, or talk to the universe. In fact, I had never talked to Bobbi about this until recently. She has a whole different take on the idea of meditation.

My sister loves being outside, so one would assume that her practice includes walking through the beauty of nature, raising her gaze to the blue, sunlit sky and thanking Whoever is listening for everything that she sees. And you would be right. However, all of us do this at one time or another, so I really didn't count her activities as anything outrageously meditative. I pushed further for some explanation. I'm glad I did.

It turns out that Bobbi also meditates every time she sits down to go to the bathroom.

"Oh, I get it," I said. "Because that's the only time in your busy day when you're actually still."

"Not really," she told me. "And I really wish you'd stop interrupting me." (Talk about a God complex.) It turns out that

Bobbi's meditation also includes athletic visualizations. As she takes her place on the throne, she first imagines that all of the little follicles involved in this process are benchwarmers because they haven't been involved in a sporting event all day. She talks to them quietly (which is a good thing because sometimes her practice takes place in a bathroom stall at Kmart) and encourages them to do their thing, coaching them to push, contract, push, contract until they've helped the "runner" cross the finish line. She is thankful when she's completed her task, and while she may not be enlightened, she feels definitely lighter, and for her, this is more than enough.

Never Hurt Ya

AFTER HAVING LEARNED THE IMPORTANCE of meditation from the High Priestess, the Fool meets another feminine archetype, the Empress, a stunning woman of royal magnificence, seated on a throne and holding a scepter. She is the Queen Mother of the tarot deck, a nurturing woman who helps us give birth to new ideas and encourages our creativity.

The Fool finds comfort in the presence of this woman in much the same way I did when Mom moved in with me. Besides being there for me with motherly advice, even at the age of 87, she was always prepared with a remedy when I had an upset tummy or a headache. The top drawer of her bureau would give a pharmacist pause, as various drugs and narcotics, some out of date, most in the wrong bottle, were waiting patiently for whoever came calling.

"I can't sleep," I told her as I entered her room one night around eleven.

"Top drawer," she answered from her bed without even glancing up from her *Woman's World*. "Look for a blue bottle marked 'Percocet.' There are some Temazepam in there. Take one of those. Knock ya right on your ear."

"OK," I said, doing as she instructed. "I found the bottle, but the pills are scattered all over the bottom of the drawer. With some old cracker crumbs, I think."

"Take one anyway. Never hurt ya."

That was one of my mother's favorite expressions, especially when it involved anything that was to be ingested into the human body. A banana peeled the day before and left on the counter overnight? Never hurt ya. Spreading peanut butter with a knife that wasn't quite clean when it came out of the dishwasher? Never hurt ya. And she knew her stuff, let me tell you. She died at 92, her last meal being an over-ripe banana with a little crusty peanut butter on it.

Not much worried my mother, and I envied her fearlessness. She would boldly walk right past difficulties without giving them the time of day. I, on the other hand, will often stop abruptly when confronted by them and hand over my hundred-dollar watch, if that's what it takes for them to leave me alone. "You think about things too much," she'd tell me. "Just let tomorrow take care of itself."

I continue to be in awe of her attitude when I recall the heartbreak that peppered the first 30-odd years of her life. She was the young girl whose family lost their home, their business, and their money in the Depression; who waited by the train tracks in the hopes that a passing coal car would drop some of its contents so that she could scoop up a lump or two to burn in her family's stove. She was the young woman whose father had a paralyzing stroke and who could do nothing but sit and shiver in the living room of the tiny, poorly heated apartment he shared with his wife and grown daughter; who became a full-time caretaker for her widowed mother when she lost her leg and eyesight to diabetes; whose first husband was killed in the war within a year after they'd married. One tragedy followed another, and maybe that's what taught Mom that worrying about the future is pointless.

Like a true Empress, she never focused on the negative. She was reticent to discuss anything bad that had happened in the past, giving my sister and me only snippets of information over the years. The conversations were short and ended with Mom saying, "That's enough of that. I don't want to talk about this." But she loved to share the good times she had growing up and, at 74 years old, agreed to my sister's request to record some of them on paper.

"It all began on January 2, 1921," my mother's short autobiography begins. "'Twas a cold and blustery day with sleet and snow (as most January days are), and I remember thinking to myself, 'It really is a little nippy. Not quite what I'm used to.' However, with all of those people *ooo-ing* and *ahhhhhing* and saying that I was the most beautiful baby in North America, I snuggled down in my blanket and basked in my glory, content with my new world, however bleak the weather."

Her sense of humor continues throughout her writing and shines most in her stories of her childhood. My particular favorite is the one involving her ineptitude at sewing, a trait she kindly passed on to both of her daughters:

"Sewing to me was the worst—I was allergic to needles and thread—and in junior high school, we had home economics where all the girls had to make dresses for themselves. There was always the teacher to help us. But even if there had been 12 instructors, Charlotte Wisner could not get her act together and was the only girl who did not have a dress to show off to her parents at the fashion show. I think my mother could have killed me.

"However, at this show, I was the pianist and played as the other girls paraded in from the locker room to the gym, just like the Miss America pageant, falling all over themselves. And me? I borrowed a dress from my sister Anna Mae. It looked quite homemade, so I fit right in.

"I made my entrance to the piano, bowed and smiled to the right, bowed and smiled to the left, and started the procession. Nobody knew the dress I was wearing was not my creation except Miss Gilbert who stood there with lockjaw. She was probably so thankful that I wasn't wearing some material pinned and basted together with a crooked hem, no neckline, and minus a sleeve. I pulled that off and ended up with an F in home ec."

When I called Bobbi to remind her of this story, she agreed that both of us inherited Mom's disdain for sewing.

"I had home ec, and I was not a fan," she told me.

"I really liked it," I said. "Except I wasn't any good at it."

"We had to take it in junior high, right? My friends Tammy and Patty still remember when I told Mrs. Weaver that Dad told me to treat a sewing machine the same way I'd treat a jigsaw. He told me it was just a tool. I guess I was scared of it and he was trying to make me feel better. So he gave me something I could relate to, you know, like the stuff in his shop."

"I'm thinking Mrs. Weaver didn't take well to that comment."

"No, I don't think she did. I remember there was a lot of laughing from the other girls in the class. And she was just trying to squelch the whole conversation so that any of the other baby lesbians wouldn't get any ideas."

"Like what?"

"I don't know. Like that we'd lead some kind of 8th-grade revolt. We'd wonder why we couldn't work with a bandsaw or a jigsaw instead of making these stupid hot pads."

There was a pause in my questioning as I tried to recollect what kind of heating elements we'd made in Mrs. Weaver's class. "Hot pads?" I asked.

"Oh, you know. Those things you use to take pans out of the oven."

"You mean pot holders?"

"Whatever. And I remember we had to make tea towels.

"No we didn't."

"Or washcloths."

"No we didn't."

"Aprons?"

"Yes. We made those."

"Boy. I really hated that class."

My sister and I then continued to talk about the rest of

Mom's memories in that little book of hers. She writes about her pet parakeet Teddy, who sang beautifully until he contracted asthma and could then only squeak, despite the medicine given to him from an eye dropper. There were her best friends Billy and Buddy with whom she played cowboys and Indians. One day, they tied her to a tree and ran away. "That was the beginning of the end of that friendship," she says. "I enjoyed my own company more than anyone else, so I took up roller skating and would fly down the steep driveway of our house."

She tells stories of her father, an accomplished organist and pianist, who would take her along to choral group practices where she would turn the pages for him as he played.

"I don't think I liked that very much," she recalls. "All those old people. They were at least in their 50s. And there was talk of a 'friendship' (if you know what I mean) between the lead baritone and Dorothy Shaw, who was the alto soloist. Dorothy was not married. George was, but we never saw his wife. I learned all of this by listening through closed doors and keyholes."

In 1938, however, the family lost their home and had to move to an apartment in the city. "We were really poor," she writes. "My father's business went belly up and we had no money coming in at all. The house was sold for back taxes. And my mother began to lose her eyesight. And Daddy had a stroke. As I look back now, all of this must have been terrible for my parents. But I don't want to dwell on the next five years. It is really depressing."

I believe that was the key to my mother's happiness. Why think about anything that's depressing? It certainly won't lift our spirits. Some may call this technique "avoidance." I'd call it survival. The Empress asks that we not only nurture others, we also must nurture ourselves; reliving painful experiences in our lives probably isn't in our best interests. Acknowledging them, learning from them, and moving on is the way to go—a point my mother illustrates in her writing:

"There were never any problems between me and my parents, but during high school, I didn't have the closeness with them that your father and I have with you two girls. My parents had a lot to contend with in the 1930s. When the business was failing, nothing was ever discussed with me. Maybe my older sisters had more contact.

"They were good parents. I loved them and took care of them in later life. But I never had the loving relationship that you two girls have with your dad and me."

The creative energy connected with this card was always present in my mom. She was able to face a bad situation and, as the saying goes, adapt, create, and continue toward something better for her and for her family. I'd be hard-pressed to find a better Empress.

It's the Friction

AFTER LEAVING THE NURTURING, CREATIVE FORCE of his mother, the Fool next encounters the Emperor, a somewhat foreboding figure complete with a long, flowing white beard and seated on a throne. Usually, we see him inside a building, a structure, if you will, because that's what he's all about: structure, discipline, logic, and reasoning. The Fool has met, for the first time, an archetype who lays down the law. The Emperor explains that creativity is a wonderful attribute but needs certain constructs in order to manifest into something useful.

Let's see. I wonder which Carmitchell sister might struggle with the idea of following the rules? To answer that question, let's go back to April 1974, when Bobbi was 17. Our family of four had just finished Easter dinner. Since it was time to do the dishes, Bobbi had disappeared from the kitchen. We thought that she had gone into her bedroom to take a nap, a clever trick of hers that she employs to this day. Shortly thereafter, however, the three of us heard screams coming from the living room.

"FIRE!" Bobbi was yelling. "FIRE! I mean it!"

I don't know why she felt that she had to add how serious she was, as all three of us went running down the hall to the living room as soon as we heard her first scream. There we witnessed the coffee table, completely ablaze, Mom's Easter decorations in grave danger. Dad ripped off his cardigan sweater and threw it over the inferno, stopping the blaze before it jumped to the couch. With smoke hanging in the air, Mom and I frantically gathered Styrofoam eggs and plastic bunnies, cradling them safely in our arms. Dad looked at Bobbi who was standing there helplessly.

"What the hell happened?" he asked.

Bobbi started rambling. "I don't know! I don't know! I was just, I was playing, I was just playing with the Easter grass and it caught fire! I was just rubbing it between my fingers and it must have been the friction or something, but it just caught fire and then I yelled 'FIRE!'"

I find it interesting that neither Mom nor Dad ever asked Bobbi if she were OK, if she had been burnt or injured during this event. It's not that they didn't care. It's just that, I'm guessing, when the word "FIRE!" is used in the same room that Bobbi is occupying, they knew something was amiss, and that it would probably be her explanation—which we could now clearly see that it was.

Dad's facial expression resembled that of a dog to whom someone was trying to explain quantum physics. "The friction," he said flatly. "That's what caused this. You picked up Easter grass, and the table went up in flames."

"Yes, yes! I couldn't believe it!" Bobbi cried, her eyes welling up. Was she crying because the fire had scared her? No. She was crying because Dad knew that she was lying. This wasn't the Empress that Bobbi was facing now. Mom's reaction would have been a bit different. She would have shown a tad more concern for her daughter's safety and emotional state, at least for the time being. The Emperor, on the other hand, would save all of that parental empathy for later. As a man, he needed the solution to the problem at hand—how does a 17-year-old girl start a fire? Might the matches sticking out of her jeans pocket provide a clue?

"What are those?" he asked her.

"Matches."

An eerie quiet settled over us. Mom and I, who had said nothing up to this point, quickly stepped away from the burnt carnage and let Dad pass, as he went down the hall and back into his study. We then looked at my sister.

Mom finally spoke. "I don't need to tell you what kind of trouble you're in," she said, and then she left the living room, too.

I looked at Bobbi. "Really? The friction? That was the best you could do?" All that she'd wanted to do, she explained, was to see how long it took Easter grass to burn, so she'd found a pack of Mom's matches and had let the games begin. She just didn't think they'd begin so quickly.

Her punishment, the Emperor had decreed, was to buy another coffee table for the family, but since she didn't have any money, she'd have to build one and let our family use it, forever and ever. She did so, in Industrial Arts class. Bobbi had learned a good lesson ("Don't get caught starting a fire") because of the fair, logical judgment of our father.

I think her teacher, Mr. Bailey, gave her a C for that project. Maybe it was a D. I don't really remember, as I was in Home Ec class making potholders that year. The thought that Dad had been in touch with her teacher and negotiated the grade entered our minds, but neither one of us was stupid enough to bring it up. When the Emperor spoke, we listened. And so should you.

Boogsla's Dream

THE HIEROPHANT

IN THIS CARD, the Fool meets another fellow you shouldn't ignore. Enter the Hierophant, an authoritative, religious figure wearing a gold crown and a sacred robe of red. He sits on a throne and points one hand toward heaven where he is able to understand the mysteries of the universe and summon them to earth. Like his predecessor the Emperor, the Hierophant represents someone in a position of authority, but this ruler has the added responsibility of seeing that the members of a group work together in order in order to function at top efficiency.

In church or in school, for example, we all share some common base. We have traditions that we follow, such as taking communion or reciting the Apostles' Creed. We have a set of rules that are assigned and to which we adhere, like having respect for the teacher or taking out the weakest kid in dodgeball. (I always hated this exercise in Darwinian natural selection, as I was constantly the species that was immediately eradicated.) Out of necessity, our independence must take a backseat when part of a group. How can we function as any kind of a team if one member chooses to follow her own path off of the playground and into the nurse's office?

Bobbi and I have a set of rules in place when we perform. We feel that these constructs allow us to be good team players, and we embrace this conformity to help the Carmitchell Sisters succeed. Our rules are succinct, yet sufficient:

1. Always ride to the jobs together.
2. Never learn new material.
3. Whenever possible, avoid songs that make us want to stick hot pokers in our eyes.
4. Don't hit a bunny on the way home.

Staying within these guidelines promotes a sense of community that I enjoy, nay, *require* in order to perform without passing out. I must be a team player. I am too frightened to entertain an audience all on my own, and I don't know how anyone can. Bobbi does not share my affliction. She is comfortable doing solo acts anywhere, even in small coffee houses, venues in which I am not at ease. Everyone sits there sipping coffee and actually listening. That is just too much pressure for me. Give me a slightly inebriated crowd any night, one whose members are more interested in dancing and mingling and not watching me too intently.

But Bobbi never loses her composure during a live performance. The closest that she ever came to a complete meltdown was when she had a nightmare about playing Radio City Music Hall.

She called me as soon as she woke up that morning. Her voice was shaking, she was on the verge of tears, and I was deeply concerned. She told me that, in this dream, she got booked at Radio City, and everyone she knew was in the audience — Mom, Dad, all of our relatives, all of her fans. She was quite excited and went backstage to prepare. There, she met a group of jazz musicians, smoking (because they were jazz musicians) and waiting to be called on stage. She asked what they were doing there, and they told her that they were performing that night.

"No," she said. "I am. I'm performing here."

23

"Not tonight, you're not," one of them told her. "Look at the chalkboard over there."

Bobbi did as she was told, and sure enough, on the board in white chalk was written, "Tonight: A Jazz Band. Tomorrow night: Bobbi Carmitchell."

I tried my best to sound concerned. "So you were there on the wrong night. Wow. That is one scary dream."

"It wasn't just that," she said. "My name. You should have seen my name. The letters were squiggly and it didn't even spell anything. It read . . . it was like . . . " She was trying to catch this part of the dream before it floated away. "It . . . it wasn't even my name. It was something like *Boogsla Carmrod.*"

I wanted to guffaw. But I couldn't do anything except listen, as Bobbi was still terrified.

"And then," she continued, "I was at my house. And I heard some noise outside. I looked out the windows and I saw Lorne Greene slowly walking up toward my house, his arms extended in front of him like a zombie. He was a body-snatcher, and he was coming for me."

I kept wondering when this dream would get scary and not funny, but she wasn't there yet. So I covered my mouth with my hand and kept listening.

"And then," she said (using the segue that all dreamers do), " . . . and then . . . then the King of Scotland was beside him, walking next to him like some kind of wind-up doll. And there was a third guy, too, in a red shirt. They kept coming closer and closer, and my windows turned into huge sheets of wet, damaged cardboard, and Lorne Green and the king pushed right through them and the king knocked me over. Then I woke up."

Her last words signaled my turn to speak. "Wow," I repeated. "Boogsla Carmrod. Then Lorne Greene. Jeez. That is somethin'." I couldn't contain myself any longer. "Bobbi, I'm sorry, but that is frickin' hysterical." I then released the hounds of laughter that had been clawing to get out of my throat, and they apparently had done some damage.

"NOT funny, Anne! Not funny. I am so scared right now."

I tried to calm both of us by dropping my voice to a lower register. "Oh, I know," I said. "I know you are. And I'm sorry. Boogsla."

That was the turning point. She saw the absurdity of it all. A chuckle popped up from her end of the phone, followed by, "Yeah. OK. That *is* kind of a funny name."

"And you know, "I continued, treading lightly at this point, "that there is no King of Scotland."

"Well, in my dream there was."

"I wonder why you put him with Lorne Greene?"

"I don't have the answer to that question," she said. "If I did, I'd be the King of Scotland."

And on it went from there. The retelling of the nightmare, the laughter, picturing the moors on a Scottish Ponderosa, even envisioning Hoss in a kilt all cleared the demons from Bobbi's head and she was able to move on with her day.

However, she never escaped the name Boogsla Carmrod. To this day, many of her buddies still use it in one form or another, either when addressing her directly or referring to her indirectly. It's such a common moniker these days that it's spoken with a straight face and warrants no reaction at all. In fact, when she and I got separated at Kmart a few years back, I asked the woman at the front desk to page "my friend" using that nickname. ("She's foreign," I explained, trying to cover my tracks.) Bobbi claims that the minute she heard the muzak pause and the words, "Attention, Kmart shoppers: Would . . . ," she knew for certain that the words "Boogsla Carmrod" would follow. Her precognition is a testament to how working well together with your sister, whether on stage or in Kmart, can make life run more smoothly. All the powers of heaven and Earth came together to bestow that knowledge upon her. The Hierophant, and the King of Scotland, couldn't be more pleased.

25

My, How You've Grown

ON THE CARD IS A MAN AND A WOMAN, both naked, standing in front of a tree with a serpent wrapped around it. If the Lovers appear for you in a reading, a loving, intimate partnership may be on its way. However, the card also presents the need for trusting relationships in all areas of your life, such as those with your co-workers or your extended family. Or, in my case, with my doctor.

I was 43 and it was time for my annual Pap test. I am always a wreck for weeks before the exam, and my brain goes in the oddest directions. Let me give you a little roadmap.

First of all, when I hear the words "Pap test," they remind me of my grandfather, Pap. For some reason, I always imagine how awful it would be to have your grandfather "down there." After that mental image and the ensuing nausea have passed, I then think of my grandmother, Mam Mam, and this reminds me that my mammogram is overdue and that I always faint when I have one of those done—not before the exam, but during. The nurse flies over to catch me when I say, "I'm going down!" and releases my breast just in time. (For those of you wondering how in God's name you can be held up by one breast when you pass out, let me tell you: God has nothing to do with it. It's the vice as big as a tectonic plate clamped down on your woman parts that's doing the magic.)

I then realize that it's been too long since I've been to the doctor's and envision some kind of flesh-eating bacteria that has been invading my body, unbeknownst to me, but that the doctor will notice the minute he walks in the room. This, in turn, gives me stomach cramps, and I'm afraid I'll throw up—again, not before the exam, but during.

All of these fears run through the core of my being, so that by the time I get to the office, my legs feel like Jello and I'm surprised that I can walk at all. This time was no different.

After the nurse got me situated and covered with a paper towel, she told me on her way out the door that the doctor would be in shortly.

"OK," I said, glancing around the room at the reading material. There was a poster on the wall of a uterus holding a baby. Not interested. One featuring a set of fallopian tubes. Nope. Beside me, a stack of pamphlets about STDs. Maybe. . . .

But just as I was reaching for one, the doctor came in. He shook my hand and introduced himself as Dr. Shirk. Since this practice included several physicians, I never knew which one I was going to get.

"So you're here for your Pap test," he said, looking down at my chart, while I looked at his face morphing into my grandfather's. "Well, let's get you started." His presence sparked a sense of familiarity in me, but before I could piece anything together, he glanced back up at me and said, "Oh, I see you're a teacher. Where do you work?"

"Cocalico Middle School."

"No kidding," he said. "I went to CMS."

Now, I've never dropped acid, but I've heard tales of trips that my friends have taken. Some say that you're aware of where you are, but that everything takes on a surreal tint, and the acid dropper finds it all incredibly funny. You seem to drift in and out of that state for a while, laughing uncontrollably until something metaphorically slaps you upside the head. Then, for a brief moment, you're back in the present where everything is normal. Other friends have told me that their trips are just the opposite, where they see everything clearly, how it "really is," and believe they can answer all the questions which have stumped humankind for years.

What I was going through was a combination of the two. On the one hand, I was well aware that I was in the doctor's office, sitting naked in front of a young man, and something inside of me found this comical. On the other, when he asked where I'd taught, the last 20 years of my teaching career imploded before me into one clear image, that of me standing in the front of my eighth-grade class, calling on little Michael Shirk in the third row.

"Oh," I said. "Uh-oh. Dr. Shirk, I was your eighth-grade English teacher."

He looked at me as if I'd suddenly started speaking Chinese.

"No, I don't think so," he said slowly. "No, no. My eighth-grade English teacher's name was . . . Ms. Emery, I think."

"That was me," I told him. "Before my divorce."

We both stared, waiting for the other to speak.

"No," he said at last, glancing at my blond hair. "My teacher was a brunette." Poor guy. He was desperate.

"Still me," I assured him. "And if we could get going with this exam, you'll see what I mean."

I thought this comment was funny. He laughed a little. Then coughed. Then stumbled on his words.

"Honestly, Ms. Emery, or, Carmitchell, if you want another doctor, I totally understand."

"I think you can call me Anne at this point," I told him. "And look, it takes me forever to get in here. So I'm here, I'm naked, you're my former student, and let's just get this over with. If you're OK with it, I'm OK with it." And that was the truth. It took all my willpower to make this appointment. I was going to take the high road, be a grown-up, and carry on as best I could. As long as it wasn't my grandfather staring up at me between my legs, I was good to go.

He agreed, buzzed for the nurse, and told me to put my feet in the stirrups. At this point, we both realized to our horror that we had some time to kill. We started chatting. Actually, he started rambling as I lowered myself onto the table.

"So, you still at Cocalico?" he asked, situating himself on the stool in front me. "Great school, CMS. Great school. Are most of the teachers still there? I loved art class. Now what was that teacher's name? Oh, gosh, I don't remember. I do remember your class, though. Those were good times. Good times."

It was incredible. This doctor was somehow able to do two things: One, talk a lot without stopping to breathe, and two, sit right in front of my nether regions and retain solid eye contact with me while I attempted to respond to his questions.

The nurse entered the room, and it was only then that Dr. Shirk's bravery returned. He picked up what has always looked to me like a medieval tuning fork — the speculum — and with a jovial, "Here we go, then!" started the procedure as I mentally escaped to Tahiti.

"So," he said, lowering his head and talking while he examined me. "I guess everything's pretty much the same down there, right?"

I caught the first plane back and propped myself up on my elbows, looking at him quizzically. "You mean, does my vagina have any new piercings or anything?"

His head snapped up, and he was mortified. "No! I meant at Cocalico. Is everything pretty much the same at Cocalico!"

Finally, here was something at which we could both laugh. I told him that nothing much had changed at the middle school, and that no accessories would ever be added to my feminine parts. He continued the exam, and before long, he had finished. Or so I thought.

"Just one more thing, he said, changing into a new set of gloves and applying some jelly to one of his index fingers. "I need to give you a rectal exam. Would you mind?" His chivalry touched me.

"You know, I've been waiting all day for someone to ask me that," I said. The tension between us had melted at this point, so I was willing to take on anything, even the gloved finger of my former student. Before I knew it, the exam was over, and Dr. Shirk and I had survived.

I was telling this story once to a faculty room full of colleagues when my principal walked in. He'd heard raucous laughter echoing through the hallway and stopped by to see what was going on. When I filled him in, he shook his head and said, "I thought you were doing stand-up."

"Nope," I assured him. "I did the whole thing lying down."

Anything We Want

A REVIEW OF HIS JOURNEY SO FAR illustrates that as a young one, the Fool takes a leap of faith and is excited to get started with whatever the world has to offer. Along his way, he meets various helpful archetypes: the Magician shows him how to create; the High Priestess explains to him the importance of meditation; the Empress encourages him to take what he's learned while meditating and put it into action; the Emperor adds a dose of logic to this action; the Hierophant encourages group conformity to enhance growth; and the Lovers introduce our traveler to the grand experience of intimacy. The Fool is now officially a grown-up, as the number seven signals the completion of his childhood. He is ready to go out on his own, and when he does, he meets this fellow, the Charioteer.

Clothed in a suit of armor, a young prince is pictured steering a chariot being pulled by two horses. They are beautiful creatures and extremely well behaved, as no reins are visible. The Charioteer is a good example of healthy ego, his yin and yang in perfect sync as he maintains control of his emotions while he enjoys success through his hard work. A hero, he has achieved his goals and is heading home.

As retired people, Bill and I feel much like Charioteers. I taught for 32 years, and he

VII

THE CHARIOT

30

worked for about the same amount of time in accounting and IT. We have both finished our races and now enjoy time in a way we never have before. It is ours, all ours, with no lesson plans to follow, and no more "meetings and beatings," as Bill likes to call them. Friends of ours who are still in the workforce look to us with anticipation, as they know that one day, they will also enjoy the fruits of their labor. But something bothers them. "This 'time' that you reference," they ask. "Without a set schedule, what do you do all day?" We're really not quite sure how to answer that, so we usually keep it simple and say, "Anything we want."

Understandably, this glib response doesn't do much to answer their question. I'm not sure what goes through their minds. They may be envisioning us lounging in our pajamas until noon, doing crossword puzzles, and watching TV talk shows. This is completely false. We do not lounge in our sleepwear until noon. Most of the time, we're fully dressed by 8:00 in the morning, and this is possible because we've slept in the same clothes that we had on the day before. We also don't do crossword puzzles, as this requires too much thought, and talk shows would be overkill, since we're sick of trying to figure out what to say to each other on a daily basis and don't need television to remind us of our incompetence in the area of conversation. And we especially don't need the commercials.

The world of advertising has painted a picture of retirement that is ludicrous and counter-productive in our household. Look at the seniors in these scenarios. They are skydiving. They are taking Zumba classes. And, inevitably, they are riding their bikes, the helmeted woman usually in front of the man, looking lovingly over her shoulder at him as they both pedal and laugh, sharing a private joke and holding their glances longer than a couple married for 30 years would ever do. Now, if Bill and I were to film the same commercial, we would begin by riding our bikes up one of the ballbusting roads around our house. He would pass me and not look back at all, since it's the first time we've been out of each other's peripheral vision for about three weeks. He might stop at the top of the hill and glance back to see me at the bottom, straddling my fallen bike, mouthing obscenities and lighting a cigarette before just giving up and walking home.

Here's what retirement is not: It is not learning a foreign language and then traveling to a country where you attempt to use this language. It is not taking electric guitar lessons and joining a garage band. Instead, it is more like picking up an English-to-French dictionary at a bookstore, paging through the preface, and losing interest because TNT is running a *Law and Order* marathon. It's playing a C chord on your new Strat for about five minutes before soaking your fingers in massage oil and developing a healthy respect for Eric Clapton's callouses. Retirement, or at least the beginning of it, is figuring out what you want to do for the next three decades of your life and being a little overwhelmed by your choices.

It's sometimes difficult, then, to answer specifically the question, "What do you do all day?" when you haven't figured out the answer for yourself. In the meantime, I find it helpful to develop a list of activities that will pass muster. For example, I often tell people that I'm working on a book, leaving out the part about not actually *writing* a book quite yet, but just reading one. Or I tell them that I take French lessons every Friday, which is true. However, I really only took about five, because my French teacher and I really love talking about clothes and food and do so, over coffee, in English. I'm not promoting lying, you understand. I'm just asking you to flex your creative muscles a little bit and come up with a few answers that can make everyone feel comfortable. Because God forbid you tell them what you really do in a day.

Our mornings around here begin with waking up, although not in the same bed. Bill and I have separate bedrooms for a variety of reasons, the most important being that neither of us can stand being in bed with the other. It's not that we don't love each other; we just don't like touching anyone, except the dogs, when we're trying to go to sleep. When we were dating and would spend the night together, we did the obligatory cuddling and pillow talk, both of us unsure of expressing our true feelings about sharing a bed. We were just getting to know each other, after all, and still on our best behavior. Once things got serious, however, we got more comfortable with the truth.

We had decided to live together, and one day, as we were on the phone planning where to put his furniture, I said to Bill, "Would you mind having separate bedrooms when you move in here?"

As a man, Bill was very aware of the trick questions that women can pose, and he paused before giving the correct answer in an effort to word his response properly. It was, and will always remain, his standard one in cases such as this: "If that's what you want."

Oh, it was what I wanted, all right. Sleeping next to a marathon runner is like sleeping next to a furnace, especially after menopause came to town. I need to keep the windows open and fan on even in the middle of winter. For about ten minutes. Then I need to shut the windows and bundle up under the blankets which had, a short time before, been kicked to the floor. None of this is romantic, unless elbow sweat is something that turns you on.

So he awakes in one room, and I, in another. Eventually, we meet in the kitchen, make our coffee or tea, and talk a little bit, asking each other how our nights were and if the dogs kept us awake. Then we share our plans for the day.

For me, these include petting and kissing our dogs, reading, checking email, watching TV, cross-stitching, and thinking about going to the gym. Bill's day is surprisingly similar, except that he runs for two hours while he's cross-stitching, which is no small feat. We don't see each other a lot as the day progresses, but we always end up in the living room at night with the pups because there is no place that we'd rather be.

Think about it this way: Retirement is the time of your life where you get to do everything you've always wanted to do, but never had the time to do it—even if it's discussing with your partner, in depth, how Maggie's tail wags a totally different way than Emma's does. You can, as a proud Charioteer, finally let go of those reins.

The Ghost in the House

THE NEXT PERSON that the Fool meets on his journey is a woman gently closing the mouth of a lion. For me, this card is reminiscent of Card 6, where Eve fearlessly talks to the snake in the garden. Equally reminiscent would be my reaction. If I were this woman, I would take off in the opposite direction of the beast, my legs thrashing about with no apparent rhythm, my head whipping from side to side as I shrieked and gasped for air. (This is actually how I look when I run, by the way, which explains my aversion to all things athletic.)

The Strength card is a symbol of work balanced with intellect. The message is a simple one: With the right amount of stamina, we can domesticate any unappealing instinct that we'd like to squelch, such as pride, greed, lust, or envy, and can replace these traits with love, forgiveness, empathy, or mercy. Like the woman on the card, we can tame our baser instincts and grow into a better person.

If you draw this card, then, you should be asking, "What scares me? And how can I overcome this fear?" Personally, my answers to these questions differ from the norm because of one important reason: I don't mind fear. Fear can be good. I respect it like my sister says she respects those Amazonian lesbians at a pride festival; they scare her, but she likes it.

I recognize fear, compliment it, and send it on its way. Roller coasters, for example, terrify me. And while I admire the people who ride those death-traps, I don't envy them. I've never been the type of person who insists on conquering every fear she has in the hopes of becoming a better "me," a stronger "me," or, in the case of flying, a stupider "me." (Don't waste your breath telling me how safe flying is. I know for a fact that if I ever got on a plane, it would crash. My cousin Marianne tells me not to worry about this because if the plane went down, I would experience three to four minutes of sheer horror, and then it would all be over. I'd be dead. "And stupid," I told her, "because I'd have known that I should have never gotten on that plane in the first place.")

I know that my aversion to snakes, lions, carnival rides, and flying might make me seem like a frightened, wilting daisy, but most of the time I'm a pretty strong woman. In fact, I have ghosts in my house, and I'm not afraid of them at all.

The first ghost appeared several years ago. Living alone, I was subject to the fears that we all have from time to time. I'd hear small noises at night while I was in bed and would think momentarily that there could be burglars at my windows or aliens on my roof. Before terror enveloped me, though, I'd turn up the volume on the TV. For some reason, infomercials about hand-hammered woks always calmed me, and I'd drift off to sleep. The next morning, I'd awaken, un-robbed and un-abducted, the light of day erasing all memory of the night before and leaving me with a strange craving for Chinese food.

One afternoon, however, I was walking through the piano room, which is so named because it is a room with a piano in it. I had to pass the stairs leading down to the family room, which is a room with no family in it, and I noticed out of the corner of my eye a woman floating down the steps. She was Victorian in nature and very graceful, wearing a beautiful, high-collared lace gown, her hair piled in chestnut curls on her head. She ignored me, and I, her, as I kept walking toward the living room. I didn't stop. I simply told myself, "If you acknowledge what you just saw; if you repeat this to anyone; if you continue to think about it in any way, you will never be able to live here. You will be too scared. Burglars and aliens may come and go, but this ghost is a deal-breaker. Bury the memory, the same way you do your skinny jeans and your dreams of being a Broadway dancer. Nothing good can come of this. Or those jeans."

And that is exactly what I did. I continued to the living room, sat down to watch TV, and never thought of the ghost again.

Four years passed. I was married now and sitting in the living room watching TV. (I know it may seem like I do a lot of this, but that's only because I do.) My husband walked into the room and stopped beside the recliner, looking at me quizzically. "You're here," he said.

"Yes, I am," I replied.

"Is your sister here?"

"No. Why?"

"Because I just saw a woman walk down the steps."

I jumped up from the couch and excitedly explained to him that I'd seen her too, years ago, and as we compared notes, we realized that we'd seen the same woman. (The fact that he'd thought he'd caught a glimpse of Bobbi in a dress with full hair and makeup didn't enter into the conversation until later.) We both admitted that this was quite the experience, but since he was a football coach, his interest in a topic not sports-related eventually waned.

Intent on discussing this further, I did what any good ghost hunter would do: I called my mom. She suggested a trip to the library, and off we went to search through files and records of any kind which might suggest that my house was built on top of a Native American burial ground. Or was the site of a factory fire. Or that, somehow, the Titanic had actually sunk off the shores of the Susquehanna River. None of this was so, however, and I was left with just a fond memory of The Woman on the Stairs. If she were the only ghostly visitor I'd ever have, that was good enough for me.

But, of course, she wasn't.

When Bill and his son moved in here, we decided not to tell Jon about the ghost. He was sixteen and old enough to handle the news, but living in a new place was a big adjustment for him, and we didn't want to make him uncomfortable. I loved it when Jon stayed here. Since I'm an insomniac and he was a teenage boy, we were both up most of the night, I, walking from room to room wondering where I'd left my sleeping pills, and he, on the computer playing video games and chatting with his friends. I usually stopped and talked with him around two o'clock in the morning, which I'm sure he found not at all invasive of his privacy.

About a month before he left for college, during one of our late-night chats, I slipped and mentioned the ghost. Not many topics can pull a kid away from a computer screen, but that one did. He stopped typing and asked me for details, which I gave him.

"I can't believe this," he said. "I saw something, too." What he saw on his way to the bathroom one night was not the woman, but a pair of men's dress shoes walking from the top of the stairs, through the piano room, and toward his room. Not a body, mind you—just the shoes. Jon immediately stopped moving, and the shoes did the same. Both entities just stood there facing each other, like two gunslingers preparing for a paranormal shoot-out. The shoes then turned and headed toward the stairs again, while Jon spun around and ran back to his room. He told me that he'd shut his door and sat on his bed for about an hour until he finally had the nerve to make the trip again.

I was stunned. "Why didn't you tell us?"

"Because I decided never to think of it again."

So who was *this* ghost? I suspect that it was my father, whom Bobbi had a seen a few years after he passed as she was working in the woodshop downstairs. Why he showed up in only a pair of shoes, I have no idea. When I think of Dad's footwear in his later years, I see a pair of tube socks with sandals. If reincarnation is true, perhaps he was coming around a second time to make up for his fashion *faux pas*.

Whoever these spirits are, though, and why they're here, remain a mystery to me. They're never a threat; every time one is spotted, it is going in the opposite direction of whoever sees it. So when Bill and I think of leaving this house and buying another, I also have to think about leaving my ghosts. Would they go with me? That answer probably lies in the audio tape that my friend Scott, a ghost hunter, made for me. We were standing in the basement, since this is where all of the activity originated, and I asked aloud to whoever was listening, "Are you happy here?" When Scott had prepared the final recording, we listened to it around my kitchen table one night and heard a male voice respond to my question clearly and gently.

"I am," it said.

This particular fear for me, then, is one that I've conquered. Going down the steps used to unnerve me quite a bit. Now, though, whenever I enter the basement, I always greet this spiritual guest to whom I have become quite accustomed. My acknowledgment of his presence gives me a good feeling. While I still have no interest in getting on a rollercoaster, I'm completely at ease with my ghost. I have overcome my anxiety. I have mastered my phobia to the point that I even ask him how he's doing. But I promise you this: If he ever answers me, I will run upstairs like a sprinter with her pants on fire.

Alone With My Lo Mein

THE HERMIT IS PICTURED in traditional tarot decks as you'd probably expect him to be: an older, wise-looking man with white hair and a long beard. A grey cloak over his shoulders, he stands alone on top of a mountain with a cane in his left hand and a lantern in his right. He is waiting on the mountaintop for the students of truth to make the trip and join him at the precipice, as they follow their own path to enlightenment and to the mentor who can help them discover it.

On the one hand, this card suggests that you are indeed the Hermit and that it's now time for you to share your gifts of enlightenment and spiritual truths with others. On the other, it may imply that you need to take some quiet time to ascertain exactly in what direction your life is headed and if its purpose is serving you well. (And remember that "quiet time" in this case does not mean binge-watching all nine seasons of *House* by yourself, with nothing but a bowl of chips and M&M's at your side. Nice try, though.)

No one likes alone time more than I, except, of course, my sister. Over the years, both of us have referred to the other as a hermit, and it's easy to understand why. It's really hard to make us leave our respective houses for mundane activities. We'll have really good intentions of getting together, but something always happens to get in the way. For example, one time she was supposed to come over to my place to work on some new songs. She was planning on being here at seven, and my phone rang at six-thirty.

"Hey," she said. "Do you really hate the songs that we're doing now?"

"You mean the same ones we've been playing for sixteen years? They're OK, I guess. Why? Do you hate them?"

"I don't know. There are some nice ones in there. People always like 'American Pie'."

"But we'd rather eat dryer lint than play that song again. Isn't that what we said?"

"No. We said that we'd rather chomp down on a ball of aluminum foil."

"OH! Right. Right. So, do you want to keep the song, or chew aluminum foil?"

She paused momentarily, realizing that her answer could mean the difference between leaving her house or staying at home. "I think I'd rather keep the song."

"Cool. Me, too. So we're good then, for not getting together tonight?"

"Yeah," Bobbi told me. "How about I call you later and we can brainstorm some new songs for the next time we plan to cancel a practice?"

"Perfect," I said. "Talk to you then."

When I look over the last 35 years, I realize that I've lived alone for about 23 of them. Bobbi's the same way. Neither one of us wants to be with our partners all the time, nor do we always need to cohabitate with them. So when I called her, I didn't even have to ask if she liked living alone, hermit-style. The more important question was, "Why?"

She told me that being alone gives her a chance to restore herself. If she doesn't get that down time, she feels irritated and depleted. I feel the same way, and I'm fortunate that Bill has his own routine during the day which doesn't involve me. I get a lot of time to myself, and I enjoy it. But again the same question nagged at me: Why?

"Do you feel," I asked Bobbi, "that when we're with our partners all the time, we have to do things we don't want to do, but we do them just to keep the other person happy?"

"Oh, God, yes."

"Like what?"

She started answering before the Coco Puffs she was eating were fully swallowed. "Like chewing good food. Driving somewhere I don't wanna go. Listening to stupid music. Going to bed when I'm not sleepy. You name it. That's why I'm better alone. I can eat what I want, listen to what I want, sleep when I want."

I pressed on. "But when you're by yourself," I asked, "do you find that you become more inspired, that you've reached a higher form of enlightenment?"

"Huh. Let me think a minute. . . . No. I really. . . . Nope."

So much for the tarot's Hermit card being personified in Bobbi. She just liked being alone. There was no hidden magic in her solitude. She just enjoyed eating that box of day-old lo mein off of her dashboard while she drove to Kmart, listening to classic Bowie, and planning which *Star Trek* DVD she'd fall asleep to later on that night when she was good and ready.

I tried one final question.

"OK. So if the Hermit showed up for you in a tarot spread, it wouldn't be because you need more private time. But could it mean that all of the time you've spent alone has been preparing you to share with other people what you've learned about life? Like you do through your music?"

"When you say 'other people,' what do you mean?"

"You'd be a teacher, of sorts. You'd lead others along their paths and help them to understand their life's purpose. You'd be just like the Hermit, waiting on the mountaintop for your students to come to you."

"I would hate that."

"Why?"

"Because then I wouldn't be alone. Was that a trick question?"

I wasn't getting anywhere with this discussion and was ready to end the call. Then Bobbi made a valid point.

"You know," she said, "it *is* possible to be with other people and help them grow, without losing ourselves in the process."

She's a lot more enlightened than she thinks she is.

Finding Equilibrium

IS YOUR LIFE RULED by God, Fate, or the choices that you make? The Wheel of Fortune asks you to ponder this question. I've always considered this card one of the most existential in tarot because it makes us wonder exactly who's in charge. Depending on your religious framework, you may think that God is at the helm, that he is holding the reins, or that he is acting in any number of cliched supervisory roles. If you're more of a New Age-ist, you may believe in Soul contracts, those agreements that we make with God before we incarnate into physical form. We might agree, for example, that, once in human form, we will insist that our stylist give us a most egregious haircut because we want to look like Demi Moore in *Ghost*. Seeing ourselves in the salon mirror after the ensuing carnage, we will have learned a valuable lesson—that a face in the shape of a shoebox has no business sporting a pixie cut—and will have grown as spiritual beings.

Then again, you may be a true existentialist who believes that life has no meaning at all. We're only here because we've hit the evolutionary jackpot, and events in our lives are nothing more than a series of random occurrences. Or, you could be like me, what I like to call an Eclectic Presbyterian, one who is open to any philosophy that keeps her away from bad hairdos. However you categorize yourself, the Wheel tells us that life is constantly moving forward, and that we have no choice but to move along with it.

The wheel of the zodiac is pictured with four icons in each corner of the card. These vary from deck to deck. Sometimes air, earth, fire, and water are depicted. Sometimes an angel, a bull, a lion, and an eagle are shown, all holding the Torah. Whatever is on the card, these symbols are all there for the same reason: to remind us that we have everything we need at our disposal to partake in the continuity of life. In fact, most of the time the bull, lion, and eagle are all drawn with wings, just like the angel, to show that, even though these are fixed signs of the zodiac, they are able to embrace change. A snake is also present, along with Anubis, that bizarre Egyptian god of the dead, with a dog's head on top of a man's body. (I'm ignoring the fact that some of you ladies out there, including me, are drawn to this deity, thinking that he may be the perfect mate for you. Let's put that aside for now.)

As if all of these symbols weren't enough, a sphinx, that great riddler, is also hanging out. This card seems to encompass a little bit from multiple religions, doesn't it? You've got your snake from the Garden of Eden, your man-dog from Middle Eastern lore, your animals from our friends the Pagans, your Torah from the Jewish tradition. The Wheel does not discriminate, and for good reason. Life goes on for *all* of us, and every day can be an opportunity for change. This idea in itself is reason enough to celebrate.

Sometimes, however, the card may be reminding you that the good luck you expected is not showing up. Your life may seem to be in quite a rut, your wheel stuck, your options, limited. So whose fault is this? Ah. That brings me back to my original question. Is it God's fault that your circumstances are dire? Could it be your soul contract manifesting itself? Is Fate enjoying a good chuckle at your expense? Or could it be, of all things, karma, showing up for a little bit of payback? You'll need to decide how to interpret this based on your own core beliefs.

But before you start making absurd promises to God or cursing fate, ask yourself if any of your past actions may be responsible for your predicament right now. For example, I could have blamed my stylist for that haircut she gave me in the 80s. She should have known better. I could have demanded that her license be revoked to save others from the same shame that I experienced for weeks, nay, months. But if I had to be honest with myself (something I hate doing, by the way), the responsibility for that pixie-do rested firmly on top of my own shoebox-shaped head.

So whether you're a Jew, an atheist, a Presbyterian, or an explorer of all things spiritual, the Wheel encourages you to expect something good to come out of something bad. Delays are not an option at this point. Keep moving forward with what's been working for you, or re-evaluate what hasn't been and change your course. Either way, your options are limitless.

I often ask Bill's opinion about God, karma, reincarnation, and why my printer doesn't work. He's always honest with me, and he sometimes even combines his answers into one succinct response that encompasses all four of the above topics: "For the love of God, Annie, what did you do to your computer yesterday, and why does this keep happening to you?" My answer is the standard "I didn't do *any*thing to it" because I'm also not good at accepting blame. But I wanted to ask him only about karma this time, so I was careful to frame my question so that it didn't involve technology. The best I could do was, *Do you believe in karma?* I repeated the question in my head several times as I entered the kitchen where he stood doing the dishes.

"Do not say anything about the computer," I said to myself. "The wording is very important here. Just ask him, 'Do you believe in karma?'" I was fearful that "Do you believe in karma?" would somehow spill out of my mouth in the form of, "Do you believe in karma and what's up with this copy and paste thing, anyway?" I'm proud to say that I was successful in my endeavor.

He pondered the question as he continued to wash the plates. "Yes. I do."

"Great," I said. I waited for him to continue. He didn't.

"That's all you got?" I asked.

"Did you want something more?"

I had forgotten that I was talking with Bill, a man who answers questions without any footnotes at all.

"Well, yeah. Like, how would you define karma?"

"I look at it like this," he said, focusing his attention only on the sink. "Everything strikes a balance in the universe. If someone is out of balance, he needs to go back to an equilibrium that's sustainable."

Since I couldn't remember any of that, I asked him to wait until I was able to grab a pen and an old receipt in the junk drawer. When I was ready, I said, "You know, all of that stuff sounds pretty accountant-y. I guess because you used to be an accountant."

"That's exactly right. The practice of accounting must have equilibrium."

"Wait. Slow down. . . . E . . . quil . . . OK. Go ahead."

"That's how you see the good and the bad in all things business," he explained, draining the water from the sink. "When you're selling a product, the accounting for cost ultimately determines the profit that you can make. You always have to weigh the cost of something against its benefit." He grabbed a dish towel and dried his hands as I finished transcribing his words.

"That's a really good analogy," I told him.

He considered my statement. "I don't know if it is or not. But that's how I look at things."

"Well, I think it's cool, and do you know why my Chromebook won't support iTunes?"

Dammit. I was THIS close.

A Tale of Two Mice

THE WHEEL TELLS US THAT we must always move forward in life, but that doesn't mean that we should step on other people to get what we want. Only in politics and Easter egg hunts does that notion apply. Now our hero meets Justice, who holds scales in one hand and a double-edged sword in the other. Both of these items are there to remind the Fool to be cautious with his judgments of others as he proceeds on his journey. There are two sides to every issue, and he must choose wisely and do the honorable thing.

And let me tell you, this "doing the honorable thing" is exhausting. Some days, I can't be just or even kind to people. Why? Because sometimes, they annoy the heck out of me. So when a long-winded friend calls, I don't pick up the phone. I'll throw my ethics aside and lie to her later, telling her I must have been washing my hair and didn't hear the phone ring. Or when the Jehovah's Witnesses show up at my door, I hide in the garage. I love my friends. I even have long talks with the Witnesses. But there are periods in my life when I become the Hermit herself and could do without people altogether.

Not so with animals. Where they are concerned, I always try to do what is ethical, especially when a critter enters my home uninvited.

Bobbi wrote a song called *Life in the Country* where she describes our hometown of Washington Boro. She sings of bucolic scenes of long dirt roads crossed by caterpillars and of slow-moving wagons winding their way through fields and farms. My sister and I are drawn to country living, and here in the Boro, we don't have neighborhood watch groups telling us that we can't hang out our wash or that our leaves can't lie on the ground in the fall. However, what we do have, as a sort of agricultural trade-off, is the occasional mouse sharing our quarters.

Now, mice are not the types of roommates to make themselves known. They are, instead, just one of those things that Bobbi and I choose to ignore, like that faint outline of a post-menopausal moustache. As long as they mind their own business, we just pretend that they're not in our houses. This strategy works most of the time, but now and then, we're faced with situations that require quick thinking and the willpower not to scream like a girl.

Many of these ordeals occur at night, as mice are nocturnal creatures who usually work second shift. As a result of an unusually mild winter one year, most of them stayed outside, enjoying the balmy temperatures or even taking family trips to the islands. Once the cold weather hit in February, though, they left their tropical playgrounds and ventured into my house. I was aware of their presence: I hadn't actually seen any of them, but I'd hear them scampering in the kitchen as I watched TV. Channeling my father, I would simply say over my shoulder, "Don't make me come out there." That was usually enough to quiet them. One particular night, though, all of that changed.

I was lying in bed when I heard the sound of rustling plastic coming from somewhere in the house. Thinking it could be a burglar or a ghost, I began to investigate, taking a marble bookend with me for protection. My sense of hearing took me closer to the bathroom, and turning on the light, I entered with trepidation. My suspicions were correct — the shower curtain was moving back and forth. Fear dissipated into relief, though, when I realized that burglars (at least the ones that I knew) didn't care about personal hygiene. And the intruder couldn't be a ghost for the same reason.

The curtain moved again. I called upon the strength that only insomniacs have and peeked inside the tub. There, looking up at me, was a baby mouse. The dogs slept peacefully, unaware of my situation, and I realized that the conflict of man vs. nature, written about so ubiquitously by Herman Melville, had come down to this, with a few literary distinctions: My symbol was not a whale, but a mouse; not in the ocean, but in my bathtub. As an animal-lover, my options were limited. I wasn't going to kill this creature because I try to be a catch-and-release kind of gal and also because I had no tiny harpoon.

Breaking his stare, he tried several times to jump out to safety. His athleticism was to no avail; his feet had nothing to grip, so he slid back down following every leap. Since all he needed was a little traction, I placed a wet washcloth over the side of the tub. He leapt, he gained his footing, and he was out.

I stayed up for a while, hoping he would find a place to bunk for the night far away from my bedroom. When I heard no stirrings, I assumed that he had gone back to his compound, so I went back to bed. I fell asleep quickly, as I assumed that the mouse had learned his lesson and wouldn't be back.

However, one night, about a week later, I opened the cabinet door under the kitchen sink to retrieve a bag of parakeet food. As I did so, I noticed that the bag was moving slightly. Since I had just taken three Tylenol PMs, I was aware of the fact that my brain was not functioning properly. But the drug had given me courage, and I knelt down to examine the bag more closely. It rustled again. Then, very slowly, a small head peaked out of the top and two sweet eyes made contact with mine. It was, as you may have guessed, my white whale.

Obviously, he was here to stay. And as long as he stayed out of sight, I didn't mind.

When I called Bobbi to ask if she'd seen any mice in her house lately, I hadn't yet told her about my recent experience. As she began to relate her tale, I was reminded of the fact that whenever she tells stories involving animals, the critters are always personified.

"I can give you a perfect example," she told me. "Last night, I was sitting in my blue chair in the living room and Berk was on the floor beside me. We heard some noise and both glanced toward my bedroom. The world's tiniest baby mouse had come out from under the bed and was slowly walking toward my kitchen. He was wearing a bandana around his neck, I think, and was carrying a little backpack. His mom probably told him it was time to strike out on his own. He saw us, and I think it freaked him out a little, but he knew that he had to cross the shipping lane."

"I don't know what that means."

"Well, when you're sailing, you have to be aware of the shipping lane. It's like a big highway on the ocean that oil tankers use. These ships are humongous, and so are their wakes. They can be three or four feet high. When you see one on the horizon coming right at you, you have to commit to either surfing it or going bow-first into it. Some scary shit."

"This happened to you?"

"Oh, sure. Couple of times."

"You never told me that. Did you ever tell Mom?"

"No."

"I guess for the same reason you never told me."

"Exactly."

Smart girl. I could picture Mom and me on the phone for hours while Bobbi sailed, sharing with each other the worst possible scenarios and debating what to do with her guitars after her certain demise.

"So the mouse was crossing the shipping lane of your kitchen floor. He saw you, but he'd already committed to crossing at that point and couldn't turn back."

"Right," Bobbi said. "He headed toward the open door and that was it. I assumed he'd gone outside."

"Your door wasn't shut?"

"Nah. The weather was great, so I'd propped it open. But the next morning, it started to rain, so I walked over to shut it, and that's when I saw him again. He was trying to get outside, but there was so much rain and wind coming in, even his umbrella was turned inside out."

"He must have taken off when he saw you coming."

"Yeah. I'm pretty sure he went under the stove. I shut the door and got a shoe box. I just put some bread and a piece of old flannel inside the box, turned it on its side, and put it next to the door. Then I went back to my bedroom to get dressed. I guess when I wasn't in the kitchen anymore, he got brave because when I came back out, he was curled up in his own personal Motel 6, sleeping. That's where he was when I left."

"You just walked over him and out the door?"

"Yep. He was dead asleep. And when I got home from work later that day, he was gone. He just left a little Airbnb note, thanking me. Gave me a good rating, too."

So Bobbi and I try to do the right thing when there's a critter in the house. Do we kill the occasional pissed-off hornet or charging rhinoceros? Of course. But if we can avoid doing so, we will. Thankfully, Bill's on board with this philosophy. I asked him about the upside of having mice in the house.

"Well, we allow the cycle of life to continue," he said. "And we're helping the environment. Mice are good at pest control. They eat insects, I think."

"Plus they're really cute," I said.

"Except if they start leaving their turds in my running shoes," Bill said. "Then we call the exterminator."

"But they're cute."

"We call the exterminator."

"For just one mouse?"

"It's never just one mouse, Annie. You know that."

Stupid Justice with her stupid double-edged sword.

The Sky Ride

HAVE YOU NOTICED HOW INNOCUOUS the cards have been up to this point? The Fool has met some lovely archetypes along his way: a magician, some religious figures, some mom-and-dad types. He's fallen in love, experienced victory, faced his fears, searched for inner truth, and has learned to be fair in his judgments. He also discovered when he encountered the Wheel that life doesn't always turn smoothly. However, even that card encouraged him to keep going because better days were sure to follow. Then he comes across this fellow, a man hanging upside-down on a cross, with one leg free and his hands tied behind his back. The image is understandingly disconcerting. I pulled this card for a friend of mine who had just broken up with her partner. Her exact response?

"Oh, dear God, Anne. That sounds just great."

She didn't have to worry, though, because all the Hanged Man is asking you to do is to look at a situation from a different perspective—in his case, upside-down. Once you're able to do this, you might notice various options available to you. In all areas of my life, when things go asunder, I attempt to replace my anxiety with the strength and stability of the Hanged Man. Unknowingly, I'd even applied his lessons during one traumatic experience I'd had as a teenager.

Friends and family over the years have asked me to retell this tale so often that it smacks of urban legend. However, I can assure you that it is all true and well documented. Refer to the sketch featured on this chapter's card illustration. My sister drew it on the last page of my high school yearbook in 1973. I offer it as proof positive of the event I'm about to relate.

When I was fifteen years old, I worked at Dutch Wonderland, a family amusement park here in Lancaster. A lot of kids my age were employed there, as the pay was phenomenal (about $1.35 an hour, I think) and the job was easy. We operated the

THE HANGED MAN

rides, which back then included everything from giant slides to a haunted, swinging house. A few of the assignments required some physical work. I remember, for example, having to walk carefully across the bumper car floor, fearing death by electrocution, to free some cars that had become entangled in others. Most of our jobs, though, involved nothing more than making sure the guest was properly placed in the ride before we turned it on.

The easiest of all attractions to operate was the Sky Ride, a ski lift that took guests from one end of the park to the other and back again. All we had to do was have the child (or the adult who desperately needed a break from this child) stand at the line on the platform and sit down in the cart as it scooped him up from behind. Nothing could have been easier. There were no start or stop buttons to push, no long-winded words of caution to offer. We simply walked alongside the cart as it moved toward the end of the platform, and we lowered the safety bar around the rider. He was on his way, up, up in the air, as we walked back to our station and performed the same task for the next customer.

One Saturday, I had been assigned to work this ride. It was late in the day and the guests were dwindling. I hadn't had a customer for over ten minutes at this point, but then a young boy of about twelve years old climbed the steps of the platform and handed me his ticket. I punched it and told him to wait at the line on the floor. Like most boys his age, he had the personality of a doorknob, said nothing, and did as he was told. The cart slowly approached him from the rear, he sat down, and I did exactly as I had been instructed during training: lower the safety bar while walking beside the cart and return to my station a few steps behind me. This would have been fine except for one small detail.

When I tried turning around, I found that I was stuck and was being pulled alongside of the moving contraption. I realized my mistake immediately. I had stood too close to the cart when I lowered the bar, and now a large wad of my vest was pinched securely under the hinge. In about five seconds, the cart would be airborne, and I would be dangling from it.

I didn't panic. I knew that there was an emergency "stop" pad at the very end of the platform so that people could change their minds about their excursion at the last minute. Step on the pad, and the ride would come to a halt.

I did. It didn't.

All I could do was wrap both of my hands around the pole on the side of the cart, hang on like Mary Poppins, and pray. The Sky Ride began its trek, slowly lifting me off my feet into the air. I was now eye-level with the boy and glanced over at him. He still said nothing. I had nothing to offer, either. I returned my gaze to what lie ahead of me—the entire park in all its Wonderland glory. We climbed higher and higher. No one was left on the platform to see this spectacle, and I wondered if I were going to have to make a round trip before anyone could rectify the situation. This awkward silence between the boy and myself was beginning to annoy me, so I turned to him and said, "I'm stuck."

I got nothing back. He never even made eye contact. At his age, girls were filled with cooties, and here I was, spreading them all over his joyride.

We continued the climb in silence. Finally, a co-worker walking through the park miraculously glanced up and saw what was taking place. She screamed, ran to the platform, and shut down the ride. The boy and I had almost made it to the first pole and were about 50 feet in the air, just hanging there. And not talking.

By this time, I was high enough for the entire population of Dutch Wonderland to see me. People ran from all over, like ants scurrying toward a breadcrumb, and stopped directly underneath me. They began shouting orders, such as, "Kick your feet into the seat!" With no upper-body strength, I tried this unsuccessfully a couple of times, while the boy made some half-hearted attempts at grabbing one of my feet. He saw the cooties, however, and gave up. I continued to hang. "Can you take off your vest, at least?" someone yelled. "Not doing that!" I yelled back. "It's the only thing that's keeping me up here!" and it was, unless one counts the stimulating conversation.

Finally, some kind of truck with an extension ladder made its way through the park and stopped below us. A maintenance man climbed up, wrapped his arms around me, released my vest from the hinge, and walked us both down the ladder to the ground.

The crowd was quiet. They all seemed to be waiting for me to say something, an explanation of what had happened, perhaps, or for me to just collapse. I looked back at them. Concern covered their faces. Finally, a large woman in the front held out her arms and said, "Honey, you just come on over here, now," and as I walked quickly to her, I began to cry. I collapsed into her arms, and her ample bosom provided a pillow for my head.

Once I was able to collect myself, I was escorted to my boss's office where I was offered a seat and a Coke. He expressed great concern for me, and after I stopped sniffling and assured him that I was fine, he sent me back out to finish my shift.

When I got home that night, I told Bobbi what happened. Had we acknowledged the difference in our sexuality at this time in our lives, she would have said how mightily impressed she was that a straight girl like me could have pulled off such a feat. Instead, she just nodded her head in silent approval.

Now, Mom and Dad were away that weekend in New Jersey, and when they got home the next day, I related my story to them. Like the crowd in the park, they stared at me.

"You know," Mom finally said, her face showing more than a hint of disgust, "just *once* I wish that your father and I could go away without one of you girls getting into trouble." And the conversation, if you can call it that, was over. At least Mom was able to form a complete sentence, as opposed to The Boy in the Cart. (I have no idea what happened to him, by the way. For all I know, they let him finish his ride.)

When I think back to that summer day in 1972, what amazes me most is that there were no discussions of a lawsuit. No parents calling my boss to complain about poor working conditions. No press releases accusing Dutch Wonderland of violating child labor laws. Just a gal getting stuck on a sky ride.

So if you find yourself wishing that things could be that simple today, remember that they can be. Just trust the Hanged Man and look at them from a different perspective.

Death Takes a Holiday

THE FOOL CONTINUES on his life's journey by discovering, right in the middle of it, Death. If I were he, after all the lessons I'd learned and all of the advice I'd taken from sages and kings, I'd be more than a bit put off. "For real?" I'd ask God. "I've been through 13 steps along this path, have been schooled in everything I need to know, and now, as a reward, I get to die? Nice. I should have trusted my instincts and taken this course online."

And why wouldn't anyone feel that way? A skeleton encased in black armor is riding a horse through human carnage. At his feet are people from every realm of life. Some are already dead, some are in the process of dying, and some are mourning the loss of their loved ones. He even brandishes a sickle just in case the idea of a skeleton on a horse headed our way isn't making its point clearly enough.

But here's the good news: Death also has a lot going for him. First, he always carries the banner of life, a flag that features a black background and white roses. The horse he rides is a white one. Like a knight in shining armor, he's coming to rescue all of us from our bad patterns. He's going to be the death of them all.

So God does have a plan for the Fool, but it's not a physical death. The card simply implies the need to change, to close one chapter of life and move on. This may not be something that you want, but the card is wise and understands that it's time for you to evolve.

All of this is just dandy unless you're someone like me who thinks about death constantly; who lies awake at night wondering what's out there, up there, or down there; who's read more than enough books about near-death experiences and past-life regressions; and who always wonders if today is her last. Bill sees pictures of me as a toddler, notices the expression on my face, and says, "You were thinking about death then, weren't you?" And he's right. Now, there was probably no conscious ponderance of death arising in my two-year-old mind, but I'm sure that it made its way in there by the time I was three.

I assumed that everyone was like me. Who wouldn't think about dying once you knew that it could happen at any minute? Well, Bobbi wouldn't, apparently, which I discovered during one of our late-night telephone interviews.

XIII

DEATH

"Don't you think about it all the time?" I asked her.

"What? Death? Not really."

"No kidding. You just really never wonder about it."

"No. Even when we were little and went to funerals, it never freaked me out."

"You didn't stare at the body thinking it would all of a sudden sit up in the coffin and start talking?"

"No. Did you?"

"God, no. I just was curious if you did. That's stupid. A body sitting up in a coffin . . . ."

Of course I thought about it. I always figured that if I stared at the dead person long enough, I could make him come to life. That's why, to this day, I just breeze past any open casket with nary a look at its contents. And the idea that my powers were greater than death came from, I'm sure, a story that our dad loved to relate about a funeral during his childhood.

He lived in the Coal Regions of Pennsylvania, and when a family member died, the body was laid out in his or her home. Mourners would come visit, pay their respects, and eat. Funeral homes were a relatively new idea in the 1930s, and apparently, my father's family looked at them the same way I look at computers: with suspicion, fear, and the feeling that these new-fangled ideas are just a passing fad.

My dad's uncle had passed away, and his body rested in the second-floor bedroom of his house. The family walked the stairs to pay their respects and afterwards returned to the dining room where the women had cooked copious amounts of food for the wake. My grandfather had eight children of his own, and his brothers and sisters also had large families, so kids were everywhere at these events. Cousins and siblings, no matter how young, were expected to view the body, and after the mourning itself was over, they played in the parlor or the yard and ran around the kitchen, generally causing havoc until one of the women grabbed them by the ear.

This was the scene at the funeral of my father's uncle, Charles, a man who died relatively young, in his 60s, as most coal miners did. Dad never told us much about Charles himself except for the fact that he played the cello and that he did so beautifully.

I'm assuming that everything had been going swimmingly until the sound of that cello came from upstairs. These weren't the rich tones of the instrument that one would hear at a concert; it sounded more like two cats mating, incorporating the cello's strings in a sort of feline "Fifty Shades of Grey" tryst. The adults put down their plates and hustled to the bottom of the stairs. Looking up, they saw my father's dead uncle seated in a straight-backed chair, his beloved cello resting between his open legs, and his hand clutching the bow that was being dragged over the strings. His expression remained the same as when he died, of course, but I'm sure that a hint of "What the fuck?"edness had made its way to his countenance.

Upon closer inspection, it was clear to those watching that a small boy was kneeling behind the chair, and that it was his hand that moved Charles' arm. My great-uncle clasped the bow in his clenched fist, but it was Dad's cousin George who was animating this nightmare. Other lads scurried behind the scene, snickering and helping to prop up Charles when he would lose his balance and sway from side to side. (This must have happened often because Charles had no balance to lose, as he was dead, despite the concert that he was giving at the moment.)

It didn't take long for the men to rush upstairs, grab the boys by their collars, and escort them down to the women where the real fun began. My father had been a member of the stage crew for this musical, and what he remembers most was his mother flicking his earlobe repeatedly while he wiggled to escape. (Unfamiliar with this type of corporal punishment, I once did the same to my earlobe. It hurts a lot. But I don't have to tell you that because you just tried it, didn't you?)

I don't know what happened next. Your guess that the men of the family placed Charles back on his bed and continued with the funeral may be correct. Or perhaps the festivities were over at the point. But Dad laughed his way through the retelling of this tale for decades after, with little regard to how it impacted one of his daughters and exaggerated her fears of death.

"Didn't that scare you at all?" I asked Bobbi. "I mean, it was funny and everything, but it always gave me the creeps."

"Oh, I thought it was hysterical," she said. "I think if it were anyone but Dad telling the story, it might have been creepy. But it was Dad."

"Yeah. I guess it was humorous. In a bizarre sort of way. But it really makes you think."

"About what? About death? Or about Dad?"

"Well, both," I told her, "since Dad's dead. And we'll all be dead, one of these days."

"Why do you keep thinking about this stuff?"

"I don't know."

"I'm hanging up. You wanna meet at Turkey Hill for some junk food?"

And this is how most conversations end between Bobbi and me. The Death card, after all, does ask that we stop what we're doing and surrender, even to a bag of chips and some ice cream.

A Solid Block of Me

SO YOU AND THE FOOL DIDN'T DIE. All of your worries about pulling the Death card were for naught. But if you're like me, you'll save any near-death experience and use it in the future when your partner is angry with you for something silly, like inadvertently turning off the crock pot when you're cleaning up the kitchen. (Bill gets so testy sometimes.) All you have to do at this point is remind the person that you "almost died." I have used this explanation plenty of times, and it has always tempered Bill's anger. He balances my mistakes with the idea that I'm thankfully still around to make them. That's the idea of the Temperance card—balance in all parts of your life, from relationships to crock pots.

The card features an angel standing by a water's edge, pouring liquid from one goblet to another, back and forth, like a cosmic bartender. What exactly is in each cup? Some decks suggest it is hot and cold water representing the conscious and subconscious mind, while others imply that the liquid is indicative of the past flowing into the present. Either way, things are mixing together amiably now, two opposites being tempered in a smooth, easy rhythm.

Temperance reminds us to take into account other people's opinions and to mix theirs with ours. I wish that the nurse at the doctor's office had mixed my opinion with hers a few years ago. I had called because I felt like a vise was twisting my insides, but since I didn't have a fever, she assured me that my symptoms were nothing serious. Perhaps it was something I ate, she said, or maybe it was just a mild case of the flu. I called two days in a row, but the nurse still didn't think that my symptoms warranted a trip to the office. To make this situation even worse, Bill was away on a camping trip, and I had no one to bitch to, no one to listen to my fears of dying, no one to just kill me and end this suffering once and for all. (This is probably why Bill goes away so often—my tendency to exaggerate any illness I may have to Kevorkian levels.)

For some reason, though, Bill decided to come home early, saw the mess that was his girlfriend, and called the doctor's office to tell him that we were coming in immediately. He went into what I call "Business Bill" mode, where there is no room for discussion or other people's opinions, and most of all, no room for temperance. I find him quite sexy when he morphs into this entity, and normally, I'd have acted on this impulse. I did consider asking him for one last fling, as I was quite sure that I was never coming home, but the pain was too much at that point.

After about 15 seconds with the doctor, he told us that I had appendicitis. We had two choices—he would call an ambulance or Bill would drive me to the hospital. Bill chose the latter and before long, I was in the emergency room. Someone was finally listening to me.

I was examined by a surgeon who pushed on my belly and confirmed my doctor's diagnosis: severe appendicitis. To this day, I am convinced that the expression I made during that exam replaced the one in the pain-face scale for "Hurts Worse." In fact, I'm pretty sure that this phrase was changed to "Fucking Hurts Like a Son-of-a-Bitch," but I can't be sure. The hospital has refused my requests for copyright information.

I was in and out of surgery in about three hours and placed in a room where I was told that not only had my appendix almost burst, but it had been leaking over the past couple of days. As a result of this, I had begun to develop peritonitis. In other words, my poo was escaping from somewhere and attaching itself to my other organs. (That's as medically specific as I can be.) I didn't care. All I knew was that a majority of my pain was gone, and I looked forward to getting home in a day or two.

But that wasn't going to happen. It seems that peritonitis can be a little complicated. Days of intravenous antibiotics were needed to clear the infection. In the meantime, due to the operation, taking deep breaths was painful, so I decided not to breathe a lot. As a result, my lungs started to collapse. Then I developed a rash all over my back from the anesthesia. I had no waistline to speak of anymore and resembled a large rectangle, as I was filled with gas from the surgery. Worst of all, my hair looked like I had gone through a screen door head-first.

Bobbi and Bill were worried. Bill says I looked grey. Bobbi says I looked dead. Day after day they came to see me — or so they say. I had lost track of time and while I remember a few of their visits, I wasn't clear-headed enough to be good company. The operation had taken a lot out of me (my appendix, my dignity), leaving me very little interest in social norms.

In retrospect, my whole hospital experience should have been an awful one for me, but it wasn't. It was actually beyond pleasant because I had made two new friends while I was there: Percocet and oxycodone. They were by my side as soon as I came out of the operating room, and they stayed with me for the week that I was in the hospital. I'd never met anyone like them. They were loyal and caring and giving, and they asked for nothing in return.

I lived for these drugs and kept a close eye on the clock, counting down the hours when the Angel of Mercy would enter my room with that tiny paper cup. These pills took away my pain and elevated my mood. They also put me into another dimension sometimes, but I was fine with that. I didn't realize, though, how quirky I was getting until Bobbi put together a list of text messages, word for word, letter for letter, that I had sent her over the course of the last four days of my hospital stay.

Bill had given me his iPad to use while I was recovering, and I was unfamiliar with how to activate the autocorrect feature. My inability to navigate this particular piece of technology made for some interesting messages. Here, then, are the top eight, for your perusal and enjoyment. You should be able to translate them easily, based on what I've written above. At the end of this chapter, you will find the corrected versions. Enjoy playing this 21st century version of "Find the Hidden Pictures" (a game that

I always hated, as I could never find anything except that stupid hammer and that damn toothbrush).

1. "Those breaths are pain little Dickrson I tell va$."
2. "So they told me that is Colleen normal sincere appendix basically bezplodexx! I'm o Per set now!"
3. "Oh, and I have a rash and itchiness from the American Institute."
4. "I'm Alleppo g a close wath on a clock. Was supposed to have pith at at 12 and the every six hours. Sibwell see what happens!"
5. "A solid block of me."
6. "Boy, I'm having Chicago vets atoms with people who aren't here!"
7. "So it no I ill walk down and yell male it stop! Nnnnnnn."
8. "She came and unplugged it! I reiterated the necessity if getting the sites Snd myedsijinbhera ASAP!"

Percocet, it turns out, bade me farewell when I was discharged, but my oxi stayed with me for another week. When its job was done, I was so grateful that I wrote a song parody in its honor. When my sister and I performed it at the Ware Center in Lancaster, the mayor and his wife approached me after the show. He told me how much he loved the song but that I'd forgotten about one side effect of the drug: constipation.

His wife interrupted him. "No, she didn't, honey. Remember the second verse? She said that it doesn't help you poo."

Oh, boy. Were the mayor and his wife actually going to start arguing about the lyrics of this song, one that covered so sensitive a topic? I held my breath.

"Oh!" he said, chuckling "I must have missed that part." And they were on their way, marital discord easily tempered.

≈

Text Messages Correctly Written

1. Those breaths are painful little dickens, I tell ya."
2. "So they tell me that all of this pain is normal since my appendix basically exploded! I'm on percocet now."
3. "Oh, and I have a rash and itchiness from the anesthesia."
4. "I'm keeping a close watch on the clock. Was supposed to have a pill at 12 and then every six hours. We'll see what happens!"
5. "A solid block of me." (This is the only correctly written message and one that aptly described my figure.)
6. "Boy, I'm having conversations with people who aren't here!"
7. "So now, I'll walk down and yell, 'Make it stop!!!!!!'" (The *Nnnnnnn's* at the end were my attempt at multiple exclamation points.)
8. "She came and unplugged it! I reiterated the necessity of getting the pills and my edsjinbhera ASAP!" (Your guess is as good as mine.)

CARD 15: THE DEVIL

Don't Get Too Happy

THE FOOL HAS LEARNED MUCH about his ability to bring opposing sides together after he encountered Temperance on his journey. Not only has he avoided the hazards of archetypes such as Death and the Hanged Man, but he can now be known as The Great Compromiser, one who can summon peace in a chaotic environment. All in all, he must be feeling pretty smug right now. Pretty cocky. Pretty self-righteous. But then he meets the Devil.

And isn't that just always the way?

Your life is going along quite nicely. Your hair looks great, your partner's cute, your house is sort of clean, you ate one pack of M&M's instead of three—aren't you just the big girl now? Why, you're so happy and in such control that you let your joy get a bit out of hand. You start to get a little too secure in this cocoon of yours, wrapped up snugly in all of your accomplishments. And then a tiny voice whispers in your ear, "Not so fast, Little Missy. I have a few surprises in store for you. . . . "

The idea of Not Getting Too Happy has been around for a while. We all go through it at one time or another. We don't want the universe to see us enjoying ourselves so much that we forget who's in control. I don't know where this thought process originated, but it clings to us the same way that an annoying middle child clings to her mother. We can't shake it, and when we try, we feel like social services is going to show up on our doorstep within the hour.

I immediately fall into this mindset when I pull the Devil card. "Just swell," I think. "Look at him with those bat wings and those horns and that goat face. Just sittin' there on that block of concrete, glowering at me, those hairy legs of his all exposed. And those claws. For the love of God, I swear I kind of look like him. I haven't shaved my legs all winter. I haven't had a pedicure in two years. But why bother getting coiffed? I drew this card. I might as well give up. No beauty regimen is gonna save me now."

My gut instincts are correct to a point. The Devil is frightening and can be a portent of doom. Not only is he beastly to behold, but also, on the block on which he sits, he has chained a man and a woman, both naked, both ashamed. They seem to be imprisoned by dark forces, held captive by bad habits and beliefs from which they can't break free.

I called Bobbi to ask if she'd ever found herself being cautious when things were really going her way.

"You've got to be kidding me," she said. "Sure I did. But I always refer to it as the Sleeping Out Syndrome."

"That again? Can't you just let it go?"

"You're the one who brought it up."

"For God's sake. The last time that happened was, what, 1968?"

"No, it didn't. It just happened last week."

This Sleeping Out Syndrome that Bobbi is so fond of reliving began in our childhood. We grew up on Locust Lane in Willow Street, Pennsylvania. (The fact that our town was named after a street should give you some idea of the neighborhood's metropolitan feel.) Farmers' fields bordered our back yard, giving us the impression that we owned about 30 acres of land. While residential, the development was a quiet one, with no streetlights or sidewalks. On any given summer evening, you could find nine- and ten-year-olds from several houses dragging their sleeping bags and pillows to one common backyard.

We'd usually start out at dusk because we could get in a good round of our favorite game, *Daniel Boone*, before settling in for the night. After our camping gear was thrown to the ground, we would gather in council to choose our parts wisely: Daniel, himself; Israel, his son; Rebecca, his wife; and Mingo, his trusted Native American ally. (I was not really allowed to pick my part but instead was handed—usually by Bobbi—the role of Rebecca. I got to stay in the homestead and pretend to cook coffee and eggs for the menfolk as they went out on adventures. Fun.)

The rest of our friends who weren't playing major characters in our little show filled in as other frontiersmen and native people. I don't remember us "killing" each other, really. We'd just run into the cornfields and hide from each other amidst the growing crop. Corn stalks are itchy, for sure, but they provided an intricate maze in which to avoid our opponents. (Not that I'd know, as I was back at the imaginary farmhouse preparing deer and rabbit and fetching water from the well. And maybe sewing.)

The game usually took about an hour. Then we'd crawl into our sleeping bags and get ready for ghost stories and hot chocolate, served to us by mothers whose grinning faces humbly expressed gratitude for a night without children under roof. Most of us fell asleep within the hour, except for me. I was always wide awake, thinking about death, aliens, and burglars, and I'd eventually go inside where I'd be safe from all of the above. This was fine with Bobbi, as she had several other comrades with her throughout the night.

Sometimes, however, Bobbi and I would get a hankerin' to sleep out on our own, just the two of us. (The vernacular into which I just slipped was a common one among us while we played our Boone game. It had to be. "Look out for that critter by the Snake Tree, Dan'l!" could not be replaced by, "SHIT! There's that big, honkin' snake under the tree, and he's coming after you again, Daniel! RUN!" We were historically accurate, if nothing else.)

"You wanna sleep out tonight?" Bobbi would ask me in the morning.

"Sure," I'd say. It always sounded like a good idea in the morning.

By the time the evening rolled around, though, I'd be thinking about my bed and the warmth of the house. Coupled with these comforts was the protection of Mom and Dad from all things dangerous and unholy, so that by the end of the day, I had lost my ambition.

But not Bobbi. I'd glance out of the kitchen window in the early evening and see her setting up for the night. Both sleeping bags were laid out, and our pillows were appropriately placed. Her joy was uncontained until she walked up to the back porch and called to me through the screen door.

"You ready?"

"Well. I don't know. I don't really feel like it, Bob."

"But you said!"

"I know. But it's cold outside."

So Bobbi would sleep out by herself, a nine-year-old girl curled up in her sleeping bag, with an empty one resting on the ground beside her. If that image isn't enough to make you weep a little, let me help you along: This scenario took place a lot—IF you're believing Bobbi's side of the story. I feel like it only happened four or five times, at best. Bobbi says that it was a recurring event that slithered its way through our entire child-hood, just like that angry snake who kept showing up in our Boone game. Whatever the case may be, the entire experience has colored her relationship with me to this day, as she made clear during our conversation.

"It happened just last week? Come on," I told her. "I haven't slept out in about 15 years."

"Yeah, but you're still doing the same thing."

"No I'm not."

"Yeah. You are. Remember you always said how much fun it would be to go grab breakfast, like I do, but you couldn't because you were working? And how after you retired, you'd be doing all kinds of stuff like that with me?"

"I do stuff."

"Yeah, as long as it's in your house. Or five miles away."

I had no retort, as she was correct. She has asked me numer-ous times to join her and her friends for dinner at a diner, or a musical event, or a gathering of lesbians summoning the Goddess of Water somewhere. I usually say no.

I felt bad about this. But then I remembered that the chains that bind the man and woman to the Devil are loose and remind us that we can break bad habits. I was determined to do that now.

"Well, I'm sorry, Bob. I really am. I'll try to do better. I promise."

"OK. So a bunch of us are going to go see a show on Broadway this summer. You in?"

"No."

"Shocking."

"Why can't we just all go to Kmart or something?"

"Because that's depressing, Anne, and so are you."

I guess in this sibling relationship, Bobbi drew the Devil card from the moment she was born. But that's probably what has made her the strong, independent woman that she is, one who laughs off disappointments and goes on her way to more adventures.

I, on the other hand, realizing how I have damaged Bobbi forever, am on my way to see my therapist. I may be there for a while. But that's OK. Her office is only four minutes from my house.

Worrying about Wildebeests

AFTER HE'S MET THE DEVIL, the Fool knows that he can break the chains that bind him to bad habits and ideas. He goes merrily along his way, his attitude uplifted. However, his journey doesn't end just because he's learned a lesson or two. He's reminded of this when the skies around him become foreboding and he sees the Tower.

Sitting precariously upon a rocky mountaintop in the darkness, this stone building is being struck by a lightning bolt. Flames are shooting from the tower's windows, and the people inside of it are being tossed out or are jumping out, hurtling to the ground as the structure begins to collapse. The tower is beginning to crumble amidst the conflagration, and the situation is out of control.

However, the Fool can find hope even in this catastrophe when he remembers what he learned from the Devil. His life must change, and he sees that it needs to do so immediately—this fire isn't going away. Its dangers are present. His former paradigm wasn't working for him, yet he did feel safe behind the walls that kept his thoughts and beliefs intact. However, his tower was nothing more than a false sense of safety, and now that he sees how things really are, his security is crumbling. If he doesn't move quickly, he'll be back to his old way of life which could be the death of him. The Tower can signify that one's life will be turned upside-down without any notice at all, and this is what had happened to Bobbi.

Her landlords decided to tear down the old house she had rented from them for almost 30 years and build one in its place for their married daughter. They were good people who had always welcomed her to their farm property as a tenant. Bobbi understood that this was something they had to do, so she held no ill feelings toward them. However, she loved her home and its surroundings. Losing it was like losing a family member, for her and for all of us. Suddenly, she had to find a new place to live, and where could she find a house with the privacy and natural setting that she needed? The turmoil that the Tower can cause in one's life happens very suddenly, and it mirrored Bobbi's experience. She did find a place that she loves, but we still can't look back on her period of transition fondly. I didn't want to relive the destruction of Bobbi's tower, and I was sure that she didn't, either.

So what to ask. What. To. Ask. I started thinking about belief systems, and I wondered if she'd ever had to shed any of hers.

"I'm not sure what you mean."

"Well, did you ever believe something to be true for most of your life, and then, one day, you realize that what you thought was so, really wasn't so?"

"I still have no idea what you're talking about."

"Really. Because I thought I was crystal clear." I knew that I wasn't. A fog had rolled into my mind and surrounded any kind of clarity I might have had. "Well, I can give you some of my own examples, but that might cloud your judgment."

"No, no. Go ahead. That might be good."

"OK. Well, for one thing, I used to think that I had to style my hair all the time. Even on ponytail days, I'd get out the curling iron. And then I realized, 'You know what? The world is not going to end if my hair isn't perfect.' See what I mean?"

"Sort of," she said. "You realized that nobody really cares about your hair except you."

"Well, that's mean."

"Sorry. I just don't even think about my hair."

I feared that I was approaching a dead end and was considering throwing *myself* out of a tower. Suddenly, a thought appeared, and I tried a new approach.

"Look at it this way," I said. "Let's talk about worry. What do you worry about?"

This is what she said: " -------------------------------------
----
---"

It was the longest pause in any conversation we'd ever had. I considered ending the call right then, but I was beyond curious at this point.

"Wow, Bobbi. You don't worry about anything, do you?"

"I try not to. I mean, if I do start to worry about something, I just put it out of my head."

I wish I could do the same. I wish I could laugh at this demon of mine and send it on its way, just like I do with fear.

"You're a lot more prone to thinking about bad stuff than I am," she continued. "And some of it is pretty out there." She was right. To prove it, here's a (partial) list of stuff that makes me worry, and Bobbi's reaction to each item.

1. If I leave the back door of the house propped open like you do, a wild animal will walk in.

   "OK. That word 'walk.' First, all I can picture is a herd of wildebeests running full-speed around Washington Boro. I can hear them yelling, 'We're so fucking hungry! Look! There's an open door!' Then they jump your fence, slow their gait, wipe their hooves on your mat, and gently walk into your kitchen. You realize, of course, that this will never happen. Or maybe you don't." (Well, I didn't, until she put the idea into my head.)

2. If I don't get at least six servings of fruits and vegetables a day, I'm convinced that I'll be dead by the end of the week.

   "Just throw some canned peaches on your cereal a couple times a month. That should do it."

3. If I sleep under any kind of framed picture, it could fall in the middle of the night and split my head open.

73

"I remember. You'd never sleep on my couch because of that cool painting I have. You know the title of it is 'Afternoon Visit,' right? You probably called it 'Death Hanging on the Wall.' You're insane."

4. When I'm done with the toaster, I always unplug it in case some kind of power surge will start a fire.

"OK, I'm with you on this one. I'll never even move a toaster if it's plugged in. Do you remember that I got shocked by the oven when were were kids and nobody cared?" (I didn't remember, I guess because nobody cared.)

5. If I don't use the bathroom before I leave the house in the morning, I'll have to use a public restroom with other people around. And I hate that."

"You know me. I can go anywhere. I don't care about the people around me. The only thing I care about now are those long toilet farts I'm leaving when I start to sit down. I'm turning into Mom."

6. I keep all clocks in my house set five minutes ahead so that I'm never late. My car's clock is set 13 minutes ahead for the same reason, and to keep me from getting into accidents.

"I don't understand any of this."

No wonder I had a difficult time discussing this card with Bobbi. She has very few chains to break and no towers from which to jump. She's pretty secure in how she runs her life. I envy that. But it also makes me concerned for her. Doesn't she need something to worry about? Isn't that part of life? How can she get up, day after day after day, without a written agenda of *Things That Can Go Wrong and Ways That I Can Prevent Them From Doing So?*

In short, Bobbi doesn't worry. And that worries me. I should probably add that to my list.

The Glasses

THIS HAS BEEN QUITE A JOURNEY for the Fool, and he needs a break. He's finally getting one in these last five Major Arcana cards, and I, for one, am happy for him. If you rounded up the directors of *The Exorcist, The Sixth Sense,* and *The Towering Inferno,* you still couldn't get a better movie than the one the Fool has survived. He finally gets his reprieve when he sees the Star resting in the sky above a woman. Vulnerable and trusting, she is kneeling at the edge of a pond and pouring water from two clay urns. One is being emptied onto the ground, forming five small streams while the other is flowing into a pond. Neither of the urns runs dry, symbolizing the continuity of Source replenishing us as we travel through life. Like all stars that act as maps of the sky, this card provides inspiration and hope for the end of our journey. Our faith is restored. The universe is good, abundant, and caring, and we are filled with self-confidence.

Any musician needs to feel this way when going on stage, and Bobbi and I are no different. When we decided to form a duo, however, it was a challenge for me. Bobbi had always performed either by herself or in duos and trios.

I, on the other hand, had fronted bands for 20 years, being the chick out front playing guitar with four or five other musicians behind me. That was my comfort zone. I could make minor mistakes and no one would notice. I could forget lyrics and make them up as I went along, or play a A minor 7th chord instead of a C. Who was going to care? Not the dancers in front of me who were gyrating and posing. Not even the band behind me; the caterwauling guitars and pounding drums masked my ineptitude, and I saw this as a gift, a kind of musical camouflage. But standing beside just one person without even an instrument in front of me? This was going to be a new experience and one that was a bit frightening.

Bobbi and I both knew that we needed something to set ourselves apart from the onslaught of acoustic duos that were invading the bars back in the early 90s. We decided to rely on our sense of humor to provide not only some originality to our show but also a smokescreen to hide my feelings of insecurity. The crowd's response was positive and added an extra shot of inner strength for me. We sang well. We were funny. What could go wrong?

We were playing the Lancaster Dispensing Company one night and were debuting a parody I wrote entitled "Bifocals." The song described my need for stronger glasses as I aged, and it could have stood on its own merit. However, Bobbi had phoned me earlier in the day to tell me that she had just bought something to make the song even better. When she pulled into my driveway that evening, she was grinning so hard, I thought she'd had a stroke.

"Just wait 'til you see this," she said, getting out of her car and handing me a paper bag. "I got these at the Dollar Store. This is gonna be great."

Out of the bag, I pulled a pair of jumbo plastic sunglasses, 11 inches wide. She told me that I should wear them when I sang the new song. "People will love it," she said.

I tried them on but injured myself when I turned to look at her, the glasses hitting the open door of her car and jamming themselves into my face. "I don't think these are going to be funny," I told her.

"Well, that was."

"*Nobody's* going to think these are funny."

"Yes, they will! They will! They will!"

Still not convinced, but deferring to her expertise, I agreed. I'd wear the glasses. What could go wrong? (One of these days, I'm going to stop asking myself that question.)

As we performed that evening, the crowd was receptive. They clapped at the appropriate times, requested a few numbers, and smiled encouragingly. Sensing that the time was right, we gave a brief introduction to the song. Bobbi started playing as I picked up the glasses from my gear bag behind me, donned them, and began singing.

People stopped talking and stared briefly at the stage. Then they went back to their conversations. There were no guffaws or even mild giggling. This joke had gone over like a tofu side dish at a pig roast. And there stood Bobbi and I, trapped on our spit, as it were, twirling about in our minds various ways of making an easy exit from the stage. However, we were still in mid-song dying a slow, painful comedic death. But mine was worse. I was the one wearing the glasses.

We had no choice but to continue and were hopeful that the next portion of the song would create some levity in the room. I forged ahead, singing lyrics that described my inability to walk without bumping into things unless I had these over-sized monstrocities attached to my face. Maybe that line would grant us a last-minute reprieve.

But the governor never called. Any hope we might have had perished with our dignity. And there were still two verses to go.

I slowly turned my head to the left—as I couldn't do so rapidly without the glasses knocking over my mic stand—and stared at my sister. I said nothing, but, as siblings are apt to do, she was able to read my mind.

"Fuck. Bobbi." The words were as clear to her as if I'd said them aloud.

We finished the song to no applause and didn't think that things could get any worse. I'm sure, by now, you know that they did.

From the back of the room, we noticed an elderly gentleman with a cane walking slowly toward the stage. As he approached us, we suspected that he was going to request a new song, or just offer condolences for that last one. But as both of us graciously leaned forward to accept his comments, he said gruffly, "Cut the schtick and just play the music."

He never stopped to hear any response that we might have offered. He just dropped that verbal bombshell in mid-stride and kept shuffling toward the men's room.

Sometimes in life, you may be feeling defeated because what started out as an inspired idea now has you questioning your original intents. But you'll find hope for the future when you encounter the Star's light, even if it is a little dimmed from the oversized sunglasses that your sister made you wear.

Little Joe's Horse

THE FOOL CONTINUES ON HIS JOURNEY, filled with the self-assurance that he received from the Star. In this nocturnal part of his adventure, he comes upon a dog and a wolf who gaze at the Moon. This is a card of psychic insights, imagination, and intuition. We're being called to tap into our subconscious, investigate what lurks there, and welcome it. Tarot has encouraged self-exploration before but only on a basic level. Now, it's time for us to go deeper into our psyche and bring to new heights what the other cards have taught us.

I've done just that with my addiction to chocolate and now, thanks to tarot, I am totally fine with eating three brownies in one sitting. I have explored the brownie options available to me, have discarded the ones made with kale, and have embraced the Betty Crocker side of life. That I enjoy these treats at night enhances the experience of the Moon card for me, and if I get any more enlightened, I might just explode.

Digging into our hidden demons can be downright unsettling, so this card often has dark overtones. We keep our fears under cover for good reason: they scare us. To make matters worse, they sometimes manifest themselves in our nightmares, and we awaken filled with anxiety and dread. Some people tell us to record our dreams in a journal as soon as we wake up and before they vaporize. I've never been an advocate of this activity. I lean toward eating another brownie and watching an episode of *Frasier* until the dream dissipates. (This is especially true for dreams in which I appear naked, usually *in* an episode of *Frasier*.) Bobbi's method of handling bad dreams, as you'll remember, is to call me.

Her nightmare about Lorne Greene and the King of Scotland had always interested me. It scared the pants off of her (if, indeed, she were wearing any at the time), but we never discussed its implications. After she had awakened, her emotions were running high and she felt vulnerable. But to what or to whom? We obviously needed to discuss it again. Since I'd once read a book by Carl Jung, I fancied myself a master of all things psychoanalytical. I therefore tried to frame my questions to reflect my genius.

"So, let's start with Lorne Greene," I began. "You watched a lot of *Bonanza* as a kid. What did you like about that show?"

"Oh, well, first of all, that green denim jacket of Little Joe's. He always kept his collar up, and this was in the '60s, you know, before it was really cool to do that."

"So your dream was in color? Interesting. Anything other than the clothes?"

"Well, there were the horses. You know, they always seemed to match the characters. Like, Ben had this really cool quarter horse, dependable, and this fit him because he was the dad. He was the one in charge."

"And these horses were tame ones, on the Ponderosa, so the dream wasn't about controlling anything in your life."

"I have no idea. I just liked the horses."

"OK, then. Let's look at the characters. Who was your favorite?"

"Little Joe's horse."

This was going to be a tough session.

"Let's move on to the next character in your dream, a human one, this time. The King of Scotland. Why do you think he showed up? You mentioned Ben Cartwright, who was in charge of the ranch. Could these two men have something to do with a possible aversion to male authority figures?"

Bobbi had to think a long time about this one.

"Wow. Huh. I don't know. I have no idea. The dream was in the '90s, right? The king had the same face as that creepy Burger King king. Maybe that's it. Maybe I just ate a burger before bed."

"So, when the King of Scotland landed on top of you ..."

"It scared the piss outta me. He was robotic. And he kept moving, sorta like that toy you got me, the cow that you wind up and it walks? And then when it runs into something, it falls on its side, but its legs keep moving? It was like that. Like the cow."

I paused in my questioning to pull together what I considered the strands of a fine psychological tapestry. Horses and cows were both important in this nightmare. I quickly jotted down these thoughts in my spiral notepad, the kind Jung was always pictured as using.

Then Bobbi spoke. "Remember, the other part of that dream was that I was playing Radio City Music Hall. But I got there on the wrong night."

"Right, but that's a pretty obvious interpretation, for me anyway. I mean, all musicians worry about showing up for a gig on the wrong night. I think that's pretty common."

"Yes, but I remember that I was ready to sign with an agent who wanted to book me for a five-day tour in New England. That's right, that's right—remember this?" My sister's sudden excitement of our analysis was palpable. "She got my name wrong on all of the paperwork. She wrote *Boobie Carmitchell* on the posters and stuff. Boobie. And the guy who ran the Red Raven in Cambridge, he highlighted my name on the poster and asked her, 'You sure this is who you booked?' I was on the fence about having her represent me after that."

"So that's it then. You were worried about having no control over your own show, your merchandise, maybe even your music, with a woman who couldn't even spell your name right. And she might even book you on the wrong night. Just like the King of Scotland and Lorne Greene, both in-charge kind of guys, were holding you captive in your own house. You just had no control. That has to be it."

"Or the burger I ate before I went to bed. Either, or."

So there you have it—my attempt at playing the all-knowing dream therapist. I lay in bed that night thinking about what the Moon asks us to do: to dig deeper, to be more inquisitive, and to reach enlightenment. Then I started thinking about my conversation with Bobbi and I realized that Freud was right. Sometimes a hamburger is just a hamburger.

The End of Innocence

THE FOOL HAS JUST COMPLETED some thorough spring cleaning, sweeping the cobwebs of fear out of the corners of his psyche. He followed the Moon's instructions, and he sees a much brighter day ahead. The nightmares are gone and the Sun is out, radiant and glorious. Creativity and freedom of expression are all on the horizon now.

The Sun brings us a new enthusiasm, one that we may not have experienced since we were young, and encourages us to relive the innocence of childhood. What we notice first, then, is a small boy, naked, riding on a white horse. He passes an orange-red banner between his left and right hand. Behind him are four sunflowers peeking over a garden wall. Perhaps this is the Garden of Eden, the perfection and peace that we're all seeking. Like the Charioteer, the boy needs no reins to control his horse. He is in command and has the freedom to do as he pleases.

If all of this seems a little *too* sunny and bright for you, you're not alone. I find this card to be mildly nauseating in its buoyancy. I'm not sure why I have such an aversion to it. In fact, when I called Bobbi, I wanted to discuss the innocence of our youth and tried to remain upbeat, but everything we talked about was

tinged with dark humor. We have many great memories sub-
merged in our past, but this particular card, for some reason,
wasn't bringing any of them to the surface.

For example, there was the story of the baby chicken that
our parents gave us for Easter one year. We couldn't have been
more than five or six, and this tiny ball of yellow fluff was just a
delight to behold. Even as children, we were extremely creative
(and gullible, as you'll see shortly), so we named her Peep. Dad
built a little home for her, a small box with some chicken wire
on the top. We just adored this little one, playing with her every
chance we got, cradling her in our palms, and loving up to her.

Then one day, she was gone. Dad told us that he had found
a nice farm where Peep could run and enjoy life. "She's getting
bigger," he told us. "So she needs a bigger home."

One spring afternoon, decades later, I was hanging out with
Mom in her living room, just chatting about life and enjoying
a smoke with her. Something reminded me of that Easter long
ago. (It may have been the ornamental grass on her coffee table
and the matches that lay in close proximity.)

"Hey, remember when you guys got us Peep? I always wondered where she ended up."

My mother raised one eyebrow ever so slightly, enough to
warrant my curiosity but not enough to arouse suspicion.

"You and Dad said he took her to a farm," I continued. "Was
that true?"

Mom hesitated. "Yes. That's what he did."

"Well, was it Kenny Garber's farm?" Kenny lived behind us,
and as kids, we'd spent many hours on his property, ice skating
on the pond and learning to milk cows.

"No. He didn't take her to Kenny's."

"So . . . where did he take her?"

"Just a farm."

"But where was it? I mean . . . wait a second."

Mom tapped her cigarette into the ashtray and glanced out
the window. "Well, she couldn't stay small forever. So your dad

. . . found a place for her."

"On someone's plate, I guess."

"Oh, now, Annie. You don't know that for sure."

"I'm pretty sure I do."

Mom just chuckled a bit. "That was a long time ago. What you didn't know, wasn't going to hurt you."

As Bobbi and I reminisced, the evolution of that childhood memory devolved into disappointment. I was hurt more than she; to be honest, she didn't recall too much about Peep. However, she did remember very clearly George the Lion, another uplifting fragment of our childhood we pieced together that night on the phone.

Back in the mid-1960s, a car wash owner in Lancaster managed to buy a lion and keep him in a cage right there on the property. Customers could have the thrill of observing a trapped animal pacing back and forth in his prison while they had their vehicles detailed. George the Lion was apparently quite the hit with most folks around here, but even at a young age, I saw the immorality of the whole situation. I felt a sense of relief when he died, knowing that his horror had ended. I even remember wishing that he'd eaten his owner before he passed away.

"But his dying wasn't the worst part for me," Bobbi told me. "I thought he got murdered."

"What? Why did you think that?"

"I remember this really well. One morning, I went out to the porch to get the paper. And George's death was on the front page. I was reading the headline as I walked back in the house. Mom was standing there in the hallway, and I said, 'Mom. I can't believe this. Somebody killed George.' Before Mom could respond, *you* came walking down the hallway, stood behind me, and glanced at the article over my shoulder.

"*Pneumonia kills George the Lion*, you read. Then you looked at me in disgust. 'That's not a person,' you said. 'Pneumonia is a disease.' Then you walked up the hallway and back to your room. You showed a huge amount of sympathy for me that day."

As a slow sense of recollection began to creep through my mind, I suspected that, once again, I had something to do with Bobbi's need for ongoing therapy.

"Well, that's a fine memory," I said.

"Isn't that what we're looking for? Memories?"

"Yeah, but I have no idea how we stumbled down this path. The Sun is supposed to be about the innocence we had as children. And fun. I think it's supposed to remind us of funny stuff. Like my tampon story."

When I was about 9 or 10, Mom sat me down on my bed to explain all things menstrual. The subject wasn't completely foreign to me at this point; my friends and I knew that something was happening to older girls that hadn't yet happened to us. I'd also seen those odd elastic belts hanging over our shower curtain rod. I wasn't clear about their use, but I did know they weren't Dad's. (Or Uncle George's. Hanging on a hook behind his bathroom door was a truss. This contraption was much larger than the belts I'd seen, and I'd asked Mom about it. She'd simply told me that these were "just for men." That hadn't answered my question, but the device certainly scared me. Knowing that, as a girl, *I'd* never have to be concerned about it was enough information for me.)

The thought of having a period every month didn't bother me, so Mom must have done a good job of explaining the facts in a calm, sensitive way. I remember hearing the part about my breasts getting bigger during this time of my life, and I found that quite exciting. My mother was very well-endowed, and I'd assumed that I would be, too. It took me about 40 years to realize that was never going to happen.

When she was finished, she asked if I had any questions. I had just one.

"What are tampons?"

A dark look of concern crossed her face, and her voice dropped to a murmur.

"You won't be able to use those," she said, leaning toward me. "They're only for married women."

Her words sounded conspiratorial and had a hint of warning in them. She closed the book that she'd been using as a guide, the one illustrated with flowers and fallopian tubes, and left the room.

I didn't know why single gals couldn't use tampons, but from Mom's scant explanation, I made the only assumption that I could: They were illegal. After all, one couldn't drive until the age of 17, drink until 18, and vote until 21. As a young girl, I probably didn't know exactly at what age I could drive, drink, or vote, but I knew that the police and judges were monitoring all of these activities, and I presumed that this was the case with tampons. Mom and I never talked about the topic again. When I finally got my period, she bought the Kotex and the belts, and that was that. There was no reason for me to consider the alternative. And I sure as hell didn't want to get arrested.

I'm embarrassed to say that I didn't see the error in my presumption until I went to college and realized that all of my girlfriends were involved in the criminality of tampon usage. They weren't storing huge boxes of overnighters in their closets, and I knew for a fact that no one in our dorm was married. Also, my roommate mentioned once how much easier it was to use tampons after she'd lost her virginity. Things then began to fall into place. I mentally replayed the conversation with my mother and saw the fallacy in my reasoning.

Bobbi laughed. "That's a good one."

"It is pretty funny, in retrospect. Do you remember Mom's talk with you?"

"Oh, she never told me a thing. I learned about it in school."

"You're kidding. Mom never mentioned it once?"

"Of course not. We had some guy — a guy, an actual *guy* — telling us about menstruation. I thought it was gross. And

I remember looking at Sally next to me and saying, '40? We have to do this until we're 40? I won't even be able to walk when I'm 40.' And Sally said to me, 'I'll be dead by the time I'm 40.'"

Sally, a loving, kind, and beautiful friend of Bobbi's, one of her best, did indeed pass away at a very young age. Remembering this made both of us very sad.

Bobbi spoke first. "That's a great card you have there, that Sun."

"Let's hang up. I'll talk to you tomorrow."

See what I mean? I can't get behind this card. It doesn't work for me.

Maybe I'll just call Bobbi back and ask if she wants to sleep out.

God Bless Pudgy

OUR TRAVELER SHOULD BE QUITE EXCITED at this juncture because his journey is almost complete. Now is the time for Judgment, so the Fool will examine all that he has learned and decide if it has served him well. The idea of self-examination appears paradoxical when we see the illustration on the card. The angel Gabriel is pictured blowing a golden trumpet, while men, women, and children below him are rising up from their open coffins. His wingspan is huge, and even if you, as a newly risen corpse, were considering avoiding this whole mess by just scurrying around him, you couldn't; mountains and large bodies of water in the near distance would put the kibosh on your plans of escape. It seems very clear that Gabriel is calling these folks to come before God where he will examine their lives, praise them for the good works they've done, and chastise them for the bad. From what I understand, there's not much wiggle room here. You don't get to say a lot of "Yeah, but..."s when the Big Guy is running down your list of indiscretions.

But in tarot, *you're* the one reading that list. God isn't doing the punishing or the congratulating; that's up to you. Look at your past and be honest with what you see. You'll need this information for your next big leap, that of going out on your own and not making the same mistakes again.

Bobbi and I had an interesting discussion on the phone about Judgment Day. Neither one of us remembers our Sunday school teachers or ministers talking about it, as Presbyterians don't dwell too much on the downside of the afterlife. Remember, other denominations refer to us as the Frozen Chosen, and since it would take a lot more than eternal flames to melt our exteriors, I'm pretty sure that God figures it would do no good to send us down below. There must be some other type of punishment for us, and I suspect that it comes in the form of endless committee meetings. Just join a group at your local Presbyterian church and you'll see what I mean. Nothing can be accomplished there without a task force put into place and agendas more numerous than John Calvin's writings.

"Do you remember Mom and Dad talking about Judgment Day?" I asked Bobbi.

She didn't, and neither did I. But she did recall Dad saying that he always had conversations with the Man Upstairs.

"And we said grace every night, too," she said, and she began to slip into the cadence of our pre-dinner prayer, a fine example of devotional iambic-pentameter:

Lord bless this food
Which now we take
To do us good
For Jesus' sake
Amen

"I don't think I'll ever forget that prayer," I told her. "Or the one we said at bedtime. Remember?"

"I do," Bobbi said. "But parts of it are missing."

"Which parts?"

"I don't know, Anne. They're missing."

I ignored her and continued. "Well, tell me what you do remember."

"OK. After we said that prayer itself, then we started asking God to bless people. Like, I remember we said, 'God bless

Mommy and Daddy.'" She paused for a while. "But I can't remember anything past that."

I jumped in. "I do. After 'Mommy and Daddy' came 'Pudgy and Bobbi.'"

Her response to the above names was abrupt and, may I say, rather judgmental.

"Wait a minute," she said. "Pudgy? You asked God to bless your doll before me?"

"Yeah, I did. And now that you mention it, that *is* kind of odd."

Bobbi said nothing. I, meanwhile, was frantically trying to come up with a reason why I had petitioned God for blessings in the order that I did.

"Maybe you weren't born yet."

"Oh, I was born. I was so born."

She was right. I vividly remember getting Pudgy for Christmas in first grade. So I was six, able to form complete sentences at that point, and apparently more than able to place my doll's well-being over my sibling's.

I told her I was sorry and gave the conversation a little nudge to move it forward. "Then we started listing our relatives' names: Aunt Mamie, Uncle Digger, Butchie, Cousin Steven . . . ."

Bobbi interrupted with a little yelp. "And Aunt Cottie! Yes. I remember that now. But why them? And where was everyone else?"

She had a point. We quickly calculated that there were 16 aunts, uncles, cousins, and one grandmother who didn't make the final cut. We could understand how the first three recipients of God's grace were included, as Mamie, her husband Digger, and their son Butchie had lived right down the street from us. But Aunt Cottie didn't live nearby, and as far as Cousin Steven is concerned, he lived in Virginia, was much older, and I don't think we saw him more than five or six times while we were growing up. The inclusion of some family members and the exclusion of others made no sense to either one of us.

"I wonder if we decided who was on the list," Bobbi said. "Or was that up to Mom and Dad?"

Neither one of us had any idea. This was the kind of question that we would pose to Mom as we got older. Her answer was usually the same: "Oh, girls, how should I know? That was a long time ago." (This *"long time ago"* of which Mom spoke seemed to relieve her of many obligations for honest responses, whether they concerned Peep or prayers.)

The etymology of our nightly prayer, then, is one mystery we'd never crack, and we'd certainly left the topic of this phone call—Judgment Day—in the dust. Trying to resurrect it was going to be difficult, as I felt that Bobbi had somehow reverted to her five-year-old self, was plotting my demise because of the Pudgy Incident, and could end the conversation at any moment in an act of revenge.

I quickly posed another question. "So you don't fear meeting God after you die and having him tell you what you did wrong?"

"You mean like standing at the Pearly Gates? And God either letting me come in or hitting the button for the trap door? Not really."

"Mom and Dad never did put the fear of God into us, did they?"

"No, they didn't. And I think we're better off because of it."

"And maybe because we were raised Presbyterian," I added. "You know, because the church is really kind of loose with some of its beliefs."

"Good thing we weren't raised Unitarian. Those people are like, 'What. EV.'"

We agreed, then, that we were both grateful for the moral structure that Mom, Dad, and the church provided us. But I needed to know more about self-judgment. "One more question before we hang up, Bob."

"Yes, Anne."

"Do you ever look back on stuff you did and feel bad about it?"

"Well, sure, but we were just kids. Kids do stupid stuff."

"Like what?"

"Well, I remember one time, in Girl Scouts, we made ceramic ashtrays for our parents. And I stole one that someone else had made because I didn't like the way mine turned out. I gave it to Mom."

"Did you get caught?"

"Somehow, yeah. I had to return it to the girl who made it and apologize."

"Holy shit. Were you in a lot of trouble?"

"I don't remember that part," Bobbi said.

"So do you feel bad about that? Do you judge yourself harshly because of that?"

"Look. Here's the deal. How many other ashtrays have I stolen in my life? A big, fat zero. I felt bad enough not to do it again, right?"

I had to admit that was true.

Bobbi continued. "We're not ax murderers. You would hope that the people who *are* ax murderers would walk around saying, 'Wow. Those were some dark times.' I don't know if they do that or not. But I do know that we can be too hard on ourselves."

As far as Bobbi is concerned, she puts as much effort into self-judgment as she does into worrying. I, on the other hand, am now worried that she'll judge me for asking her too many questions. It's amazing to me sometimes that we came from the same parents. Or maybe we didn't. This is going to keep me up all night.

A Noun Is an Action Word, Right?

"YOU KNOW," I TOLD BOBBI one night on the phone. "We've discussed 20 tarot cards up to this point. I was just wondering if you were getting more interested in them."

"So weird you brought that up," she said. "I got out my Motherpeace deck the other night, just to see if I could do a reading."

"Cool! How'd that turn out?"

"Well, I really didn't do anything with them. The phone rang or something. But I did pull one out of the deck quick because I needed a coaster."

"You used a tarot card for a coaster? You don't even use coasters."

"I do when I have to put a glass down on that end table of Mom's. She used to put the fear of God into me about water marks on that thing."

I was suddenly struck with a bit of inspiration. Tarot calls to us in mysterious ways. And what way could be more mysterious than using a card as a coaster? I wondered if the universe weren't prodding Bobbi into doing her own kind of reading.

"Is the card still around? Which one was it?"

She told me to hang on while she did a quick search of her living room. "Found it," she said when she returned to the phone. "It says it's the Three of Cups. It shows a bunch of people dancing around."

"Oh, that's a good one. So, let's give this a try. What does the card say to you?"

"That there's a bunch of people dancing around."

"Yes. I know that. But what does it say to you?"

"You mean like in a totally 'out there' kind of tarot way?"

"Right. Does it reflect anything going on in your life right now?"

My sister paused. When she spoke again, there was a hint of irritation in her voice. "Well, I don't dance," she said. "And I never will. Because the last time I tried, someone told me I looked like I was marching. I never danced after that, and I'm never dancing again."

That someone was a former girlfriend. I remembered the story well. And obviously, we hadn't come as far in my sister's understanding of tarot as I'd hoped. "But why do people dance?" I asked, getting back to the matter at hand and hoping to push her into some deeper understanding.

"Because their girlfriends make them,"

"Don't you think it's time you let that go?"

"Nope. It's burned into my brain. I'm never dancing again."

I ignored her. "Why do people dance, Bob? Think about it."

"I don't know. Because they're happy, I guess."

"Right! Good. And so, this card is about . . . ?" I let my voice trail off, hoping she'd finish the sentence and see the light.

"Happy people."

"Exactly. So, it's a card about . . . ?" I waited for more. She finally came through.

"About being so happy, you could dance. So, I guess it's what you'd call a 'good' card. Not a negative one."

"Bingo!" I said. I was so proud of my new tarot student. "You know, I bet if you really tried, you could figure out more cards. I could help you."

"If you want," she said. "Sure. That might be kinda fun."

I had a feeling that Bobbi was doing this just to humor me, but that was OK. I was excited to see if I were able to actually "teach" tarot to someone. But where to start? I thought that the conversation we'd had was a good one because I didn't just hand her the answers to the questions I'd posed. She'd come up with them on her own, with just a little help from me. Maybe we could continue this way: I would give her incomplete sentences based on my description of the card, and she would supply the missing words.

Bobbi was interested. "Oh, you mean like that word game where the players just shout out random words."

Ah! This was a new twist on my original idea.

"Sure," I told her. "We could give that a try, too."

"And the words I give are based on their . . . oh, you know what I mean . . . what the hell are those things called again?"

"Their parts of speech?"

"Right . . . And again . . . one more time . . . what's a part of speech?"

I explained adjectives, verbs, and nouns to her again. One. More. Time.

"But if I don't see anything that you've written," she asked, "how will I know if the words I pick are the right ones?"

"That's the beauty of it. I want to see if the universe will move you toward picking the right ones."

"And you really think that's gonna happen."

Well, it wasn't what I had in mind initially when I'd called my sister that night. But nothing involving Bobbi goes the way one would expect. And since I do enjoy a humorous approach to everything, I could think of no better way to discuss the World, the last of the Major Arcana cards.

After we hung up, I deleted random words from my description of the card and called her again.

"So here we go," I said. "Give me a noun."

"Person, place, or thing, right?"

"Yep." And we went from there.

Here, then, is Bobbi's description of Card 21.

> *Finally, the Fool's journey is finished. This is a time for **trombones**, even for entitlement, because he has mastered the **dog bone** put before him when he was a **jittery** young **paperhanger**. He has learned to skip and grow in a way that is positive for him and for*

*Poughkeepsie. He used the **sticks of dynamite** he'd been given at the start of his adventure to **jump, smoke, and work well with others**. The importance of **sweaters, tomatoes, and paint brushes** helped mold him into a fully actualized **nurse**, so that when life became challenging, he was able to move on and make important **sticks of butter**. All of his experiences, **sultry and slimy**, were important in shaping the **egg** that he's become.*

*The image on the World card is a **funny** one. A young woman **pukes** in the sky. She is surrounded by a **wine bottle**, that familiar symbol of victory, and holds in each hand a **crayon** symbolizing the balance she's achieved. The **toilet, horse, coffee mug, and tampon** that are pictured on the Wheel of Fortune card are featured here as well, reminding us of, perhaps, the four **green beans** of the Bible or the four **ice cream cones** of the Earth. He is ready to move ahead, after some well-deserved time off, and is in perfect balance with **Germany**.*

And here is the original description. You decide if Bobbi is a tarot master:

Finally, the Fool's journey is finished. This is a time for celebration, even for entitlement, because he has mastered the task put before him when he was an innocent young one. He has learned to evolve and grow in a way that is positive for him and for the world. He used the gifts he'd been given at the start of his adventure to create, organize, and work well with others. The importance of determination, strength of character, and solitude helped mold him into a fully actualized being, so that when life became challenging, he was able to move on and make important decisions. All of his experiences, good and bad, were important in shaping the person he's become.

The image on the World card is a celebratory one. A young woman dances in the sky. She is surrounded by a laurel wreath, that familiar symbol of victory, and holds in each hand a staff symbolizing the balance she's achieved. The angel, the bull, the lion, and the eagle that are pictured on the Wheel of Fortune card are featured here as well, reminding us of, perhaps, the four evangelists of the Bible, or the four elements of the earth. He is ready to move ahead, after some well-deserved time off, and is in perfect balance with the world.

I sent Bobbi her finished paragraphs and she read them back to me amidst much laughter from both of us.

"So, after reading this, do you have any idea what the World card is all about?" I asked.

"Sure. It's about everything the guy's learned on his journey and how he's ready to take a little rest before he starts another one."

"You nailed it," I told her.

"But the part about the four green beans of the Bible. That part I don't get."

"That's because there are no green beans in the Bible, Bob. But there are four of something else. What do you think they are?"

"Wise men? No. Wait. There were only three of them."

I sighed. "The four gospels, Bob. The four gospels."

My work was done. I wasn't going to get much further with my sister on this one. I could have continued the conversation, but, like the Fool, I needed a break, too.

"Well, we're finished with this card," I said. "And in keeping with the theme of it, it's time to celebrate. So, what are you going to do?"

"Well, right now, I'm making a bologna sandwich with mayonnaise and lettuce."

"Iceberg, I take it."

"Oh, hell, yeah."

"Green beans on the side?"

"Goodnight, Anne."

"Goodnight, Bob."

THE MINOR ARCANA

The Minor Arcana are 56 cards that represent the day-to-day events in our lives. They address situations specific to our personal routine rather than ones shared globally. There are four suits in this group of cards: Wands, Cups, Swords, and Pentacles, representing creativity, emotion, actions, and material possessions. Each suit features 10 numbered cards and a Royal Court of four cards at the end.

"Say to wisdom, 'You are my sister'..."
— PROVERBS 7:4

"You girls knock if off. Somebody's gonna get hurt."
— DAD

*"You sure you haven't been playing with your tarot cards,
or burning sage, or doing whatever it is that you do?"*
— BOBBI

THE SUIT OF
WANDS

THE ACE OF WANDS

A Couple of Enterprising Young Gals

ON THIS CARD WE SEE A HAND COMING OUT OF THE CLOUDS. It is grasping a wand, which is actually a tree branch sprouting some budding leaves. Behind this image a castle rests on the landscaped horizon, offering us a glimpse of the riches that await us. As with all suits in the Minor Arcana, the ace card represents the best of what the suit has to offer, and in this case, a passion for going forward with enthusiasm and creativity is in your forecast. Life is offering you a new direction, and through your actions and enthusiasm, you have the excitement and energy to grab what is yours. This is your chance for a fresh start, and success is on its way.

When I called Bobbi that night, we began to discuss the different directions that our lives had taken over the years, and we agreed that one of the most memorable was when we both found ourselves moving back in with Mom and Dad. I had left my husband for the second time. Bobbi's relationship with her girlfriend was over. And by some quirk of synchronicity, we both ended up at home on the same day one December. When Bobbi walked into the house, she found Mom in the kitchen frying chicken and told her that she needed a place to stay.

Mom greeted her, listened to her story, and kept cooking. "Oh, that's fine, honey. Your dad's in his shop. Go on down and tell him you'll be sleeping in the spare room in the basement. Oh, and Annie's taking the couch in the living room."

"Anne's here?"

"Yes. She and you-know-who had some kind of to-do. I think she's out back on the porch. Now scoot. And tell you father and Annie that dinner's almost ready."

As Bobbi walked down the steps, she heard Mom humming. Nothing seemed to faze that woman. Look-

ing back, I realize that she and Dad were understandably concerned about our situations, but neither of them was overly worried. There were no lectures given at dinner that night, just conversations about our future plans. Our parents were obviously sad that our lives had been disrupted, and they were sad for the people we'd left. But they knew that we always landed on our feet, no matter what direction we took.

After talking to Dad, Bobbi found me on the porch.

"Hey, loser," she said. "Merry Christmas, and welcome home."

"Back at ya. Mom told me what was going on with you when you were downstairs. Loser."

After comparing notes, we found ourselves excited to be hanging out for a while. There was, as to be expected, a fair amount of heartache involved in leaving our partners, but it was tempered by the realization that we were both in the same boat. And in our parents' house.

"This card reminds me of a *Star Trek* movie," Bobbi said, continuing our conversation on the phone. My sister's obsession with *Star Trek* rivals that of mine with Hugh Laurie. For her, any film inspired by Gene Roddenberry offers fresh analyses of the human condition that would make those written by Shakespeare pale in comparison.

She then explained to me that Nicholas Meyer, the director of one of those films, followed his own path by killing Spock and then bringing him back to life. She credits Meyer with saving the entire *Trek* franchise, and she even began throwing around words like "foreshadowing" and "characterization" in her verbal dissertation. Her terminology dazzled me a bit since I had no idea that she was so well-versed in the world of literary devices. Of course, I also didn't know that she'd almost died in The Oven Electrocution Incident of 1968, so I was glad to be writing this book. All kinds of surprises about my sister were being unearthed.

Within a few weeks, we moved out of Mom and Dad's and into our own places. Determined and excited to start our lives again, we each embraced the meaning of this card and found our new beginnings. There would be other upheavals in our lives over the years that followed, but we always used our wands as walking sticks to help guide our way. Now, despite what life throws in our path, we're able to lightly step around it and know that we will live long and prosper.

Sorry. You know that had to be said.

Cheaters

A MAN IS STANDING ON THE PRECIPICE of a castle and is holding a wand in one hand. In his other, he holds a globe, and behind him a second wand rests against a wall. His posture implies self-confidence as he surveys the expanse of land before him, the mountains on the horizon, and the blue sky above. All is right with his world, and after the bold step he took with the Ace of Wands, he feels even more empowered. This card indicates that you are ready to move forward fearlessly with your plans.

However, if this card shows up in a reading about your love life, beware. These new horizons that your partner's seeking? Another love interest may be waiting for him on one of them. And this empowerment he's feeling? He might use it to start dating her at the same time that he's dating you. After all, he has two mighty fine wands at his disposal. Why not use them both?

Had I only been familiar with tarot as a younger woman, this card could have saved me the heartache I'd experienced with my boyfriend. We had been dating for about two years, and I was certain we'd be getting married. One afternoon, Susan walked into my office where I worked as a graduate assistant. I glanced up from my desk and recognized her as someone who'd always been in my periphery of friends and colleagues. The two of us had never actually met, so I was surprised to see her standing in front of me, her eyes on fire, her body language a tad threatening.

"I want you to leave Brian alone," she stated.

I had no idea what to say. He was my boyfriend. Why would I leave him alone?

"What? What do you want me to do?" I was completely flummoxed.

"Leave him alone. Stop calling him. The two of you broke up, and he's with me now."

I considered the possibility that this girl might be insane, and criminally, at that. "I honestly have no idea what you're talking about. Brian and I are still together."

"No, you're not."

"Yeah. We are."

"You are not."

"We are, too."

Obviously, some breakdown in communication had occurred, and its reduction had caused both of us to lose our ability to respond to each other's statements in an adult manner. Before we took this outside to the playground, I suggested that we talk the whole thing over and compare notes. She took a seat in front of my desk.

As it turns out, she was correct. Brian and I had broken up, at least according to the story he'd given her. But after hearing my side of things, she began to see the light, and the more we talked, the more we realized that we were both being played. The ice between us started to melt, and we needed to decide what to do.

"Well, I know what I'm doing," I told her. "I'm breaking up with him. He's all yours." I don't know where I found the courage to make that decision, but I meant it. I was emotionally flattened, to be sure, but now I could see him only as a two-timing turd. How exactly a turd could two-time anyone, I didn't know. But the imagery worked and gave me the bravery I needed. "What about you? Are you still going to see him?"

"I am," she said. "I love him. But you know that he's going to deny that any of this is true."

"I wish he weren't in Philly right now. We could confront him."

I will never forget that little smile she gave me. It was wry, coy, and telling, the female equivalent of a dastardly villain twirling his moustache.

"He's not in Philly. He's playing poker tonight at his friend's place. I'm supposed to meet him after the game's over."

And right there in my office, we plotted his demise as only two pissed-off women can.

In the early evening, we drove separately to a development in the suburbs. We arrived at our destination, and there, in front of the house in question, sat Brian's car. Susan and I both parked behind it. As per our plan of attack, she entered the house while I searched for a place to hide. I saw some shrubbery and dove into an arborvitae bush where I crouched down and waited impatiently.

Within a few minutes, I heard a screen door open, and out came Brian strolling beside Susan, his arm slung over her shoulders while the rest of his poker buddies walked behind the happy couple.

"I missed you," I heard him tell her.

"I missed you, too," she said, "and I brought a friend with me."

That was my cue. I stepped out of my hiding place just as they passed the arborvitaes.

"Hello, Brian," I said.

I don't know which dropped more quickly, his jaw, or the arm that he had wrapped around Susan. If the ensuing cacophony of female voices weren't enough to deafen this man for life, the laughter of his fellow poker players was. They scurried to the safety of their cars, however, because while they seemed to enjoy seeing one of their herd being taken out by two predators, they sensed that there was more than enough danger to go around. Susan and I continued our diatribes, each allowing the other ample time before proceeding with more of our own indignities.

When the yelling was over, he had little to offer. He looked at me and said, "Annie, I love you." Then he looked at Susan and told her the same thing. Before we knew it, he was acting as the injured party, throwing himself on the mercy of the court, and citing "Loving Too Much" as his only defense. His entire demeanor was nauseating.

"Good luck to both of you," I told them, and walked back to my car.

"That was it?" Bobbi asked me on the phone. "You just left?"

"From what I remember. I was really hurting, but I didn't want him to know it."

"Right. But you sure let Mom know."

I paused, remembering the horror of it all. "Yes. Yes. The Toilet Scene."

I had come home that evening and told Mom what Brian had done. She was shocked and sympathetic. For some reason, as we were talking, we ended up in the bathroom. I sat on the toilet (not to use it, mind you, but just as a resting place, as the lid was down), and she sat on the edge of the tub, facing me. I cried. She listened. I cried some more, and she agreed that what I'd gone through was awful. I slowly realized that I was bonding with my mother in a way I'd never had before. She was sharing stories of her heartbreaks over the years and was assuring me that what I was feeling would pass.

I sensed the maternal wall between us starting to crumble, and behind it sat not my mother, but a friend. I assume this feeling of familiarity allowed me to slip into the type of vernacular most used by my peers. Either that, or I had somehow damaged my frontal lobe while diving into the arborvitaes.

"He is such a fucker," I said flatly.

Without missing a beat, Mom slapped my face so hard, the tears on it flew across the room. After I was able to wrench my neck back into a position to once again make eye contact with her, she declared quite firmly, "I hate to add insult to injury, but never use that word in my presence again."

I was fairly sure that my mom got it wrong, that she had instead added injury to insult, but now was not the time for semantics. She abruptly left the bathroom.

"Wow. She really nailed you," Bobbi said.

"I know. And you know what really had me confused? Dad used that word from time to time. Or a form of it. And Mom always laughed."

"Yeah, but that was Dad. And he only used it when he was telling a joke."

"Did you ever say it around Mom?" I asked her.

"Are you kidding? What kind of an idiot would use that language in front of her mother?"

I hung up the phone.

Lust for Lists

IN THE THIRD CARD OF THIS SUIT, we see a young man standing on a cliff. He has taken the necessary action to develop his ideas into something concrete, and his efforts are beginning to show results. As he overlooks the ocean, he sees three ships coming his way carrying the additional resources he needs to bring his initiatives to fruition. This card represents not only the imminent completion of goals past, but also the contemplation of those in the future. Symbolizing good things to come, the three wands behind him show that this guy is probably the original multi-tasker who is thinking, always thinking, about his next activity, career, or adventure.

Ah, multi-tasking. It is five of my favorite things to do. Bobbi and I have often discussed how we approach the setting and accomplishment of our individual goals. As for me, I love a good agenda, one written on paper, with a beginning, a middle, and an end, and one that would, if possible, follow *Robert's Rules of Order*.

Henry Martyn Robert, as you probably know (and if you don't, you can Google him like I did, and then you can pretend that you knew him all along), wrote the *Rules of Order* to guide people's conduct during meetings. Apparently, he saw a need to remind a lot folks how to behave when they find themselves trapped in a room with no viable means of escape until they have accomplished their assigned task. Since I'm only a body of one, I couldn't use his ideas unless I was including all of my personalities. Furthermore, his rules don't apply to written agendas, and I find that sad. But, oh, had I the means to follow such a procedure, I surely would.

I came close once. Bill had recently moved in with me, and we were both getting to know each other's routines. He learned quickly that one of mine was to start each day with a list of things to do, my order of the day, as it were. Below is a typical one that Bill would see if he were to glance at the paper on my desk:

1. *Do wash*
2. *Call Laura*
3. *Get broccoli (recipe)*
4. *Work out*
5. *Learn new songs*

He would chide me from time to time about this habit of mine, not because he was averse to making lists; he simply enjoyed the fact that I wrote everything neatly, sometimes in a beautiful cursive, and placed the paper squarely on the middle of my desk under a lovely Victorian paperweight. (I was going through a *Downton Abbey* phase at the time.) However, one spring, he considered filing commitment papers on my behalf. I am thankful that he instead approached me first to find out just what the hell was going on.

He noticed that my lists had taken on a multi-dimensional aura. Instead of only four or five items, there were now 15 to 20. And no longer was I simply writing random thoughts on a Post-it note; I was now underlining those items that needed the most attention. I used asterisks. I started experimenting with color. First-line indents were suddenly critical, as my individual items grew into paragraphs describing in exquisite detail how each goal was to be completed. I switched from cursive to block-lettering. I used so many exclamation points that the Commonwealth of Pennsylvania, had it been aware of my writing style, would have promptly revoked my teacher's license. What had frightened Bill the most one particular morning, however, was the item at the top of my list:

1. *Wake up.*

Why, Bill wondered, did I feel the need to remind myself to do this? Wasn't this just something everyone did without any prompting?

I was in the middle of signing up for an online calligraphy class to make my lists more attractive when Bill interrupted me.

"Are you sleeping OK?" he asked me.

"You know, honey, I'm really not." This came as no surprise to him since he knows I'm an insomniac. "But lately . . . wow. I just can't sleep at all. My mind keeps racing and I can't wait 'til the morning comes so I can get up and do stuff."

"Are you taking any kind of medication?"

"No, nothing new. Just those little pills you buy. I take them every day now."

"What, the pseudoephedrine?"

"Yeah, those little red ones you said were so good. The ones for my sinuses."

"How many of those are you taking?"

"Just what the box says. Two of them every three to four hours."

Bill's countenance revealed two expressions: one of relief that he could cancel my competency hearing, and one of wonder at how I had so badly misread the instructions on the box.

"You're only supposed to take one of those every six hours to eight hours."

"I am?"

"You know what's in those things, right?"

"Of course I do." I had no idea.

"You know people use them in meth labs, don't you?"

I *had* heard Bill mention that he had to show the pharmacist his driver's license when he purchased these little wonders. But I'm also the gal who used to think that tampons were illegal. I probably wasn't the best judge of anything bought in a drugstore.

"I know what your problem is, honey," he continued. "You're on speed."

Good grief. That explained it all: my inability to sleep, my increased physical activity. Why, even the lists themselves appeared nervous and anxious. I should have noticed the warning signs.

When I stopped overdosing, my routine became a lot less manic. But I still enjoy organizing my day in a written manner. Bobbi does this, too, but only during the week. She can't get enough of those little tablets, the kind with the spirals at the top which allow the pages to flip easily. She told me that she has several of these placed around the house, one by her bed, a couple in her car, a few in her art studio, even one by the toilet. Since she works three jobs, it's important that she keep track of what she needs for the day. If making a stained-glass window, putting in a floor, or learning a song for someone's wedding is on her agenda, she'll write down everything she requires in order to complete her tasks. But on weekends? Forget it. Then she suffers from CSHD.

CSHD (chicken-steak-hot dogs) is a mental disorder common among artists and other creative types. It presents itself as an inability to decide what to do with one's free time. I began to diagnose Bobbi's problem when I asked her one night what her plans were for the weekend.

She didn't have to work, so her options were unlimited. She rattled off about a hundred things that she wanted to do, but we both knew that she'd end up doing a hundred different ones. This indecision of hers was especially evident when I once inquired about her dinner plans.

"Well, it's a beautiful night, so I think I'll get some chicken at John Herr's and throw it on the grill." Bobbi paused. "You know what?" she continued. "I haven't had any red meat since last week. I think I'll get a steak." She paused again. "No, not a steak. I'm not in the mood for steak. Maybe a pack of hot dogs. Yeah, that's it. I'm going with the hot dogs."

When I called her the next day, I asked her if she enjoyed her evening.

"It was a blast. Tam and I saw that new Sigourney Weaver film."

"How were the hot dogs?"

"Oh, I didn't have time. I just opened a can of Spaghettios."

"Tell me that you heated them up."

"Nope. Had to run. Ate them cold, right outta the can."

"You have a problem," I told her.

"I do?"

"Remember the chicken-steak-hot dogs?"

"What the fuck are you talking about?"

I explained CSHD to her, and a new personality disorder was born. I emailed my findings to the American Psychiatric Association in the hopes that it could recommend some effective treatment for Bobbi's issues. But, alas, there was none. No ships filled with ideas for what Bobbi should have for dinner were sailing toward Washington Boro. But that's a good thing; they'd probably be filled with shrimp, salmon, and tuna, and that would make her head explode.

The St. Valentine's Day Massacre

THE FOUR OF WANDS IS A FUN CARD showing a band of merry-makers, their arms upraised in jubilation, approaching a canopy supported by four wands connected at the top by a garland of greens and flowers. These folks are ready to kick up their heels, for it's time to celebrate their accomplishments.

Bill and I had a memorable celebration for Valentine's Day a few years back. He took me to my favorite five-star restaurant, and instead of the full-course meals that we usually ordered (which were delicious but left us feeling like slugs), we decided to limit ourselves to only appetizers and drinks. The waiter served us small plates of artisanal cheeses, tiny cups of cream-based soups, and a variety of fresh bread accompanied by sweet butter, tapenade, figs, walnuts, and olive oil. Since I was convinced, or deluded, that the spread in front of us was low in calories, I decided to splurge a little on the alcohol and had a chocolate martini. Then I had another. It was a satisfying, delightful meal. We congratulated ourselves on our restraint and decided that, from then on, appetizers were all we really needed.

Walking with Bill out of the restaurant, I felt a mild rumbling in my stomach. As we made our way to the parking lot, I told him that I probably should use the restroom before we left.

"Well, go ahead," Bill told me. "I'll get the car and meet you here."

We both stopped walking for a second while I considered his suggestion. "Nah. I'm fine. We're, what, 20 minutes from my house? I can hold it."

"You sure? I don't mind waiting."

"Yeah, I'm ready to get home and out of these heels."

As we continued to the car, the sense of urgency I'd felt a minute before had dissipated. I really was fine. No need for worry here; everything was just dandy. We got in Bill's SUV, buckled our seatbelts, and off we went. We chatted about the evening, the food we'd had, the beautiful surroundings, and how glad we were that we'd found each other. Really, the amount of romantic and culinary gushing on our parts was enough to make one nauseous, and before long, that is exactly how I felt.

The rumbling had returned, stronger now, and soon my lower intestinal tract began to contort and expand in such a way that I felt sure it was lecturing me on the rich food I'd enjoyed such a short time ago.

"Uh-oh," I said.

Bill glanced over at me from the driver's seat. "What's the matter?"

"Oh, my God. I don't feel good."

"What's wrong?"

"I really, really have to go to the bathroom. Oh, boy. This is bad."

"Do you want me to stop somewhere? There's a McDonald's straight ahead."

I explained in hushed tones (because I didn't want to speak loudly and give my bowels any ideas) that if we *did* stop and if I *were* to shift my position to get out of the car, I couldn't be responsible for what came out of my pants.

Bill was mortified for me. "Oh, honey," he said. "I know how that feels. I remember one time when—"

I sharply held up my hand to interrupt him. "No talking!" I whispered rapidly. Then my voice softened even further. "No talking." I stared straight ahead. All of my concentration had to be spent on keeping everything in its place. I unbuckled my seatbelt and unbuttoned my pants to remove pressure from my abdomen. I clenched my teeth, my stomach, and my buttocks and focused my attention on the road before me. Every pot-hole, every turn threatened to undo my plans for a successful ride home, one which I hoped would conclude with both my relationship and my dignity intact. Bill, I suspect, understood my situation and was trying to drive carefully; however, he also understood the need for acceleration.

I'd motion for him to speed up. Then I'd grasp the dashboard so he knew to slow down. My non-verbal clues allowed us to communicate for a short time, but eventually, I had to speak forcefully.

"Pull over," I told him. "Right here."

We had only been in the car for five minutes and were now winding our way through one of the most esteemed neighborhoods in Lancaster, School Lane Hills. Several inches of snow covered the ground, the moon was full, and it was a fine night to violate one of the most beautiful roads in the county. Without the constructs of a seat belt or a top button, I was able to open the car door, step onto the side of the road, and drop trow in one graceful motion. I crouched down without a modicum of embarrassment and let the games begin.

Holding onto the open car door with my right hand, I reached between my legs and grabbed the back of my pants with my left hand. I pulled them forward, as far away from Ground Zero as possible, and right there, under the moonlit sky which delicately covered Lancaster's prime real estate area, I released the hounds.

Between the explosions, I looked up at Bill, who was staring out the windshield and pretending to admire the scenery. I figured that I had to break the ice somehow. This was starting to get awkward.

"Sorry," I said.

"No problem," he said, finally making eye contact. "You OK?"

After another violent anal outburst, I said, "I am now. Do you have any toilet paper?"

He did have some tissues, which he promptly passed my way.

As I pulled up my pants and observed the damage I was leaving behind, I was reminded of a line from *The Night Before Christmas*: The moon on the crest of the new fallen snow did indeed give the luster of midday to objects below. I hoped that no neighborhood watch group, equipped with some high-tech DNA testing kit, would stumble upon my blunder the next morning and have me arrested.

Bill and I were able to laugh as we finished the ride home. He assured me that, as a long-distance runner, he had experienced my trauma many times, as did most of his running friends. I appreciated knowing that he understood the need for this type of roadside assistance, but I honestly wasn't embarrassed. The only reason I can propose for my lack of shame was, I assume, the same reason that women who give birth in front of their partners can offer: I was in a great deal of pain, the thing inside of me had to come out, and I didn't care who witnessed the carnage.

When we got to my place, I warned Bill about walking behind me. I had no idea what the back of my pants or the sides of my shoes looked like. I unlocked the front door and entered the house with Bill following behind me, surveying the damage.

"Wow," he said. "I don't see anything out of the ordinary. I mean, there's nothing there. You are a true master."

I smiled smugly. It was one of the best compliments anyone had ever given me.

R.I.D.E.S

SO MUCH FOR COOPERATION AND CELEBRATION. Remember the glory days at the beginning of this suit, where everyone was getting along and helping each other? When everyone had a common goal, worked hard to reach it, and then enjoyed the fruits of his labors? Well, say goodbye to that idea of community and replace it with conflict, competition, and controversy.

The five men on this card are fighting, each using a wand as his weapon. However, this is a most disorganized conflict. All of the men appear to be confused about who started the fight, or how to proceed with the fight, or even how to win it. In fact, with their wands raised over their heads in a haphazard fashion and intermingling with the wands of their opponents, these fellows remind us more of the cast of *Monty Python* than that of the movie *Gladiator*.

The uncoordinated brawl pictured here is indicative of some type of discord in your life, to be sure. But the Five of Wands is also asking you to look inside yourself to find the root of the problem. While the card is indeed acknowledging that you may have to defend yourself against an opposing force, it's insisting that, before you pick a fight with your partner, file a lawsuit, or write an angry Facebook post, you should examine your situation carefully. The problem may be you.

And who wants to think about *that*? Not I. Not Bobbi. And certainly not both of us put together, especially when we were kids. It was always so much easier to deflect blame for our bad behavior on someone else. And in this case, it was our father.

Mom, or Bubbles, as she was known to close friends and family, played bridge every other Tuesday evening. When she was away, Dad took advantage of his free time by working downstairs in his woodshop, and Bobbi and I were allowed to have Pillow-and-Blankie Night. This event was celebrated when Dad let us drag the aforementioned pillows and blankets from our beds into the living room where we were allowed to crash in front of the TV. This was a big deal for us, since we were only seven or eight years old and normally had to go to bed relatively early. But twice a month, we could stay up as late as we wanted. We'd watch our favorite shows until Dad brought us a snack. Then we'd end up falling asleep on the floor and be awakened when Mom came home.

In addition to staring at the screen while Mom was away, Bobbi and I enjoyed playing our favorite game, R.I.D.E.S., our secret code for the word "rides." (Oh, we Carmitchell girls were clever ones.) We'd also employed this cryptograph if we were bored at the dinner table, for example, and would exchange sly glances at each other as we'd mouth the letters.

The game itself had been around for a few years, but once we learned to spell, the individual letters would be our covert signal that we'd use in front of Mom and Dad. How uneducated we thought our parents were, I cannot say. But we were convinced that they were baffled by our furtive language, and we'd sneak off to our bedroom where we'd engage in rounds of Horsie, Airplane, and Trampoline.

Apparently, the game was born from our limited knowledge of carnival rides and circus acts, and it involved much ruckus and tomfoolery. It was especially fun to play R.I.D.E.S. when we had bunk beds, where one of us would lie on the bottom and use her legs to push the top mattress, and the sister on it, as far into the air as possible. (We had bunk beds for only a very short time.)

R.I.D.E.S could be played in the living room, too, although our options were somewhat limited by the unavailability of bedroom furniture. On Pillow-and-Blankie nights, Bobbi would act as the horse and let me climb on for a ride, or I would lie on my back, extend my legs into the air, and balance her on my feet while she took a spin on the airplane. All of these activities would have been fairly innocuous if it weren't for the fact that sometimes the horse bucked, and sometimes the airplane crashed, taking the coffee table with it.

119

Dad's shop was right underneath the living room, and hearing the hullabaloo upstairs, he'd bang on the ceiling above him with a hammer to get our attention. Sometimes we'd actually feel the living room floor vibrate. Then we'd freeze and await the warning that would ring out from below:

"You girls knock it off. Somebody's going to get hurt."

One of us (usually me), would yell through the floor, "OK, Daddy." We'd then let a reasonable amount of time pass before continuing.

This particular night, however, we were especially boisterous. The banging of the hammer had resonated through the house at least three times, and each accompanying verbal command became more threatening. The first was just one word, yet it carried with it a declaration of intent:

"Girls."

The second, in more formal, complete sentences, was delivered with much gusto:

"Girls! I mean it. Knock it off."

And the third, the most dire of the three, should have given us ample cause to end the games:

"KIDS! Right now. Don't make me come up there."

Figuring that Dad was in the middle of something and couldn't be bothered to make good on this final threat, we carried on with much frivolity. Bobbi jumped from the couch to the recliner, trying to recreate some kind of Flying Wallendas act, but she miscalculated and ended up on the floor with a thud. We held our positions, looking at each other with wide eyes, and waited for retribution. But it didn't come. For a few seconds, everything downstairs was quiet. We thought we'd dodged a bullet. And then we heard the worst possible sound of all—my father coming up from the basement. His gait was quick, and his footsteps on the stairs, forceful.

He stormed down the hallway into the living room and ordered us to pick up our pillows and blankets and get the hell to bed. I'd never seen him so angry and knew that this was serious. I quickly gathered my things and began to leave the room. Bobbi, however, was moving more slowly and obviously had something on her mind. As I glanced over my shoulder, I saw her look up at Dad, our looming, furious, six-foot-two dad, and say with all earnestness, "But we didn't have our snack yet."

The sonic boom that was his response echoed through the neighborhood, and Bobbi and I hightailed it to our room. We spent the next hour or so whispering to each other from our twin beds, bemoaning our fates, and sobbing a little from time to time.

When Mom came home, we were still awake and could hear Dad telling her about the evening's events. She came into our room to say goodnight and, I assume, to make sure that we'd survived the crisis. We were still teary-eyed, and Bobbi relayed to her that we were hungry, and that, yes, Daddy had made us dinner, but he didn't let us have any goodies before bedtime.

"You girls settle down," Mom said. "I'll be back with a little something for you. Just don't tell your father."

Our glee was uncontained as she stealthily returned shortly with one of our favorite treats, a piece of bread spread first with a thick layer of butter and then, on top of that, a layer of peanut butter. (Stop judging. Nobody even knew what an artery *was* in the 1960s.) She kissed us goodnight and left us in the dark, where we enjoyed our bread and giggled quietly.

Suddenly, we heard voices in the hallway outside our door. Dad was telling Mom that he was remorseful about what had happened that evening. He just couldn't go to sleep angry at his girls and was going to give us a kiss before he went to bed, something that he did each night without fail. The door opened and a sliver of light shone through as Bobbi and I looked at each other in horror. What were we going to do with our butter-peanut butter bread?

"Stick it under your pillow!" I hissed to Bobbi. "And pretend you're asleep!"

She did as I instructed, and I followed suit. Dad approached my bed and sat on the side of it. I first feigned sleep and then pretended to awaken. I looked up at him as he explained how much he loved us and that he couldn't stay mad at us. Everything was all right now, he told me, and leaned in to give me a hug.

Dad's hugs were the best, but neither Bobbi nor I wanted one that night. He would never just embrace his girls; he'd also embrace the pillows under us, bringing both daughter and pillow close to his chest in a loving way.

He ran his arms under the pillow behind me and abruptly stopped, a look of confusion and disgust on his face. He pulled his hands up to the light, saw on them an unrecognizable glob of molten goo, and filled the room with a barrage of inappropriate language.

"What the hell? Shit! Goddammit! Bubbles!!!"

He stomped out of the room. We lay there, wide awake now, listening to Mom telling Dad the same thing she'd told us, to "Just settle down." He eventually did, and the house was quiet as we fell asleep.

I remember feeling rather guilty that we didn't take any responsibility for our actions that evening. Bobbi could have at least told Mom that we'd been acting up, that we had pushed Dad's patience to the limit, and that this was really our fault.

"Boy, we kind of made things even worse," I told Bobbi as we reminisced on the phone. "I mean, it's a funny now, but we really should have owned up to what we did. Ya know, instead of making Mom feel like we were starving to death or something."

"At least we weren't ax murderers," Bobbi reminded me.

And with that comment, my guilt was assuaged.

95th Percentile

IT'S VICTORY TIME AGAIN! The Six of Wands repeats this theme of success that we've seen before in cards like the World. But this time, recognition from others plays a part in the celebration. A young man on a horse is holding a wand with a garland around it, and another wreath sits on his head. People are surrounding him as he enters the town, and five of these folks are holding wands in recognition of the horseman's success. Draw this card, and you should be basking in the adulation of others.

However, the card can also suggest that you're getting a little too big for your britches, Little Missy. You're allowing your new-found fame to define you instead of appreciating the acclamations and moving on. Your ego is taking over, and your friends are getting annoyed. Just who do you think you are, anyway?

I try to apply each card in the tarot deck to myself in the hopes that I can learn from it. But I was stuck on this one. I tend to be pretty self-deprecating, and I don't like to think that I'd ever acted in an egotistical manner. I talked to Bobbi about this, and she could understand why I was stumped.

"I hear ya. Who likes to admit to being an asshole?"

"That's true. But . . . wait. Are you saying that there were times when I was one, but didn't want to admit it? Like, did you ever see me walking around thinking I was better than everyone?"

"Well, I didn't, but I'm sure someone did."

She made a good point. You can't reach your 60s without giving someone the impression that your ego was out of control. I've ended my share of relationships for what I thought were really good reasons. But what about the guys who broke up with *me*? I'm sure they had their reasons too, and one of them may have been that I was just a big egomaniac.

I started to think about dates gone wrong and partnerships gone awry. One of my boyfriends left me primarily because he felt that all I cared about were books and dogs. "Books and dogs, Annie. You're always reading, and the stuff you read is way out there."

"Like what? What am I reading that is so offensive to you?"

"Like that, right there." He pointed to the *Ms.* magazine on my lap.

"THIS bothers you? Why?"

"It's too radical. And it has stupid articles in it."

I began to get defensive. "It does not. Just tell me what is so wrong with this," and I opened to a random page for his perusal. It was an article on gay nuns.

"Oh, my God. I seriously think that you're a lesbian."

That started another brawl, and I, like the fellow on the Six of Wands, was certainly on my high horse for this one. When I look back, I realize that I climbed on that animal a lot during arguments, especially when I was more verbally adept than my opponent. This wasn't fair, and I can see now how I may have come off as haughty and pretentious.

All of this soul-searching reminded me of a poem I wrote once, comical in nature, about not being able to find the right man. When I read it now, I'm a bit put off by my requirements. Was I being too obsessive in my demands, and was this stringency really just a mask for my conceited nature? You be the judge:

I want to date someone who leaves me alone
Who's not at my door every time I come home

Who doesn't call me after work when I try
To just settle in for a long winter's night
Who doesn't send voicemails or texts on the phone
I want to date someone who leaves me alone

I want to date someone who has half a brain
To know when I'm tired that I'm not insane
Who knows that my job takes a lot out of me
Who knows that I need quiet time when I pee
I want to date someone who's just like my cat
Can't someone just please give me someone like that?

I want to date someone who has his own life
Completely devoid of all problems and strife
Who knows just exactly what he wants to do
With no need ask me, "What's up?" or "What's new?"
Who knows when it's time to get up and leave
Without asking permission from someone like me

I want to date someone who has his own spine
Who's not always asking if he could use mine
One who, when I call to break plans, doesn't think
That doom and disaster are right on the brink
Who can put his own ego up high on a shelf
So I might as well say it . . .
I'll just date myself.

Oh, boy. Forget about my asking your opinion. This poem just screams, "Look at me! Look at how balanced and centered I am. You don't stand a chance, pal. Move along. Nothing to date here." No wonder I got dumped a number of times in my younger days.

At this point in my life, I like to think that I've grown. However, in all honesty, one bad habit that I employ from time to time is the occasional fishing for compliments. I'm not brimming over in self-esteem, and I like to be reassured that I'm still attractive, or that I still can hit those high notes on stage, or (and you knew this was coming) that I still satisfy in the boudoir.

Bill is not the guy to fall into my trap easily. His compliments are always welcome, and he's quick to comfort me if I'm feeling down about myself. But he has his limits and won't let me wallow in self-pity for very long. I have a couple of stories to illustrate my point.

Once, I had just come home from the gym and was greeted by the dogs, who were very hungry and quite insistent that they be fed immediately. I started looking for their food bowls and ended up in the living room, where Bill was watching TV.

"Have you seen the dogs' bowls?" I asked him.

"Yeah. They're right there on the coffee table. Hey, how was your workout?"

"Good. I did my legs and arms today. I feel like I'm getting in shape. At least my body is." I glanced at the mirror behind him. "I just wish I could say the same thing for my face."

"What's wrong with your face?"

"It's fat. It's a fat, fat face."

"You do *not* have a fat face."

"Yes I do. It's doughy. There's no definition anymore." I looked in the mirror again. "I'm getting older and everything's dropping. I'm even getting jowls. I'm just disgusting. I don't know how you can stand to even look at me."

"Annie. You look fine."

"But not *great.*"

"Yes. You look great. You look, I don't know, enter the highest superlative you can think of into that sentence. That's how you look."

"Yeah, but you love me. You have to say that." I started to leave the living room and then stopped.

"Shit. I don't remember why I came in here."

"You were looking for the dogs' bowls, and then you started talking about your fat face."

That was funny. That got me laughing. The other story? Not so much.

Bill and I had only been together for a couple of months. We had just finished having sex, and it was an especially good romp. We both lay on our backs, exhausted and panting, staring at the ceiling. I thought that I'd performed especially well and was waiting for him to compliment me on my agility. Since patience is low on my list of priorities, I decided to go first.

"Wow. THAT was awesome. You know, I think you're the best lover I've ever had."

Still breathing heavily and making no eye contact with me whatsoever, Bill replied, "Well, you're definitely in the top 95 percentile."

I was stunned and speechless, and instead of focusing on the great score I was given, I couldn't stop wondering what I could have done to cover that last five percent. Bill never did tell me, but he remembers that when the words came out of his mouth, he was trying to reel them back, in the way one would a fish. I'd cast out the line in the hopes of a compliment, but Bill didn't take the bait.

So if you find yourself enjoying the applause and thinking you're all dat, be careful of setting the bar, or, in this case, the wand, too high. 95 percent of the time, it's going to come crashing down.

The Agreement

PUT AWAY YOUR PARTY PANTS and forget about all of those folks who surrounded you with praise in the last card. They've left the scene and are now replaced with foes who expect you to see life their way. The Seven of Wands is about defending yourself against these enemies, and that's why we see a young man with a wand, fighting against six unseen opponents whose wands are all around him, attacking him, trying fervently to knock him off of his precipice. But he's standing his ground, sticking to his convictions. The card suggests that you do the same, even if the opposition is in a position of power. You have the strength to fight this battle and to hold tightly to your principles.

"Any thoughts?" I asked Bobbi one night on the phone.

"Well, this is a pretty easy card because you and I aren't shrinking violets. We're not afraid to put ourselves out there."

"Especially you. Look at how early you came out. And you didn't just come out; you've been involved in the LGBT community ever since, for decades."

"So have you, Anne. You come to the pride days or the rallies or the festivals and aren't afraid to speak up."

"Yeah, but it's a lot easier to do that as an ally, don't you think?"

And it was. I didn't face the fear of being fired, being denied housing, or being beaten up because I was gay.

"But I always wanted to be a Gay-for-the-Day at those things," I continued. "I wanted to be right out there in the front lines, arguing with those Bible-thumping protesters who always showed up."

"And you did that. A lot of times."

"You're right. I did. But I also wanted to dress the part so nobody could tell the difference."

"You did that, too. Remember *The Agreement*?"

Wow. I'd forgotten about *The Agreement*. It grew out of the fact that one of my boyfriends and I, knowing that we were close to a break-up, actually went to counseling where we were told to make lists of each other's faults and to bring these lists to our next appointment. This agreement was to be a series of deal-breakers, behaviors that needed to be changed before we'd even consider continuing the relationship. If we both agreed to each other's demands, we'd get along much better. At the top of my boyfriend's list was this nugget:

Stop dressing like Bobbi's friends.

It seems that he was uncomfortable with my choice of clothing, specifically parachute pants. (For the record, these were the most awesome pants I'd ever worn, and I wish some designer would pull the Seven of Wands card and have the guts to bring the parachutes back into fashion. I can't even find them at Goodwill anymore.)

"The lesbians wear them," my ex said. "Bobbi always has them on. And her friends, too."

I don't know how the concept of lesbianism always worked its way into our altercations. But the boyfriend was quick to throw the L-Word around when he was losing an argument. One time, his behavior was so egregious that I told him he was an asshole.

"Oh, yeah?" he countered angrily. "Well, you're a bitch. And a slut. And half-a-lesbian."

"Which half?" I asked him. And Round Two commenced.

I had no idea how the words *bitch*, *slut*, and *lesbian* were related, but in his mind, they were and had all probably originated from the Greek root word *femsexuslesbos*, a not uncommon etymological find used primarily by men in situations requiring the need for high verbal skills and functioning grey matter. (But here I go again, being all pretentious and haughty.)

"How could you have forgotten that one?" Bobbi asked me. "My friends still love that story. And it fits well with this card

129

that you're writing about because you held your ground and kept wearing those pants."

And my sister can be as assertive as I am. When it comes to defending our beliefs, neither one of us backs down easily.

"Yeah, I was like that even in high school. Remember Mr. Davis? And that whole pocketbook thing?"

Mr. Davis was one of Bobbi's teachers, and she had no idea why he'd asked her to stay after class one day. She took a seat in front of his desk and tried to figure out what kind of trouble she'd gotten into this time.

He began talking as he reached into the bottom drawer of his filing cabinet. "We'd like you to carry this for one day," he said, and he pulled out and plunked down between them a pocketbook. "We think this would make you feel more comfortable."

"I had no idea what he was talking about," Bobbi told me. "None. I just kept looking at him. And then he put the fucking thing over his left shoulder to show me how to carry it."

"He was actually parading around in front of you, carrying a pocketbook?"

"No, he never stood up from his desk. He just sat there, wearing this purse. And I remember thinking that this was most bizarre thing I'd ever seen, that he looked as out-of-place carrying a pocketbook as I would have."

"Did you say anything at that point?"

"Nothing. But then he said, 'Don't you want to fit in?' and I said, 'I think I already do.' It was like he had an agenda, and I felt like I was being corralled into this little pen, and he was saying, 'C'mon, Little Dykey, hip-hip-hip! Over here.' It wasn't one big smack-down; it was like a series of little taps, and before I knew it, I was fenced in. So I wasn't going to say a whole lot. I did tell him again that I already *did* fit in, that I had a lot of friends. But he didn't respond to any of that."

"This whole thing is horrible."

"It was. This idea that *'they'* thought carrying a purse would make me more comfortable was bullshit. It would have made *them* more comfortable, and that's what I started to figure out."

"So what happened after that?"

"Well, when he took off the purse, he picked up a pile of three books on his desk and said, 'Another thing. We'd like you to carry your books this way. Like a girl does.' And he wrapped his left arm around the stack and brought it up to his chest."

"OK. This thing just keeps getting more and more bizarre."

"And I wasn't having any of it. After that meeting, I know I didn't carry my books any differently, and I sure as hell didn't leave with that purse. Oh, and I remember that my next class was band, so that was good. We were getting ready for our concert."

"I loved band. You had a lot of friends there. Hell, Bobbi, you were so popular, you made friends with everyone, the musicians, the jocks, the cheerleaders, the stoners."

"That's what was so crazy about all of this. I remember thinking that, here I was, picked by my friends to be the student director of the band, and this guy thinks that I don't fit in. It wasn't like I was marginalized or anything."

"Mom and Dad never found out about any of this, did they?"

"No, and it's a good thing. They would have raised holy hell. They were sure defensive when it came to the family. I guess that's where we get it."

"You know what?" I told my sister as we ended the conversation. "It's good you didn't have a wand back then. That's one thing you *would* have carried."

She chuckled. "And I probably would have used it."

Totally Pinkerton

THE EIGHT, NINE, AND TEN OF WANDS are about moving forward to face a challenge quickly, with courage and stamina, only to be met with heavy responsibilities. The initial card assures you that success is on its way as eight wands are flying through the air, moving quickly towards their destination.

The Nine of Wands indicates that you're facing a challenge. An exhausted man holds one wand for support as the other eight wands form a wall behind him. His bandaged head suggests an injury, but his stance reveals perseverance. He's ready to do battle again, but first he must rest and gather his wits and his energy.

Our final card shows the man carrying all ten wands as he trudges toward home. His head is down and he is obviously burdened with responsibilities. It's been a long trek for him, and while the card hints that the end of his journey is close at hand, it didn't come without injury or concerns.

These three cards are reflected in what Bobbi and I now call the Pinkerton Event. One night a few years ago, she and I were flying high on our way back from a job in a nearby town. We were happy musicians because the gig was over and we got paid. As we drove along, we passed a sign we'd never noticed before that read "Pinkerton Rd." Both of us found this amusing, for some reason, and at the same time shouted, "Peeeeeeenkerton!" Our voices were nasal in tone and mimicked those of two sopranos who had just inhaled nitrous oxide. That we'd both noticed the sign and responded in kind increased our merriment, and over the next half hour or so, we said the word repeatedly, even inserting it into songs that were playing on the radio. We drove down Anchor Road under starlit skies, approaching Bobbi's house with a feeling of contentment.

This emotion was short-lived, however, when, from the cornfield on our right, a skunk sauntered directly into the path of my car. (I will never understand the slow pace of skunks in situations like this. It always seems to me that they have other things on their minds, like what to make for dinner that night.) I slammed on the brakes but felt a slight impact. "That," Bobbi reminded me on the phone, "is when things started to go dark."

I checked my rearview mirror for signs of carnage. "I don't see anything," I told Bobbi. "I don't think we killed it. I think we just rolled it."

Bobbi opened the car door and glanced behind us to get a better look. "Yeah, I don't see anything, either," she said. "But good God. That smell."

She shut the door but didn't do so quickly enough, and the essence of skunk permeated the inside of my Toyota, settling on the upholstery, our clothes, and, worst of all, our PA equipment. (The expressions on the faces of the bar's patrons at our next gig answered our question as to whether or not the smell was noticeable.)

We just sat there for a while, trying to gather our wits. We looked at each other and exhaled deeply. Our previous gaiety had dissipated.

"You sure you didn't see anything on the road?" I asked, as I slowly put the car in motion.

"Nope. Nothing. She's fine. She'll have a headache in the morning, but she's fine."

"Boy. That sure wasn't very Pinkertonish, was it?"

"Talk about a change in mood," Bobbi said. "We just went from 'PEEEEENKERTON!' to 'Peeeeen . . . . .ker . . . . .tonnnnn-nnnn . . . .' Her voice dropped to a low bass as she dragged out the last syllable of what had been our new favorite word.

We both started laughing, and I glanced over at her. "This has been the oddest ride home that we've—"

"RABBIT!" Bobbi yelled, and I slammed on the brakes again.

In the road in front of my headlights was an injured bunny who had been hit by a car but had not been killed.

"Oh, no, no, no," I said. "Oh, God, he's still alive." I was devastated and completely beside myself.

Bobbi took the lead. "Just drive," she said. We were only minutes from her house. "Just drive. Drop me off, and I'll take care of it." I didn't know specifically what she had in mind, but I did as I was told, guiding my car around the rabbit, down the road, and into her driveway.

"I'll call you later," she told me as she got out of the car. "Just go on home."

I did as I was told. Not long after my arrival, Bobbi called.

"Is he dead?" I asked.

"Yeah," Bobbi answered. She had walked back up the road to the site of our second animal encounter and had used Dad's over-and-under shotgun to end the rabbit's suffering.

I'm always in awe of Bobbi's courage when she has to do something like this, and she's had to do it a few times. Putting down an injured animal found alongside the road is a responsibility that she sadly accepts.

"Shit," I said. "What a night. I'm glad we're both home."

"Yeah," Bobbi replied. "Pinkerton."

"Totally Pinkerton."

What a ghastly story. The only bright spot found hidden in this tragedy is that we would continue to use the word *Pinkerton* for any situation that is comically mundane. We'd never use it to describe, for example, a funeral or a broken arm. But when we perform at a benefit that has attracted, say, eight or nine people, the word is whispered between the two of us as we set up our skunk-scented gear. A blind date could be Pinkerton-esque. A failed casserole, one which took hours to prepare, tasted rather Pinkertonish.

You are welcome to use the word in any form you wish during any occasion that warrants it. In fact, one of my students picked Allan Pinkerton (the founder of what is now the Secret Service) as the subject for her research paper, and I couldn't help but share my story with her. To my delight, she didn't mind that I stopped calling her Jessica at that point and instead referred to her as Pinkerton for the rest of her eighth-grade year.

"So the word has been passed on to the next generation," Bobbi reminded me. "That's a good thing."

"And not Pinkertonish at all," I told her.

The suit of Wands encourages us to take action, often propelled by little red pills or Klingons; set into motion by a meal of rich appetizers; cleverly disguised by secret codes; made necessary through self-examination; thrust upon us by teachers; or deemed unavoidable by mortally wounded animals. So pick up your wands and get to work.

Too Too Too Fine

THE ROYAL MINOR ARCANA CARDS of all four suits refer to people or personalities rather than situations or events. If the Page, Knight, Queen, or King shows up in a reading, he or she could reflect someone in your life. These cards are not gender specific; the King could symbolize a woman who is causing you problems at work, for example, while the Queen could alert you to a fellow who's warm and comforting and is trying to get your attention. Or the characteristics of the Knight could mirror some flaw in your own fabulous self that needs work. It's all about how receptive you are to what the deck is trying to tell you.

Four members in a court. Four members in my family. It's no wonder that I find myself drawn to tarot. This picture of us, taken around 1958, remains my favorite. My mother is elegantly beautiful, my father is dashingly handsome, I'm miserable, and Bobbi looks like a football. And that, dear reader, is as accurate as I can be without some explanation. Let the explaining begin, then, with how my mother reflected the Queen of Wands.

This card describes an attractive woman, one who is hospitable and outgoing. She is friendly and welcoming and can brighten anyone's day. This is how I remember Mom. Throughout her life, she loved to entertain and had countless friends with whom she played bridge, lunched, shopped, and had coffee. Even when she was in the nursing home, she was adored by the staff, and her agreeable nature drew other residents into her room. However, Queen Charlotte, as you know from previous chapters, was more than just a pretty face. She was also a leader and quite assertive when she needed to be. Her commanding presence could, at times, over-power her affability, and Bobbi and I knew when enough was enough. It was a lesson that my sister learned at a young age.

The Legend of the Fly Swatter, embedded in the Carmitchell collective unconscious for decades, was born out of Bobbi's bad behavior when she was five years old.

"Mom was really mad at me," she said, "and I hadn't done *any*thing. Not one thing." Her words echoed those of children throughout history who have been punished for no good reason.

"Then why was Mom mad?"

"I don't know," Bobbi replied, her voice tinted with indignity.

"So you did nothing wrong. She was just mad enough to smack you on the butt with a fly swatter. You weren't working on her last nerve. You hadn't been told several times to stop doing something."

Bobbi paused as only the guilty can. "Well. Yeah. I guess I must have done something."

"I really don't see Mom chasing you around with a fly swatter because she was bored with housework. Or with killing flies."

"Well, whatever I did must have set her off. Because all of a sudden, she hits me on the butt with that thing, and it stung. Lemme tell ya. She didn't just put her wrist into it. It was a full-arm swing, like one you'd see at Wimbledon."

So the details preceding Bobbi's suffering have been lost to the ages. However, she distinctly remembered the rest of the story.

"I started to cry and went into the kitchen and crouched down in a fetal position under the windows. I tucked myself behind the curtains and just stayed there until Dad got home.

He walked in the back door from the garage and put down his briefcase on the counter. Mom must have met him there and told him what happened."

"How long had you been under the curtains at that point?" I asked.

"I have no idea. I think Mom said I hid for about an hour."

"So then Dad walked over to your hiding place. Did you run out to meet him and plead your case?"

"Nope. I just stayed there like a fetus and could only see Dad's dress shoes. I never looked up to see his face."

"Maybe you thought that was more dramatic and would make him sympathetic to your cause," I added.

"Probably. He asked me what was wrong. 'Mommy thinks I'm a fly,' I said."

I started to laugh. "That, right there, is the punchline that always killed at family reunions."

"I know, but here's the worst part. I don't remember Dad doing anything about it. He just walked away, leaving me there."

"He didn't pick you up and cuddle you? No hug or anything?"

"Nope. He just turned around and walked down the hall."

"Wow. That is *cold*. Seriously, Bob. You must have done something really, really bad that day for him to ignore you like that."

"I guess I did."

"Mom must have been warning you for a long time to knock it off. But you wouldn't listen until she gave you a little tap."

"Yeah, right on my ass, Anne. With a fly swatter. And it stung."

Bobbi was repeating herself now, still a touch of the wrongly accused enveloping her words. I decided to give her a bit of a pep talk.

"You know, Bob, I do believe that was your first joke. And at such a young age."

She had to agree. Bobbi and I are funny (at least we like to think so), and we get our sense of humor from our parents.

Mom was more understated in her wit than Dad, who was charismatic and theatrical when delivering his lines. A true King of Wands, he loved to take center stage. He was the glue that held our extended family together, telling stories that produced guffaws from his listeners and encouraging us to do the same.

"Don't be so dumb," he told us when we were kids. "When someone asks you a question, answer it. Don't say, 'I don't know,' or 'I don't care.' Have a personality, not like some of your friends who come over here."

Nothing irked our father more than our peers who wouldn't talk, who would simply shrug when asked if they'd like some Kool-Aid.

"Cat got your tongue?" he'd ask them. "What's the matter? Forget how to form sentences?"

Eventually they'd answer, probably just to shut him up. But that was one thing my father never did for very long. He was raised with a slew of siblings and relatives, all of whom talked non-stop until the day they died.

I'm not exaggerating here. During the last week of his life, Dad continued yakking it up with his doctors, nurses, and friends in his hospital room until the Tuesday he passed away. I even asked our minister about this behavior when he stopped at the hospital to visit my father once. His explanation didn't disappoint.

"Your dad always loved an audience," he told me, "and that isn't going to change just because he's dying." Pastor had a point.

My aunts and uncles, in addition to being verbose, were also a tight-knit group with a set of social mores specific to the Coal Regions of Pennsylvania, including the correct way to enter each other's homes when visiting. The family simply barged through the front door, loudly announcing their arrival. No knocking was required.

This type of behavior continued after everyone moved to Lancaster and my parents got married. Mom, a Lancastrian, found it quite unacceptable. She was happy to entertain and she loved her in-laws, but knocking on the front door and waiting patiently for someone to open it was the proper way to be received. Dad blamed Mom's Pennsylvania Dutch heritage, her German background, for her reticence in accepting his family's lack of decorum.

"Lancaster County. The most closed-off people in the world live right here," he used to say. "Nobody talks to anybody. When you try to start a conversation, they just look at you. What are they? Stupid or something?"

Dad wasn't far off the mark in his evaluation of our homeland. The "natives" here have always been standoffish, and especially so toward "outsiders." I wouldn't go so far as to call their behavior rude, but Dad didn't have a problem doing so. He loved to engage people, and when they didn't respond accordingly, he'd chalk up their lack of charm to their unfortunate county of origin.

Once, though, some Lancastrians surprised him. My parents were walking down Orange Street on their way to church. Dad always tipped his hat to couples whom he and Mom would pass on the street, and he'd greet them with an exuberant "How are ya?" or a "Beautiful morning, isn't it?" More often than not, the strangers would nod without emotion or verbal response. This time, though, the exchange was different.

A man and woman were walking toward my parents, and before my father had a chance to utter a greeting, the woman smiled brightly. Her companion made direct eye contact with my father and said in a hearty voice, "Good morning! How are you?"

Dad was dumbfounded, and in an attempt to say, "I'm fine! Hope you are, too!" he merged both responses into one conglomeration of acknowledgment and stuttered, "You, too too too fine!"

Whether or not the man and woman assumed that they'd just encountered someone with neurological issues, no one can be sure. The strides of both couples continued, unbroken. Mom started to chuckle, and Dad had a new story to share with all of us. He remained convinced, he'd later say, that these people were from out of town, or that he'd finally met the two people from Lancaster who weren't stupid. Either way, the King of Wands was pleased with his subjects.

Since we were raised by parents who valued humor as much as ours did, one would think that Bobbi and I would have reveled in it. And we did, for the most part, but there was a period of time when I was immune to anything funny. Take another look at that family photograph. Have you ever seen such an unhappy child? Mom certainly hadn't, and she was concerned.

"You were just miserable back then," she would tell me. "Miserable. No other word to describe it. I didn't know what was wrong with you. So I took you to a doctor."

"You mean Dr. Huss?" He was our family physician, the doc who made house calls, and the model, I'm convinced, who posed for Norman Rockwell more than once.

"No, not him. I took you to another kind of doctor. A psychiatrist."

"You took me to a psychiatrist? Are you kidding?"

"I'm not kidding. You were miserable. I didn't know what to do with you."

I was stunned. How awful was I, really? I don't remember being so despondent. Thoughts of death had always occupied my young mind, but I never thought that these ideas translated into some type of psychosis.

"It wasn't anything like that," Mom said. "The doctor told me that you were just going through the Terrible Twos. You were my first child. What did I know?"

Had my mother pulled the Page of Wands in a tarot reading back then, she'd have known plenty. When this card is the first one drawn in a past-present-future spread, it indicates a spoiled, whining child, one who is inclined toward temper tantrums and who is not maturing at a steady rate—in other words, me. However, it also represents someone with self-image problems.

When I look at the picture and see what Mom had done to my bangs, I'm not surprised that I looked so blue. Her attempt at creating a pageboy haircut left something to be desired.

"Wow. She really thought that you were sort of mentally ill," Bobbi told me on the phone.

"Right. Like *I* was the one who was going to be the problem child. I guess she changed her tune a few years later when she thought you were a fly."

"At least I wasn't miserable."

My sister was right. She's always been an energetic, enthusiastic person, even as a kid. Just look closely at the picture. Her little fists are balled up, ready to start this adventure into life, and her countenance joyfully ponders her next move. She is so tiny and does look like a football in Dad's arms, one ready to be thrown into the world where she can create, explore, and travel. A true Knight of Wands, her bravery and spontaneity have served her well.

Knights like Bobbi are not afraid to travel into unknown territory, so it came as no surprise that after graduating from high school she decided to drive to Florida to visit Aunt Anna Mae and Uncle Paul.

She was hoping to drive straight through to Florida, but since she got a late start, she thought it best to stop at a small motel outside of Washington, D.C. When she was checking out the next morning, she noticed several travel brochures stacked at the front desk, and one of them caught her eye.

"Skyline Drive," she read. "Huh. I remember going there with Mom and Dad when we were little . . ." And just like that, Bobbi was headed for Shenandoah National Park where she secured her first job as a musician, playing guitar and singing in the bar at Skyland Lodge for the next two years.

Life leads us where we need to go, doesn't it? Kings and Queens, Knights and Pages; we like to think we're in charge, but there's something else at work here, directing our way. Royalty indeed has its perks, yet the synchronicities of life always seem to level the playing field on which commoners and nobility romp. Fly swatters, psychiatrists, actors, even travel brochures all take part in our adventures, our performances.

Shakespeare wrote that, in the end, all of this signifies nothing. I disagree. These tiny pieces of our past, tucked away in our minds and brought to life through conversations and story-telling, are far from inconsequential, whether we strut like a King or fret like a Page. When it's all over, the myths we've lived and the archetypes we've embodied make us who we are. And for the Carmitchell Clan, at least, that is more than significant. It is blissful.

THE ACE OF CUPS

The Most Annoying Requirement

WELCOME TO THE SUIT OF CUPS, where determination takes a break and emotion is in the forefront. Love, compassion, generosity, and happiness are offered here, as the same hand pictured earlier in the Ace of Wands comes out of the clouds, this time holding a goblet overflowing with water. The card indicates that your heart should be as full as this chalice, teeming with the good stuff that makes us human: the need to connect with others, to feel compassion, to empathize, to love.

The Ace of Cups is a harbinger of positivity, especially if you're beginning a new relationship. However, just like sea rises and falls, so do our emotions, and when a new romance begins, it sometimes ends. When that happens, our job is to go with the flow, even to drift for a while until the waters calm. Moreover, we may have to forgive the other person, and the Ace of Cups encourages us to do so. I find this requirement most annoying.

Jesus and the Buddha told us to forgive. Hindus practice the concept of forgiveness, as do Muslims and Jews. And you don't have to be bound to any particular religion to embrace the idea of mercy. Most folks, including atheists and agnostics, understand the importance of letting go and moving on. This many people can't be wrong. But couldn't they just have picked an easier tenet to share?

Everyone knows that the main reason we forgive others is not to grant them absolution or to guarantee ourselves a prime spot in heaven. Forgiveness is actually a form of self-preservation. Holding on to anger only makes us feel worse about everything.

Why, then, is this whole process so difficult? I'll tell you why. Because, at first, it feels so much better *not* to forgive.

Be honest for a minute: When someone does you wrong, usually in a romantic situation, don't you just love calling your girlfriends and processing the whole mess, ad nauseum? "Can you even believe he did that?" you'll ask them. And they will respond appropriately by assuring you that he is, indeed, an awful person, and that you just deserve so much better. You'll end these conversations hours later, still seething, but at the same time feeling pretty damn good about yourself. The five friends whom you called couldn't have been more clear: You are a better person than your ex-boyfriend could ever hope to be.

You will smugly hang on to this thought long after you've hung up the phone. It will sustain you for weeks as you ponder his demise. The thought of forgiveness may enter your mind, but it morphs quickly into that of surrender or weakness. Holding on to your power right now is tantamount to anything Jesus might have suggested on the phone, had you called him instead of your friends.

"Have you ever had to forgive an ex-girlfriend for anything?" I asked Bobbi.

"Have I ever had to forgive an ex-girlfriend . . . ." Our conversation took a brief hiatus as my sister contemplated the query I'd put before her. Just as I was about to start painting my nails to kill some time, she responded.

"No. I don't think I have."

"Huh. So they were all pretty good people, I guess."

"Absolutely."

"But when one of them left you, weren't you hurt?"

"Sure I was. But I didn't hold a grudge. Remember when Amanda broke up with me?"

My sister and her girlfriend had been dating for six months when our mom died. This was also the time that Amanda ended the relationship, which wasn't a complete shock to Bobbi; she had sensed that something was wrong the week before.

"I had told her that I was at the bottom of my grief barrel," Bobbi said, "and that if she were going to leave me, that was the time to do it since I was numb, completely tapped out, and wouldn't feel a thing. Of course, she didn't break up with me then. But she did a week later."

"I remember that. She came over to your house."

"Yep. And she explained that we'd be better off as friends. I was just like, 'OK, then. Thanks for stopping by,' and I kind of hurried her out the door."

"You were pissed."

"I was because I'd given her the chance to do that a week earlier, when I felt more in control of things."

"Well, here's where the forgiveness part comes in," I said. "You were mad, but I don't feel like you were carrying any anger around with you. You weren't picturing her as a big turd or anything."

"Why in God's name would I picture her as a big turd?"

"I don't know. It was just a brief thought." (And apparently one that only straight women entertained.)

"Like I said, I just didn't think about it. But when we got together later and talked, I realized that she was the right person for me to be with at that time in my life. Mom was really going downhill then, and I needed someone who'd support me through all of that stuff. And Amanda was great with that."

Ah, yes. Bobbi's words, [w]hen we got together later and talked, reminded me that lesbians break up completely differently than straight girls. There is always a process involved as the gay gals work their way through the infamous twelve-step program of Relationship Transitions. Bobbi explained to me the difference once by using two of our favorite foods, the mozzarella cheese stick and the pretzel stick.

146

"It's like this," Bobbi had said, pulling apart the former at an Italian restaurant one night. "See how the cheese takes a long time to completely break? Lesbians are like the cheese. We get farther and farther away from each other, but we do it slowly. Thoughtfully. There's a lot of talking about the relationship, a lot of processing. So by the time the cheese stick does come apart (both of her arms were fully extended at this point, and long strings of melted mozzarella were hanging from each end of battered crust), it's not as painful. We usually end up as friends."

I knew where she was going with this as she picked up the pretzel stick. "But you guys," she continued, snapping the stick in two, "you guys just break up and that's it. No talking about where things went wrong. No discussion about how each of you could have made it better. It's over. Done."

That analogy made clear to me Bobbi's ability to forgive a former girlfriend rather easily. She does so not by herself, but with the help of the other person. And until the other person is ready to have the conversation, forgiveness doesn't enter Bobbi's mind. She knows that, when the opportunity presents itself, she and her ex will find time to talk, and in doing so, she'll be able to overlook any transgressions that may have hurt her. Moreover, she's able to acknowledge the part that she herself had played in the deterioration of the relationship.

What a mature way to handle things. It's enough to make me want to become a lesbian. Alas, I am a straight woman who always carries a pretzel stick in her purse. This was the case when I asked my friend Keith once if he knew of any men whom I might date.

"There's no one around here who doesn't hunt," I told him. "Don't you know any single vegetarians?"

"Not really. Everybody I know is either married or lives out of town."

Keith was the cruelty officer for Lancaster and played a vital part in helping the district attorney prosecute cases of animal abuse.

"All the time you spend in court, you don't know any-body?" I asked. "You don't run into fellow vegetarians? Single ones? Male ones?" I was trying to condense my requirements to include as small a portion of the population as I could, but nothing was doing the trick.

I then attempted to expand my base. "What about judges? Lawyers?"

"Well, there is one guy who doesn't eat meat. An assistant district attorney. Bruce Roth. But he's kind of an asshole."

My mind couldn't conceive of a vegetarian being an asshole, so I told Keith to call Bruce and ask if he were interested. He was, and we went out a few times. I really enjoyed his sense of humor, his knowledge of the law, his love of jazz. Things might have worked out for us, but his behavior on our fourth date incited a bit of anger in me, even malice.

He told me that I looked nice when he picked me up that night. I thanked him, but, because I never feel worthy of accept-ing a compliment of any kind, I apologized for my hair. It had been a while since I'd had it colored, and I told him that I appeared to have a racing stripe running right down the middle of my head.

He laughed. "I can't even notice it," he said. "You look great."

We went to a jazz club to hear Keith's band. He was taking a break when we arrived, and he walked over with his girlfriend to where we were standing at the bar. He introduced her to Bruce first. Gretchen was a thin, stunning woman with long dark hair and an accent that even I found sexy.

She shook hands with Bruce, and he turned to me to continue the introductions. "This is Annie," he said. "Check out her hair. Looks like she has a racing stripe running right down the middle of her head, doesn't it?"

I have no idea what Gretchen's response was, nor do I remem-ber anything about the rest of our time at the club. I was too busy mentally planning Bruce's murder, and I knew that I had much to consider; his ties with the legal system were firmly in place, and I had to make sure that I left nothing to chance.

When the night was over, we rode home in silence. I stared straight ahead as he tried to make conversation. I'm not sure whether or not he broached the subject of his intentional verbal blunder. It wouldn't have made any difference if he had; I was too occupied with thoughts of resigning from my job and having my passport updated, two important parts of escaping arrest for my imminent crime.

After he pulled into my driveway, he had barely put his Mazda in park before I opened my car door and got out. Walking around to the driver's side, I looked at him through his open window.

"Don't ever call me again," I said flatly, and I turned and walked into my house.

Of course, I couldn't call Keith. He was still at the gig. But I did reach him the next day, explained vehemently what had happened the night before, and assured him that I'd never distrust his instincts again; Bruce Roth definitely was an asshole.

I'm sure that my girlfriends heard about my plight, too, but I honestly have no recollection of my relating the story to them. However, judging from how long I held Bruce in contempt, I'm sure that I'd made contact with quite a few of them and that we had exhausted the use of every possible adjective we knew to describe his behavior.

Now, to understand the rest of this narrative, you must be aware of a few facts. First, Bruce and Keith had extremely developed senses of humor. Second, and more importantly, because of their involvement with animal abuse cases where they'd seen the worst side of humanity, everything else took a backseat and couldn't be taken too seriously. Some guy busts on his date's hair to impress another woman at a bar? Big deal. So over time, all three of us were able to laugh at Bruce's insensitivity and my abrupt reaction to it.

One night a few months later, Keith and Bruce came to hear the Carmitchell Sisters at a local bar. When we took a break, I walked over to their table and started to sit down. I didn't even have a chance to properly greet them before Bruce spoke.

"Sounds good," he said. "But what's with the outfit? It looks like something Omar the Tent Maker designed."

I thought I looked good. I thought I looked like Stevie Nicks. My cheeks weren't even in the seat before I straightened up, glared at Bruce, and walked away.

Keith later told me that he'd looked at Bruce the same way one would look at an accident victim, with disbelief and pity.

Bruce just shrugged. "Well," he said to Keith, "if you're gonna go down, might as well go down in a ball of flames."

Many years have passed, and, believe it or not, Bruce is now one of my best friends. In fact, I'd call him my best "guy" friend, a title originally reserved for Keith, who has since passed away. (Bruce and I continue to argue over which of the two of us Keith liked better, and Bruce, being an attorney and a district judge, usually wins). Keith's death was hard on both of us, and it's important that we keep his memory alive. One way we do so is to relate the above story to anyone who will listen. Bruce even prodded me into telling it at Keith's memorial service, and I'm glad I did. The mourners loved it.

Bruce still retains his dusty, wicked sense of humor. We were texting each other recently, and I wrote that I was really missing Keith that day. Bruce texted back the following:

"Me, too. I think about him a lot and how disappointed he'd be in you if he were still here."

The preceding was one of many conversations I would have missed had I not forgiven Bruce. And compared to the death of our best friend, I now understand that no social *faux pas* is so serious that it can't be laughed off. I would gladly be the recipient of a myriad of insults from Bruce, and he would similarly accept a tirade of angry retorts from me, if we could have Keith back here with us.

I try to remember this when I feel slighted by one of my friends or loved ones. It's still cathartic to fantasize about what I should have said in response to an insensitive comment, or how I should have reacted to a bone-head move. Now that I'm older, though, that catharsis is brief, and I try not to let it control me. I'll never be as good as Jesus was at forgiving people, but, in all fairness to me, Jesus never dated Bruce Roth.

Keith Mohler, 1952–2014

151

Explain to Me Again Why We're Together?

SIMPLY PUT, THIS CARD SHOWS a deepening relationship between two people. A couple is seen making a commitment to one another, each holding a goblet and standing on either side of a staff adorned with a winged lion's head and two intertwining serpents. The card symbolizes the next step in a partnership, such as an engagement or a wedding, where respect, love, and appreciation are reaching new heights.

Romance oozes forth from the Two of Cups, and before I go any further, I must explain to you that the word "oozes" produces the same type of visceral reaction in me as does the word "moisture" or "seeping." Therefore, my use of it here is intentional. A couple staring into each other's eyes, kissing each other excessively, or wrapping their arms tightly around each other as they drift off to sleep are all necessary and enjoyable components of romantic comedies. But stick one of these elements into my relationship with a man, and I tend to throw up.

I'm sure that a therapist would tell me that I have problems with intimacy, or that I view surrender as some sort of character flaw. Neither of these diagnoses would be correct. I am quite intimate when it comes to sharing my deepest thoughts about politics, for instance. (Just ask anyone who follows me on Facebook, if, indeed, anyone still does.) And as far as surrender is concerned, I will fold like an origami crane when a box of buttercream chocolates is placed in front of me. So why do deep expressions of physical intimacy make my skin crawl? The answer is two-fold: 1) I don't know, and 2) I don't care.

This is not a new revelation brought on by age or repetitive dating. I've always felt uncomfortable when men got too close, and my affliction has nothing to do with sex. I was dating a fellow once who asked that I not take a shower before he picked me up for dinner. Instead, he wanted me to wait until he got there, saying that he'd like to draw a bath for me.

"His exact words were, 'I'd love to bathe you,'" I told Bobbi on the phone.

"Oh, that would have made me puke my guts out."

"It almost did."

"You didn't let him do it, did you?"

"God, no. I told him just to pick me up in an hour. Gross."

I was glad to discover that my sister also has an aversion to this type of conduct, although I can't say for sure how deeply hers runs or what behaviors it entails. Finding out these particulars would involve asking her specific questions about her love life, and neither one of us wants to go down that road. And if for some reason the road were one on which we chose to travel, I can guarantee that we'd find the nearest cliff and throw ourselves off of it. Our loved ones would grieve our deaths, to be certain, but they'd understand completely. I can visualize Bill right now, speaking at my funeral: "She just asked too many questions for which she didn't want answers," he would say. "And she had no choice after gathering that information but to off herself. I can't tell you how much I respect her for that."

He certainly would because Bill and I share a genetic code that rejects this type of familiarity. To prove my point, I stopped writing a minute ago and found him in the kitchen emptying the dishwasher. Interrupting him, I placed my hands on either side of his face and, saying nothing, I looked longingly, lovingly into his eyes for several seconds.

"Are you okay?" he asked me.

I couldn't hold my gaze any longer and released his face. "I just wanted to make sure that you weren't into this kind of stuff."

"Oh. This is for your book, isn't it?"

"It is. Can I throw a couple of questions at you?"

We sat down at the table and got to work. I asked him about respect and honor in our relationship, and he told me that we achieve both by not getting in each other's way.

"You let me," Bill began, then stopped. "I hate to even use the word *let*. But you 'let' me run, do my stock market stuff, take naps."

"Watch your violent, blood-infested zombie movies on the Sci-Fi channel. Listen to prog-rock."

"Right. And I don't mind that you play music, write, and do your church-y stuff."

In other words, Bill and I do what we want to do without either of us being judgmental or whining about lack of time together. We give each other the freedom to explore our own interests without any *quid pro quo*. We're able to achieve balance, too, by taking turns folding the laundry, mowing the lawn, or cleaning the house. Our plans for the future don't conflict because, at our age, the only course we can propose is staying alive as long possible. Reflecting on all of this, I wondered what made us any different than roommates (except, of course, for the sex part).

"So, what makes us a couple?" I asked him. "I mean, everything we just discussed would describe how I'd live with a good friend. We're not married, so there's no legal commitment that defines us. Is sex the only thing that makes any two people a couple?"

He thought a minute. "No, it isn't. We have a depth of sharing life that defines us, one that goes beyond friendship. What you and I have, we don't have with anyone else."

"I like that a lot," I said. "How about feelings? Do you think we share our feelings?"

He conceded that we do.

"Do you want to share some feelings now?" I asked him.

"Not really." I figured I was pushing a little too hard here, so I decided to wrap things up.

"Just one more and then we're finished. Are you glad that we're living together?"

"That doesn't sound like a tarot card question to me."

He was right. It wasn't.

"I can't believe what we've just done," I told him. "We had a 10-minute conversation, and neither one of us stopped talking to look at the dogs."

"Yeah," he said. "We're really growing."

Luckily, I have found a man who doesn't require continuous hand-holding or gentle stroking of arms while we watch TV. We're much more comfortable staring into our pups' eyes, bestowing massive amounts of kisses onto their little heads, and wrapping our arms around them as we fall asleep. As one of my friends observed, we really are a match made in . . . somewhere.

Badge of Honor

HERE WE SEE THREE BEAUTIFULLY DRESSED WOMEN, each raising a goblet in the air. Celebrating life and toasting their friendship, they dance in a bucolic field of colorful vegetation. A feeling of revelry is present as these friends celebrate the beauty that surrounds them and savor their love for each other. Pure joy emanates from the Three of Cups, one of the most enthusiastic, happy cards in all of tarot. It represents the importance of community and lasting friendships and the delight of being with the people you love.

This card reminds me that I've been blessed with many friends throughout my lifetime, those I've known since childhood and the ones I've made through playing music and teaching. But I must admit that my best girlfriends have always been my mom and my sister. I mentioned this to my therapist once, and she looked at me like my hair was on fire. Apparently, she didn't find it healthy that my familial relationships were taking precedence over those I made outside of my "tribe." I didn't know what to tell her. I've always had the most fun with Mom and Bobbi. We were a small community, but a mighty one.

Back in the 80s, though, things became a little strained between the three of us. Bobbi was living in York, a town about an hour away from us, and it was difficult to reach her. Yes, she was very busy playing music four or five nights a week and was sleeping while we were awake. However, she'd always managed to keep in touch no matter where she lived. Even when she was working on Skyline Drive, she found a way to connect by phone or mail on a regular basis.

But now she was letting weeks go by without any contact at all. Mom and I were starting to get worried. Had we done something to offend her? We didn't recall any kind of argument taking place. Had she run away and joined the circus? This wasn't possible, since we saw her band's name in the paper from time to time. Had she eloped with Little Joe? That seemed to make more sense than any of the scenarios that we had envisioned. However, I had lent Bobbi some of my records; surely, she wouldn't leave for the Ponderosa without giving them back.

Parting with Elton John and Billy Joel had not been easy. Jim Croce had joined them as well, and my concern over my sister's lack of contact was now turning into annoyance. Initially, losing touch with one-third of my family community was painful, and my bereavement only deepened as I also mourned the loss of Elton, Billy, and Jim's comforting words.

The realization that Bobbi had left me and taken with her my three favorite singers now stuck in my craw. To add to my frustration, I didn't know what a craw was, so I couldn't un-stick anything that was in there. When she finally decided to answer the phone, our conversation was far from pleasant.

"Where have you been? Mom and I had no idea if you were dead or alive."

"What are you talking about? I'm alive. I've just been busy." Her voice had a lilting nonchalance that irked me.

"Busy? Really. You've been too busy to return any of our calls? We haven't heard from you in weeks. And you've had my records for months. I want them back."

She started defending herself with a lot of nonsense about traveling and gigging, none of which addressed my missing albums, nor did it make her argument any more valid.

"Are you trying to tell me that you lost my albums or something? Is that why you haven't called me?"

"I have your albums," she said. "Good God."

"Yeah, well, you've had them for a long frickin' time. What the hell, Bobbi?"

Her tone suddenly shifted to one of arrogance and condescension.

"Fine, Anne. I'll get your albums back to you." She was addressing me now as a parent would speak to a child having a tantrum, and she was on the right track: I was livid.

"Forget the albums, Bobbi. What is going on with you?"

"Nothing is going on with me."

"That's bullshit." I was getting more and more agitated with her refusal to acknowledge that anything had changed in our family dynamic. "You never call us anymore. We used to be so close, and now you've completely cut yourself off from all of us."

She said nothing. If this were part of her plan to shut me up, it wasn't working.

"It's like you just pushed us out of your life, Bobbi. What is your problem?"

I heard her voice catch a little, and suddenly she began to cry. "I'm gay."

"I don't care," I said definitively. "I just want my albums back."

Had I ever suspected that Bobbi was gay? Nope. Never even thought about it. She was always a tomboy, of course, and maybe, back in the 60s when we were growing up, this label was what defined her. She wasn't interested in boys, except to roughhouse or play baseball with them. As we went through high school, she was popular and funny, and I guess I'd assumed that all tomboys took the same road, one filled with friends and work and hobbies but void of romance.

My parents and I never discussed Bobbi's love life. If they had any suspicions, Mom and Dad kept them hidden from me. When she finally said the words "I'm gay," her lack of dating boys, her settling down far away from the family, her drifting away from us emotionally all made sense to me. (All of that, plus the fact that she had moved in with Mary and had been living with her for a year. I must plead ignorance as to why that small detail escaped notice.)

Now that the lesbian was out of the bag, we had a lot to talk about and met at a Burger King in Columbia to discuss the matter. She assured me that she'd answer all of my questions honestly, so I asked if she'd ever been with a man. No, she said, she hadn't. But once, when she was living in Virginia, a stable hand who had a crush on her tried to kiss her. She avoided lip contact and took one on the cheek. To her credit, he was impressed. She, however, was not.

"So do you have a girlfriend or anything?" I asked her.

She looked at me like I had grey matter seeping out of my ears.

"Yeah. Mary."

"How in the world did I not figure that out?"

Realizing that I was quite slow on the uptake of all of this, Bobbi knew that her work was cut out for her. With the patience of a grade school teacher, she took me through her journey. It was a painful one, and I was ready to go back in time and beat up anyone who had been mean to her.

"So your friends," I said, and I began listing them, one by one. "They're gay, too?"

"Yeah, pretty much."

"Holy shit. I never knew." I had thought they were all tomboys.

People have asked me over the years if it was hard to accept that my sister is gay. I think it's an irrelevant question primarily because I don't define anyone by whom she chooses to love. Doing so makes as much sense to me as categorizing people based on whether they prefer elephants over dining room tables. Or shopping carts over volcanoes. However, I can understand the concern of others. Being gay in a close-minded society can be difficult and dangerous. But Bobbi's sexuality had nothing to do with how much I loved her or how much fun we had together. Why would I care about her love life? If she were dating her toaster, I'd have a difficult time understanding her choice, but considering Bobbi's fear of that particular appliance, I knew the likelihood of that coupling was out of the question.

My circle of friends widened once Bobbi came out. Her lesbian buddies accepted me as an ally, and I loved hanging out with them. They impressed me with their knowledge of mechanics, their athletic abilities, their casual dress and manner. As my sister was quick to point out, though, not all gay women fit into one mold. As she explained it, "You've got your butch, your fem, your separatist, your radical." I remained in awe of all of them and was a bit envious that they didn't seem to rely on men to get things done. Why couldn't I be more like a lesbian?

I got my chance when my first divorce was finalized. Completely on my own, I had to learn to take care of things around the house. My first successful venture into a lesbionic way of life came about when I purchased a lawn mower. My husband had bought ours, it had tanked, and now it was up to me to replace it. I thoroughly enjoyed my time at the hardware store and was amazed at how well I understood the differences between a mulching blade and a regular one. Maybe I was, as that boyfriend of mine had implied, a secret lesbian. I knew that wasn't the case, but still, I thought I deserved a little credit.

"I'm proud of you," Bobbi had told me.

"I know. Me, too. I wish there were some type of recognition for straight gals like me."

"Right. Like, if you were a Girl Scout, you'd get a badge or something."

"If only," I muttered dejectedly. In the end, I understood why Bobbi had been a bit removed from the family. She eventually told Mom and Dad what was going on, and it took them some time to get used to the idea. Soon, though, all was well. I can't say that the three Carmitchell girls ever danced around with flowers in their hair, but our circle was once again complete. Interestingly, the Three of Cups can also herald a reunion with a friend or loved one who has been distant for some time. I'm happy to say that this was the case with me. My records and I were finally back together.

A Phone Call Away

AT FIRST GLANCE, this card is reminiscent of the Hermit, that wise old man standing with a lantern on a mountaintop and waiting for his students to come to him for enlightenment. Here, a younger man sits under a tree with his head bowed in a contemplative pose. However, unlike his counterpart, this man appears to be waiting for no one. He wants to be completely alone and is so cut off from the world that he is unaware of the cup being offered to him by Spirit. The three other cups sitting in front of him also go unnoticed, implying that, rather than being deep in meditative thought, this fellow could be depressed or bored. His crossed arms and legs indicate his unwillingness to accept the help that's being offered him.

Bobbi and I can be extremely independent, and we love to see what we can get done without asking anyone for assistance. Our parents enjoyed a certain degree of autonomy, so perhaps their daughters inherited this sense of self-reliance. However, my sister and I tend to take an excessive amount of pride in our abilities. When I rearrange the living room furniture, for example, and call Bobbi to tell her about it, I act like I deserve the Medal of Honor. She's the same way. She'll text me first to let me know that she'd just finished mowing the entire yard in one hour flat. Then she'll notify the newspapers.

Sometimes, though, out of necessity, we have no choice but to accept the help offered by others. Bobbi learned this lesson a few years ago when 13 sheets of drywall weighing close to 900 pounds fell on her legs. She had two knee surgeries, and the first one went well. The second, however, required that she remain immobile for months, icing her knees while she stayed on the couch. She lost a year of work, and during that time, she had to depend on the kindness of friends to bring her food, to help around the house, and to keep her company. Unlike Blanche

DuBois, Bobbi was used to a very active lifestyle and did not enjoy relying on anyone.

"That must have driven you nuts," I said to her on the phone.

"It did. You know, I used to be a moving target. Now, here I was, almost completely immobilized, and people were coming to my house to help. I couldn't have recovered without my friends and family. I kinda hate to say that, but it's true."

And there it was, that small caveat tucked into her willingness to admit that, now and then, Bobbi needed the outside world. She also needed painkillers, but she refused to take them. She had finally acquiesced to the fact that people were cooking meals for her. But taking a drug? That would imply that she was as weak and helpless as a straight girl. Ironically, that's exactly whom she called to complain.

"I cannot tell you," she told me a few days after surgery, "how much my knee fucking hurts."

I asked if the doctor had sent any medication home with her.

"Yeah, she sent . . . let me see. Hang on a sec." I heard her put the phone down and rifle through some papers on her coffee table. "Here it is. Percocet. She gave something called Percocet."

"Oh, you should take that," I told her. "I took that once and it really worked."

"Yeah, but you . . . " Her voice trailed off a bit, and when she continued talking, I noticed that it even began to falter. "Ya know. It's just that . . . you seem to have a lower pain tolerance than I do."

"Right," I said. "Because I'm not a big ol' lesbian. Look, just take the drugs."

"But aren't they going to make me woozy or something?"

"They might, but you won't care. And your pain will go away."

"I don't know. I just don't know about this. Will I hallucinate?"

"You will if you're lucky." My sister was not amused, so I quickly provided more encouragement. "Bobbi, I'm right down the road. Just try the Percocet. If you start to feel funny, call me, and I'll come right over."

We bantered some more and she became agitated. Finally, the pain reached a new level, and she agreed to take the pill. When the phone rang 20 minutes later, I didn't know which Bobbi to expect: the militant, angry lesbian who would curse me for prompting her to ditch her principles of self-sufficiency; or the scared, younger sibling who needed her big sister to come make the boogeyman go away. To my surprise, I was greeted by neither.

"Wow," she said. Then she sighed heavily. "That is some good shit. I mean . . . wow."

"So you liked it?"

"Hey. Listen. I just took a Percocet. Did you ever try this stuff?"

Oh, boy. This was comical. "Yes," I told her. "I did."

"Well, you should try it sometime."

"Did your pain go away?"

"You know what's funny? My pain went away."

"I guess you don't need me to come over."

"Hey, would you mind not coming over? I think I'll just go to sleep now."

I bid her pleasant dreams.

It turned out that Bobbi only needed that one pill to get her pain under control. Her experience was a successful one for both of us; she had accepted some pharmaceutical help, and I was able to write a parody called "Percocet," a song that remained a family classic for years. Our mom especially loved it. One afternoon, the three of us found ourselves sitting on my patio, enjoying iced tea and singing *Percocet* in perfect three-part harmony. When the last note was sung, Mom looked at both of us with delight and said, "Hey! How about that! A three-way!"

We didn't have the heart to tell her. We just agreed heartily and raised the cups in front of us to the love we shared and to the help that was always just a phone call away.

The Inevitable

UP TO THIS POINT, ALL CARDS in the suit of Cups have celebrated the romance, friendship, acceptance, and forgiveness that make up the human experience. However, life also includes loss and mourning, primarily because everyone we know will eventually die. If that thought depresses you, you'll be able to relate to the man pictured on the Five of Cups.

Wearing a long black cape, he bows his head as he stands under a bleak sky, three overturned cups in front of him, their contents spilled on the ground. The card indicates that you are grieving some type of loss, perhaps the death of a loved one or the end of a relationship. Moreover, you seem to be stuck in the past, just like the man on the card; he is so focused on the three capsized cups in front of him that he doesn't notice the two behind him which are upright. He also doesn't recognize the bridge to his right that can lead him safely across the river in front of him.

I am fascinated with the subject of life-after-death and contemplate it from every conceivable angle. What was I taught about it as a child? What does quantum physics have to say about it? Are the Buddhists correct? The Jews? My experiences with ghosts had assured me that something's going on after we croak. And my visit to a psychic confirmed this belief.

Marjorie is a well-known oracle who lives in Lancaster. She has seen dead people her entire life and was recommended to me by my therapist (which is why I adore my therapist, a woman with a doctorate in counseling who believes in just about everything other-worldly). I went to see Marjorie about Keith, who had recently passed away. Before we began, she explained to me that she never knows who's going to show up in a session and that a client may be surrounded by several loved ones from the other side. However, Keith came through loud and clear, and the accuracy of the reading assured me that he was right there in the room with us.

After talking for about an hour, I thought that we were finished, but Marjorie asked if I had other questions for loved ones who had passed over. I took a shot and asked her if Mom were okay.

"Oh, she's right here," Marjorie said, looking over my shoulder and slightly above my head. She began to smile. "Your mom says she's fine. Just fine. Stop worrying about her already."

I laughed. This woman had perfectly articulated my mother's tone of voice. Even her inflections were exact. "Is my dad with her?" I asked.

"Well, she's with a dog." This captured my attention.

"Is it Atticus?"

"I don't know," Marjorie replied, "but he's a big boy."

That he was, the biggest boy I ever had, a large chocolate lab. Mom was especially fond of him, as she'd gone with me to pick him out of a litter of seven. She'd even loaned me half the money I needed to buy him. We both adored dogs, and the fact that Atticus had been born with severe arthritis which he never let dampen his spirit endeared him to us even more. My vet, Brenda, had never seen a young dog so severely afflicted with joint pain, and when at two years old he tore his ACL, she wasn't surprised.

After his surgery, he came home in a great deal of pain. His leg was in a cast and he was wearing an Elizabethan collar that had to stay in place for weeks. I can say in all confidence that seeing him suffer like that was the worst experience of my life. Yes, I'd seen my father dying in the hospital, and I'd eventually watched my mother's slow decline. But when a person is sick or even facing death, he is aware of his situation. I'm not sure our pets have this understanding. Not being able to explain to Atticus what was happening reduced me to tears, and I sobbed all the way home from the clinic.

When the two of us walked into my house, Mom met us in the living room. My emotional devastation was apparent, and I soon realized that it was one she shared as well. Her expression of helplessness and sorrow made my heart break. My mother was one of the most stoic people I've ever known, but as she watched Atticus try to walk on three legs, as she heard him whimper in pain and confusion, she broke down, too.

The difference between my mom and me, however, is that her breakdowns always had an expiration date. The next day, I continued to sob and collapsed into her arms.

"Why did God let this happen?" I asked her. "Atti's the sweetest boy. And he was born with arthritis. He's always in pain, every single day, and now this? And Brenda said that he'll probably blow out his other ACL, too, and will have to go through another operation. Where is God in all of this?"

Mom steered me to the couch and sat me down. She released the hug I had around her and placed her hands on my shoulders.

"Honey, you can't look at it that way," she said, and her eyes held my attention. "I don't know if God had anything to do with Atti's disease. But he *did* have something to do with the fact that you're Atti's mom."

And I cried even more. After all of the heartbreak my mother had endured in her lifetime, she sat beside me, loving me, as if my sadness far exceeded anything she'd ever experienced.

"Do you see why God wanted you to have Atticus? Think of the money you've spent on his pills, the expensive dog food you buy for him. The surgery cost you thousands of dollars, and you didn't care. Do you know how many people wouldn't do this for him? He has the best home, right here, because of you. And the best care. No one could ever love him as much you do."

As you can guess, none of this stopped my tears, so Mom let me cry for a little while longer. Then it was time to move on. I could almost hear Lady Capulet saying to Juliet, "Now weep no more," as Mom hustled me out of the living room and told me to bring back a couple of cigarettes and an ashtray.

Atticus healed from his surgery and lived for several more happy years until he tore his other ACL. True to an earlier promise I'd made to myself, I was not about to put him through the torment of another operation and the ensuing recovery. Bill and I held him in our arms as he passed away peacefully in Brenda's office. To learn that Atticus and Mom were together in heaven didn't surprise me, but what happened next did.

"You know, your dog is morphing now," Marjorie said. "Huh. I don't see this often. But he's . . . yes. He's changed into a black man. He was your husband. You were slaves on the same plantation."

I'd always had the notion that in a past life I had been a slave. Furthermore, I instinctively knew that I was the kind of slave who kept her head down, who did what she was told. I can't explain these feelings. I can only relate them to you as honestly as possible. That Marjorie knew all of this shocked me; it also cemented my belief in her abilities.

She spoke almost methodically now. "He was always there to watch over you, to keep you safe. You died in the fields. You were a hard worker and just collapsed one day. He carried you back to the shed you shared with him. He never remarried, and he died a few years later."

Of course, I was speechless. I'd shared no musings with anyone about my past lives. The time never seemed right to start a religious uprising among my Christian friends, nor did I relish the thought of being institutionalized against my will.

"That's why he came back to you when he did, as your dog. He wanted to help you and protect you. Had you gone through some tough times before he died?"

I had, indeed, and Atticus was right there with me through them all—Mom's declining health, her multiple surgeries, and her death. He was also by my side when Bruce called to tell me that Keith had died, so the fact that all three of my loved ones were present that night during my reading at Marjorie's made sense to me.

Mom, Keith, and Atticus, all gone within two years of each other. It could have been I on that Five of Cups card, looking at the three empty chalices in front of me. Those were some dark times, as my sister would say, and my Christian belief in heaven comforted me a great deal. But not until my session with Marjorie did I come to know, without a doubt, two things: First, all of us were together before we incarnated into this life, and, more importantly, all of us will be together again in the next. These two cups of mine, standing behind me, waited patiently until I had the strength to turn and face them, to pick them up and accept the hope that they offered.

Of course, I'll face more of these dark times of which Bobbi spoke, as loss is inevitable. What I hope to remember when they do occur, though, is that there will always be something that brings light to this darkness, something that will lead me across the river to my loved ones on the other side. My intention is that I will grieve as long as I must, but that I will then reach for those two cups in back of me. And with any luck, there'll be a cosmo in one and some iced tea in the other.

The Bank

AFTER THAT LAST CARD, some comic relief is sorely needed, and here we have it in the Six of Cups. Under a blue sky, an older child hands a cup filled with white flowers to his younger playmate. They are standing in a garden or courtyard and are surrounded by five other cups filled with the same delicate blooms. These kids are happy because they have been left alone to romp and won't be bothered by the adult who's walking into the house behind them. The imagery of this card represents the joys of youth, whether through reminiscing or reconnecting with someone from your childhood.

Bobbi and I share many memories of our times together on Locust Lane. One of our favorites involves the 20-foot bank in our backyard. This monstrosity was the only part of the property that gave my father pause when he was considering buying it. He and my mother had started their married lives on South Plum Street in Lancaster, and after my sister and I were born, our parents searched for a house with a larger lot outside the confines of the city.

Everything that the house had to offer far exceeded their requirements, from the two-car garage to the picture windows in the front. That bank, though, was going to be my father's undoing, his Achilles' heel. He knew that trying to mow it in the summer was going to be a nightmare. But he put aside his hesitations and decided that the benefits of the property far outweighed the mowing challenges it presented. Before long, the four of us had a new home.

When Mom decided that we were old enough to venture out back on our own, the great hill, named The Bank by our father, became our focal point for all things mischievous. Our creativity knew no bounds as we devised ways to incorporate this mound of earth into our games. The top of The Bank, which Dad called The Top (his mowing frustrations stifled any imagination and reduced his naming of our property's landscape to mere nouns), became Davy Crockett's fort where he stood ready to fight the Indians as they slowly crept up the side of the mountain.

When snow was on the ground, The Bank served as a ski slope in the Alps. We owned no skis, but our trolls did, and we'd send the plastic dolls down The Bank at record speed. These little fellows would accelerate straight down the fall line, across The Flat (the more traditional part of our yard which my father again showed no originality in naming), and into the field that buttressed our property.

As we got older, however, seeing our trolls have all the fun was just too much to bear. We knew better than to ask for skis. We might as well have requested a pet rhinoceros or actual Taskykakes instead of the vastly inferior sweet snacks that my mother insisted on buying to save a little money. No amount of pleading would change her mind. "Do you know what those things cost?" she'd ask me. I had no idea how much anything cost. I just knew that the one time I had a Tastykake at a friend's house, I had been transported to Snack Heaven and had no interest in returning to the Snack Hell to which I'd become accustomed.

The snow was piled at least eight inches deep in our yard one winter and, to add to our bliss, a slight rain had fallen on top of it, covering it with a coating of ice. We couldn't wait to get outside with our skiing trolls, and with just one tap on their backs from Bobbi and me, off they went, flying down The Bank, across The Flat, into Kenny Garber's field, and out of our sight altogether. This particular storm prevented us from following their trek, as the snow was knee deep. We knew that we'd find them in the spring (and we did, covered with cow manure and alfalfa), but that didn't help our immediate predicament. We couldn't ski vicariously through our dolls anymore. We had no skis of our own. The Bank itself wasn't conducive to sledding, as the slope of it ended abruptly at The Flat and would cause the sleds to buck. What were we going to do now?

"I have an idea," Bobbi said. Those four little words would eventually come to signal familial chaos and its ensuing, inevitable punishment, but I was young and hadn't the experience of hindsight.

"What?"

"We can just tear off the cardboard on the walls inside the garage and use that."

The garage at Locust Lane was never finished. Instead of walls, we had studs, and between the studs, Dad had stapled heavy sheets of cardboard atop panels of insulation. I was a little leery of Bobbi's plan at first, but I followed her lead as we stealthily removed two sheets of cardboard from parts of the garage that we suspected were unknown to our father. Sure enough, these blocks of heavy, corrugated paper did the trick. We'd decided against making them into skis, as we had nothing to strap our feet into place, so instead, we used our new inventions as magic carpets and were transported from The Top to the middle of the field in a matter of seconds.

I'm sure Dad was none too pleased with our creation, as he prohibited any further deconstruction of the garage. But he must have purchased more cardboard because, when the two sheets that we used that winter became wet and ragged beyond repair, he supplied us with two more to use in the summer. Sliding down The Bank was easy once Bobbi wet it with the hose. It was a sloppy, sloshy mess we got ourselves into, but our parents didn't seem to mind. Dad must have been hopeful that all of our activity would kill the grass underneath us as he encouraged us to constantly change our course and to use as much of The Bank as possible. Try as we might, though, the grass still grew, and, as my father lay dying, his last words included a blessing on his family and a curse on The Bank. He'd see it in Hell, I think he said, although, to this day, I can't be sure.

In addition to summer sledding, our backyard mountain also became the setting for one of Bobbi's creations called Killer Bee. This sport involved one person (me) standing on The Top, turning on the hose and spraying its water forcefully on the other person (Bobbi), who was trying to climb up The Bank from The Flat. It was an aggressive, violent game whose premise was that the city had come under attack by a swarm of murderous insects; the only thing standing in their way was gushing streams of water (which she called "acid"). Bobbi insisted that I spray the bee (her) directly on the top of her bowed head as she approached me. The bee had to be stopped, she explained, or else the city and everyone in it would perish.

"I will never understand," I told her one night on the phone, "why you enjoyed that. Didn't the water hurt your head?"

"It did. When I first invented the game, I'd tell you to aim for my forehead, but after a while, that gave me a big headache. That's when I started looking at the ground as I made my way up. That didn't seem to hurt as much."

"And the funniest part about this is, you were always the bee."

"Yep. Always the bee. You had no interest at all in trading places."

"Well, can you blame me? I didn't feel like getting maimed."

"But you also didn't feel like playing with your little sister. So all you had to do was stand there and hold the hose. You actually looked pretty disgusted the whole time you were doing it."

Bobbi went on to explain that she couldn't take credit for the concept behind this sport. After all, she said, Mexican killer bees were making the news that year.

"Remember they were coming into the country? It was on TV. It scared the shit out of us."

172

So really, this game was a combination of child's play and current events, a fact that, in retrospect, I find quite impressive. All we Carmitchell Sisters needed were a couple of trolls, some pieces of cardboard, a hose, and a head of steel to while away the hours of our youth and, at the same time, stay focused on world affairs. Bobbi was always the driving, inventive force behind these charades of ours, and the games she produced were as varied as the cups on this card. I was lucky to grow up with such a creative sister, one I could count on to make my childhood fun, and who never, ever asked me to be the bee.

The Shopping Gene

THE PICTURE ON THIS CARD is one of the most thought-provoking in tarot. A man is surprised to see before him a cloud on which rest seven cups with a symbol rising from each one of them. These icons vary from deck to deck, but the most common are a tower, a collection of jewels, a laurel wreath, a dragon, a human head, a shrouded figure, and a snake. These items are representative of the needs that we all share, such as security, success, wisdom, or freedom from fears and temptations.

Trying to pinpoint exactly what is symbolized in each cup is fruitless; there is no definitive answer here. As in all of tarot, the possibilities are endless, and that's the point: The man on the card is faced with unlimited options that are specific to him, in the same way that the card will be specific to the querent who draws it. The overall theme, though, hints at the danger in being offered too many options, most of which won't serve you or are out of your reach. Your job is to pick the one that is attainable and to ignore the others that may sparkle and tempt you, but are in no way right for you at the moment.

Too many choices can be overwhelming, as Alvin Toffler explains in *Future Shock*. He calls this cognitive paralysis "over-choice," and I suffer from a chronic case of it. While I embrace living in a country that allows me personal freedoms, I would love to employ personal assistants to take care of all of my needs, particularly shopping for clothes.

I was born without the gene that allows one to dress fabulously no matter what the occasion, and two of my girlfriends, Stacy and Jody, fashionistas both, understand my plight and are sympathetic. They cannot cross the border into empathy, however, because for them, shopping is a joy that culminates in a myriad of outfits suitable for work or play. They can select and wrap a scarf like nobody's business. They are comfortable with the subtle nuances of distinction between "dressy casual" and "casual dressy" sportswear. They have mastered the art of layering. They own shoes to match each top that they wear, and they understand that calling a handbag a *pocketbook* is a rookie mistake, as is calling pants, *slacks*.

All of this is taken into consideration when they agree to take me shopping. I don't know which store is best, so I follow behind my friends like a lost hiker, trusting that the rangers in front of me will find water and shelter before it is too late. Jody and Stacy learned early on that accompanying me to a large department store such as Target or T.J. Maxx requires a first aid kit complete with an oxygen mask and a defibrillator, as they've witnessed my shallow breathing and the bulging of my carotid artery. Once, when a group of my teacher friends (shoppers all, except for me and one other poor soul) visited Macy's in New York City, I remember almost flatlining until Stacy pulled the paddles from her Coach bag.

"I think it's time for some cocktails," Jody suggested as she helped me from the floor. She glanced over at Stacy. "We should have known better than to bring her in here."

"Why can't stores just have sections for clothing?" I later asked over dirty martinis in Times Square. "Like, you'd walk into The Gap, and you'd seen a sign hanging from the ceiling that reads *PANTS*. And then you'd see another sign that says *TOPS* and one that says *DRESSES*."

"I feel like that's kind of the way stores are already set up," Stacy said.

Jody nodded her head in agreement, realizing for the first time, I think, that they were dealing with a special needs shopper. "You know, let's start out more slowly when we shop next," she offered. "We'll go to the mall when we get home and just stick with one wing."

The sweat that beaded on my forehead didn't go unrecognized.

"OK, OK," Stacy said, calmly stroking my arm. "How about we visit just two stores in one wing? And we'll be with you the whole time."

Always the teachers. These women had the perfect lesson plan, complete with differentiated instruction for every learning level. They'd managed to create for me my very own IEP (Individualized Education Program) that modified their original curriculum to include reachable goals for their student, allowing me to achieve success. Not to be corralled by state standards, they even provided extra-curricular activities in the form of alcohol. I couldn't ask for better friends.

My sister, on the other hand, needs no help in this area because, in her words, "I don't shop for clothes." This, of course, is somewhat of an exaggeration since she's generally dressed when I see her. She does actually purchase items to wear, but she does so on an irregular basis.

"I buy a pair of shorts after the ones that I'm wearing start to get . . . what's the word . . . threadbare?" She seemed to be as deficient in her clothing vocabulary as I am, and that thought made me feel less alone.

"And then?"

"Then I go to Goodwill and find another pair for five bucks. And don't forget, I barter for clothes. When I play at Pam Cummings' pottery show, the guy who owns ArtWorks is also selling his stuff there, and he knows how much I love the pants that he designs."

"Yes," I said. "You always come home with a pair."

"Yep. He tells me that I bring people into the show and it's good for his business. I don't get paid, so he gives me pants and Pam gives me pottery."

"Pants and pottery. Nothing better."

"And remember, Anne, I don't care about how many clothes I own. You look at a picture of me playing at Chestnut Hill Cafe in 2002? I'm wearing the same top then as I was when I played there in 2016."

"That's true. But sometimes, depending on where you play, you have to get dressed up a little."

"And that's when I go with the black pants I've owned since 2001. I call them my 'stage pants.' And if I want to really get fancy, I'll wear my black shirt. I've had that one since the 90s."

Bobbi never has to worry about getting fancy too often. Her day job as a contractor involves a lot of painting, so the clothes she wears really take a beating. She is currently mourning the loss of her favorite pair of contractor shorts. "They had holes in the butt and holes in the crotch," she told me. "I had to get rid of them. If I fell off of a ladder and someone came to help me, they'd get a lot more than they bargained for."

If I were to draw the Seven of Cups, then, out of one goblet would float a pair of high-rise, low-rise, and mid-rise jeans. Out of the second, a camisole, a tank, and a spaghetti strap tee shirt would appear. A tunic, a sheath, and an A-line dress would hover over the third. And I couldn't tell you what would be rising from the other four cups since I'd be passed out on the floor at that point, my head exploding with options.

I'd regain consciousness eventually, and would long for a utopian society where jeans were jeans, tops were tops, and dresses were dresses. Until the powers-that-be simplify women's fashions, however, I will rely on Stacy and Jody to work their magic, and on Bobbi to snap me into a more realistic approach to clothes shopping.

"Just dress for comfort," she'd tell me. "Hit Goodwill, then Kmart, and don't wear anything with holes in the crotch." Those are three options I can live with.

Homebody

THE EIGHT, NINE, AND TEN OF CUPS are about changing your course in life and enjoying the fulfillment that this change could generate. The first of the three cards shows a younger man walking away with a rather dejected gait from eight cups that are aligned and stacked in two neat rows. His back is turned on them because he is symbolically leaving behind the neatly structured life that he's built for himself. The Eight of Cups suggests that you are satisfied with the life you've constructed for yourself, but you want something more. You may be a bit fearful and sad as you depart, but you're willing to take the risk.

Leaving the comfortable surroundings of my home for a new adventure has never been my strong suit, probably due to my upbringing. We didn't take many vacations when Bobbi and I were young because our family didn't have a lot of money. Now that my sister and I are grown, neither of us travels as frequently as a lot of people do.

"Maybe that's because Mom and Dad never took us a lot of places," I suggested to Bobbi. "Traveling wasn't something that we were accustomed to, so we didn't factor it into our adult lives."

"That's a good point," Bobbi said. "And here's something else. When I think about it, most of the traveling I've done has been job-related."

"I look at other people's vacation pictures on Facebook, and I feel like a loser."

"Total loser," Bobbi agreed. "But do you really want to go anywhere, anyway?"

Of course I didn't. If you've been reading this book in chronological order, you are well aware of my aversion to leaving my house. My love of staying home has been passed down to me by my father, who liked nothing better than working in our garage or his woodshop. Mom, on the other hand, enjoyed getting away from time to time, and after Dad died, she'd take trips with her girlfriends and her sister Louise. Bobbi liked traveling with Mom, too, and their excursions to places like Arizona, New York City, and Skyline Drive were all critical successes. I loved hanging out with Mom, but I wasn't willing to get on a plane with her. Then I'd be responsible for her death in a fiery crash as well as my own. It was a risk that I was not willing to take. Mom and I, then, had to come up with something closer to home than the West Coast and easier to navigate than Manhattan.

We decided that short, overnight trips were our best bet. Actually, they were only "trips" in the sense that we'd get in my car and drive somewhere. Furthermore, the outcome of our adventures was always a comedy of errors. The vacations that my sister and mother took went swimmingly, and they had the photographs and stories to prove it. But the small treks taken by Mom and me never fulfilled their original intent.

We first went to a bed-and-breakfast in New Hope, Pennsylvania, a small town about two hours from home. An artist's colony in its conception, New Hope is filled with shops and galleries and landscaping that can make even a homebody like me forget the fact that she was leaving her dogs at her house where they would surely die of broken hearts before her return. We had a grand time driving there, I behind the wheel and Mom navigating.

When we checked into our room, we both loved its Victorian decor and the thought of an elaborate breakfast in the morning. After we dropped off our bags, we hit the town to do some shopping and have dinner. However, we lost track of time, and before we knew it, all the restaurants were closed. We had to resort to buying food from a convenience store and ended up in our room eating packs of peanut butter crackers and candy and drinking cans of Sprite. Our visions of an elegant dinner in a nice restaurant were squashed, and the fancy clothing we'd brought with us for said dinner was left hanging dejectedly in the armoire.

"Whoever heard of a town rolling up its sidewalks at 8:30 at night?" Mom asked me as we sat facing each other on the sides of our beds.

"I know. This is really kind of pathetic. There's not even a television in here."

So we talked for an hour or so before bedtime, and as we bade each other a fond goodnight and tucked ourselves in, we agreed that our trip had been successful so far, despite the fact that Mom had acid reflux from the M&M's she'd eaten. We fell asleep, but within 20 minutes I was wide awake with restless legs.

Restless Leg Syndrome, as it's now called, is something I'd inherited from my mother. It presents as an inability to keep one's legs still while trying to sleep, and it is absolutely maddening, this need to get out of bed and walk around, or to stay in bed and move your legs as if riding a bicycle turned on its side. Not one to suffer in silence, of course, I insisted on waking Mom so that I could complain about my discomfort. She, a fellow RLS sufferer, was empathetic and stayed up with me until I was able to calm my legs and go back to sleep. As a result, we stayed awake most of the night, missed breakfast the next morning, and stopped at a Denny's on the way home.

A few years later, around Christmas time, we agreed to try New Hope again, convinced that our second attempt could not possibly go over, as Mom put it, "like a lead balloon." The internet had recently made its entrance, and I decided to book a room online. What we discovered when we checked in, however, was that pictures of hotels on travel sites could be as misleading as those of people on dating sites. Our room's decor made us both question whether or not we had time-traveled to 1965 and were now vacationing not in "a quaint hideaway in the hills of historic New Hope" but instead in something resembling a condemned Howard Johnson's. The place smelled musty and moldy, and the two bath towels hanging near the shower stall in our room were tinged with grey. Mom and I looked at each other in disbelief and disgust.

"This place is awful," she said.

We agreed that even Norman Bates had his standards, and we needed a way out. Mom had a plan.

"OK," she said. "Here's what we're going to do. You grab both suitcases and walk me out to the car. I'm going to bend over and look as old as I can. Then you go back to the front desk and tell them that I have back problems." She didn't, of course, but it's the only affliction which would be visible to others and ensure our departure.

I did as I was told. After depositing her in the front seat, I entered the hotel lobby looking distressed.

"I am so sorry about this," I told the front desk clerk. "But my mother had back surgery a few weeks ago. She thought that she was up for this trip, but she isn't. Is there some way that we could get our money back? I have to take her home."

To my surprise, a vacationer beside me yelped. The hotel was booked for the holidays, and he had just been turned away. "I'll gladly take her room," he said to the clerk.

Everyone agreed that we thought we'd heard the angels singing. There was no room in the inn this Christmastide until my mother faked an illness and unwittingly provided safe shelter for this gentleman and his family. Two hours later, Mom and I were home.

"What was up with you two?" Bobbi asked. "You get sick. Then Mom fakes being sick."

"I don't know. We just never had any luck traveling."

"Yeah, but you act like it only happened when you had big plans. Remember the other stuff, like the musical you went to see?"

Yes, Mom and I had walked out of *West Side Story* at intermission because we didn't like our seats. "But don't forget," I told Bobbi, "that the three of us also walked out of *White Christmas*."

"You're right. It was the musical version, and we hated it. Wasn't it kind of sexed up or something?"

181

"Yes, I think there were some overtones. And I didn't like thinking about Bing Crosby having sex with anyone."

"I guess Mom didn't, either. Or I didn't. But we all hated it and left after the second act."

Then there was the time that Mom and I were excited to try brunch at an upscale restaurant in Marietta, a small, historic town close to Millersville. After the hostess seated us and we looked at the menu, we could not camouflage our alarm.

"Twenty-five dollars for two eggs, toast, and coffee?" Mom whispered.

I perused the rest of the choices. "And that's the cheapest thing on here."

We glanced furtively around us. No one else was sitting in this part of the dining room. No waitress had approached us with a greeting.

"There's a side door over there," Mom said, and with that, we were gone, back in the car and on the road.

Like the man on the Eight of Cups, I had tried my darndest to change my course. I had wanted the same experiences that Mom had with Bobbi, and I was willing to leave my home and expand my horizons to do so. But it was not to be. Mom and I always had fun together, even if the trip turned out to be a bust, but the best part was coming home to white towels and a refrigerator that was open all night. And this is where the next two cards of this suit come into play.

The Nine of Cups is the card of wishes fulfilled. A portly fellow sits happily on a bench, nine cups behind him, joyful that he has everything he's always wanted. Similarly, the Ten of Cups continues this theme of contentment but expands it in a familial sense. A young couple with two small children stands in front of their home, with 10 cups forming a rainbow overhead and a bucolic setting surrounding the family. I could always relate to the feelings that both of these cards emote when I'd return home from a trip. I was glad that, like the fellow in the Eight of Cups, I had left my comfort zone and tried something new. But getting back home, being with my dogs and my books (and my partner, if I had one at the time) also represented for me the contentment symbolized in the Nine and Ten of Cups.

"So how do you explain all of that?" I asked Bobbi. "You go away with Mom, everything goes smoothly. I go away with Mom, and things kind of tank."

"Well, it doesn't take a flowchart to figure that one out." I found the hastiness of her reply, even her eagerness to share it with me, more than a bit demoralizing.

"I guess you're saying that whenever I plan a vacation, the whole thing's a bust. But why do you think that's so?"

Bobbi's voice had a good amount of gentleness in it, but it also teetered precariously on the edge of condescension. "I think that you tend to be more particular in your expectations when you travel."

"Like how?" I asked.

"Like what you eat. Where you sleep. The type of mattress in the room. How far away you have to park the car."

"I get it."

"How far you have to drive to get there. The wallpaper in the room. Whether or not the front desk clerk has his hair parted the right way."

"Bobbi."

"If the color of the tablecloths in the restaurant matches the cloth napkins. If the tables actually *have* tablecloths. Whether the air conditioning in the room can be set as low as 61 degrees. The political affiliation of the guy who parks your car. If the weather is . . ."

She may have continued with her diatribe, but it was hard for me to tell. The phone had suddenly and mysteriously been disconnected.

Who Made Mom Mad?

THE QUEEN OF CUPS REPRESENTS a woman who is a loyal wife and a protective, loving mother. Mom was both of these. She and Dad had their share of marital discord as all partners do, but their marriage was one built on love. And while Mom would be the first one to break out the flyswatter if the need arose, she was also the first one to come to the defense of her daughters. She could be direct in her requirements and forthright in her opinions, but Bobbi and I never doubted her love for us.

However, she had a hard time expressing emotions that she felt might leave her vulnerable to criticism from family or friends. The Queen of Cups can sometimes indicate the need to repress one's feelings, and Mom could do that like nobody's business. Therefore, her way of dealing with any internal agitation was simply to stop talking. And then the game of "Who Made Mom Mad, and What Did You Do, Exactly?" would begin, Bobbi and I eyeing each other with suspicion while at the same time rallying our army of two into a mighty regiment.

An example of such a skirmish took place one summer at my sister's home. She was hosting a picnic for the four of us and was setting the table as Mom relaxed in her lawn chair and Dad tended the grill. As I pulled into the driveway and walked toward the three of them, Mom promptly got up and walked into the house.

"What's wrong with her?" I asked Bobbi.

"I have no idea. She was fine until you got here."

I was a bit shocked that my sister could so readily blame me for our situation. I reminded her that any discord between the troops would lower morale and that perhaps she needed to review the rules of war; after all, she, too, could fall under attack at any time and would value my support. She immediately acquiesced.

I turned to Dad. "Do *you* know what's wrong with her?"

"Your guess is as good as mine," he said, not looking up from the grill.

"Why don't we all go inside and act like nothing's wrong?" Bobbi suggested. "We can just pretend she didn't do anything rude."

Denial. The master plan of dysfunctional families everywhere, and the tactic that would have made even General Patton's invasion of Sicily pale in comparison. I liked it.

We walked into the kitchen through the front door and Mom immediately walked out through the back.

"That went well," I said.

Dad chuckled a little, shook his head, and lit his pipe. "I'll see you girls outside. The food's ready."

Bobbi looked at me blankly. "Did you two have a fight or something?"

"Absolutely not." I was frantically searching the recent past and could find nothing. "Are you sure she wasn't pissed off when she got here?"

"No. Like I said, she was fine until you . . . she was fine."

Bobbi cut short her second attempt at making me complicit in this matter. I let it slide.

"I guess we should just go outside and just . . . I don't know. Just act normal?" she offered.

"I guess. You go first." I was scared now. I had somehow angered The Queen.

Mom had seated herself strategically at the head of the picnic table where she would face Dad at the other end. As we ate, none of her comments were directed toward me, and any laughter that she shared, she did so with Dad and Bobbi. My sister and I exchanged glances of disbelief across the table.

Any eye contact made with Dad, however, was short-lived and eventually dismissed. He was a brave soldier, my father, and a crafty one. He had met the enemy years before, and she was his. As he'd told us many times while we were growing up, "You girls know how much I love you. But your mom? She's the one." I knew that I could find no paternal shelter from this particular storm.

By the time dessert was served, I could endure no more. Turning to my left, I faced my adversary, my voice harsh.

"Can you please tell me, Mom, what exactly I did to piss you off? And don't act like you don't know what I'm talking about."

Bobbi's eyes widened as she slightly leaned back from the table. Dad made the sign of the cross.

Bubbles met my gaze. "Where were you last Monday?" she asked me evenly.

"Last Monday? I have no idea. What are you talking about?"

"Just think about it for a minute. Last Monday."

My mind was blank. At 33 years old, I was beginning to question my cognitive skills.

"I don't know. I give up. Where was I last Monday?"

"You were with Jim. On Monday." Jim was the young man I was dating at the time. And apparently the guy I was with on Monday.

"OK. If you say so."

"And last Monday was Memorial Day."

She was correct. I then remembered that I had, indeed, gone with Jim and his family on a day trip to Gettysburg.

"Yeah?" I said. "So what?"

"Memorial Day is the day you're supposed to spend with your family. But you didn't think about us. You just went off with him."

It was then that I noticed that Bobbi and Dad, cowards both, had left our company and were now nonchalantly sauntering down the lane on an afternoon stroll. My only option at this point was surrender. I apologized to my mother, or at least I tried to do so. But as I turned to face her, I realized that my words were floating in the air above an empty picnic table, as Mom, once again, had walked back into the house.

"She was so mad at you that day," Bobbi said on the phone. "You lost major points when you went away with that guy."

"Yeah, but on Memorial Day? I mean, it wasn't Christmas or anything."

"Hey, I don't care if it was Arbor Day," Bobbi said. "You know how she was."

"Right, but at least we always had Dad there to lighten things up."

UNLIKE THE QUEEN OF CUPS, the King is able to deal with emotional issues more calmly than his bride. On the card, his throne rests on rocky waters, yet his face bears the calm demeanor of someone able to ride out the storm. We could always count on Dad to provide humor in a tense situation. One of his favorite methods of doing so was to perform The Pointer.

Neither Bobbi nor I has any recollection of how dad's impersonation of a hunting dog came to be. But we were always relieved to see it emerge when things had gone a bit awry,

especially with our mother. This pose of his, not easily described, began with his standing at attention, turning his head quickly from right to left in an attempt to mimic a dog, its senses on high alert as it tracked a rabbit. This in itself was enough to make Mom giggle, as my father's long, slender frame became rigid with the anticipation of a hound stalking its prey. He held the pose anywhere from a number of seconds to a full minute; the duration of time involved was directly proportionate to my mother's mood.

Then, without warning, he would slap his hands together and push his left arm in front of him and his right arm behind him, his right leg following suit while his left one remained stationary and bent at the knee. He would lean forward slightly, his eyes locked on his imaginary victim and his head quivering with anticipation. The Pointer made its appearance at the picnic and Dad's dramatic flair had achieved its goal. All of us laughed and forgot what we were mad about in the first place.

OBVIOUSLY, THE KING AND QUEEN of the Carmitchell Cups struck a balance that most couples should envy. Their court would not be complete, however, without a knight in shining armor, and that would be my sister. Bobbi has always rescued us in our time of need. After Dad died, Mom knew better than to call me if The Bank needed to be cut or a shelf needed to be hung. And I can't tell you the number of times I've called Bobbi, panicked because I'd heard a strange noise in the house. I would be certain as you well know that an alien or a burglar had found its way into my rancher, and since my sister was only five minutes away, I'd call her in the hopes that she could calm my nerves by talking some sense into me.

"Tell me again what you think you heard?" she'd ask me.

"I don't know. It was a loud thud or something."

"OK. Did the wind blow the door shut?"

"I don't think so. The doors are all closed. I have the air on."

"Are you doing a big load of laundry? Maybe the washing machine's making the noise."

"No. That's not it."

"Where are the dogs?"

"They're right here, looking around. They heard it, too."

"Do you want me to come over?"

Ah, those magic words. Yes, I wanted her to come over. Just hearing that she was on her way made my fear subside, and I knew that shortly, when I'd see her headlights in my driveway, I could release my grip on the butcher knife I'd been holding.

Of course, Bobbi found no burglars or aliens anywhere as she looked in the closets and underneath all of the beds, and more often than not, we'd never find the origin of the thud. But a visit from the Knight of Cups had cleared any negative thoughts from my mind. After she'd leave, I would be able to sleep peacefully, the knife by my bed and a bureau in front of my bedroom door.

Once, though, both of us were so unnerved by one of these experiences that Bobbi ended up staying overnight. Looking out of my kitchen window one afternoon, I took a picture with my cell phone of the dogs playing in the yard. When I looked at the photo a few minutes later, I was terrified. A woman's face was clearly present. She resembled my Aunt Mabel, a middle-aged matron with her hair in a bun and a strand of pearls around her neck. I texted the picture to Bobbi right away, and my phone rang instantly.

"What in the name of God is that?" she asked me.

"I have no idea, but it is freaking me out."

"I'm coming over."

She didn't even wait to be asked, and I was relieved that my terror had been shared. When she arrived, we examined the picture closely, even using a magnifying glass to enhance the image.

"That looks exactly like Aunt Mabel," Bobbi said. "Have you been thinking about her lately?"

I hadn't.

"Well, it could also be Aunt Marg. Or Aunt Jeanette. You sure you haven't been playing with your tarot cards or burning sage or doing whatever it is that you do?"

I assured Bobbi that all I'd done so far that day was watch TV and hang with the dogs. We continued to theorize why any of our deceased relatives would make an appearance now, decades after they'd passed. Perhaps they were trying to warn me about something. Or maybe Mom and Dad were trying to get in touch but were too busy to stop by, so they had sent a proxy instead.

"You know," I suggested, "the woman also looks like Eleanor Roosevelt. Maybe we're approaching this the wrong way."

"But why would Eleanor Roosevelt show up in your kitchen?"

"I don't know. I've always admired her. You did, too, right?"

"Yeah, but I never expected to see her."

"Maybe this is the ghost I saw on my stairs, but she's older now. You know, time doesn't mean anything on the other side. But maybe she's stuck here, and she's aging."

"But why would she look like Eleanor Roosevelt?"

"I have no idea." I tried a different angle. "Was Eleanor born around here?" I asked.

"No. I think she was born in New York."

"Well, that doesn't make any sense. Why would she come to Washington Boro?"

"Maybe because she was always traveling as an ambassador?"

None of this was adding up. "I don't know who this is, but I can tell you one thing for sure. You're staying here tonight."

Bobbi didn't argue with me. She had no more interest in going back to her place than I did spending the night locked in my bedroom. For all she knew, the woman in this picture had fully expected me to call Bobbi (since ghosts are psychic) so that she, the spirit, could lure my sister away from her house and be waiting to attack her when she got home. We weren't going anywhere until we could find a logical reason why Eleanor Roosevelt would want to ambush one of us. We put the phone away and spent the rest of the evening in ignorance, watching TV and promising each other that we'd find the answer in the light of day.

The next morning, we approached the kitchen with hesitation. Everything seemed to be in order. My home had not been transformed into Val-Kill Cottage. I didn't notice a United Nations flag hanging from the ceiling. What I did notice, however, was something I hadn't seen the day before.

"Oh, dear Lord," I said, as I approached the sink.

"What?" Bobbi asked. "What do you see?"

"This," I said, and I pointed to a suction cup with a small hook adhered firmly to the kitchen window. I had forgotten that it was there. I couldn't remember *why* it was there. I think that, a few years back, I had hung a small indoor thermometer on it.

"That doesn't even look like Eleanor Roosevelt," my sister said flatly.

"I know. Dang. I really thought she was here."

"Can we just not tell anyone about this?" I could understand Bobbi's concern. After all, her reputation as the voice of reason was at stake, and it now hung delicately in the balance.

I assured her that we would tell no one, but before long, the picture along with our experience made its way to my Facebook page. By that time, any sort of public recognition of our encounter didn't bother either of us. Bobbi and I don't mind sharing our self-deprecating stories with other people. I'm a little hesitant to admit, though, that some of our favorite tales involve my acting like the Page of Cups.

THE PAGE OF CUPS CARD represents someone prone to temper tantrums and childlike behavior. I'd like to think that I'm past the age of exhibiting the former, but I know better than to assume I've outgrown the latter. Committing immature pranks is one of the characteristics I'm loathe to shed as I age, especially if the recipient of these jokes is my sister.

Dog sitting for Bobbi is something I love and have done so countless times over the years. Our dogs have always gotten along so well that having my sister's pets here seems like camp for all concerned. The only requirement I'd ever asked of Bobbi is to please make sure that her dog Chance (or Jessie or Berkley) was flea-free before coming to Aunt Annie's for an extended stay.

"Are you sure Chance doesn't have fleas?" I'd asked Bobbi when she dropped off her dog before leaving for Michigan.

"Yep. I checked. Not a flea in sight."

I looked down at her dog. "Really? Because she's scratching a lot."

"She's just getting used to the flea meds. She's fine. Just a little hyper right now."

I'd never seen a dog take so long "getting used to the flea meds," and after three days of watching Chance scratch and three nights of hearing her do so, I took her to see Brenda, our vet.

After a brief examination, Brenda told me the prognosis. "Chance has scabies," she said. "Not a big deal, but it's good you brought her in. This isn't going away on its own. I'll give you some meds, and this should clear up in a few days."

For all I knew, after she pronounced her diagnosis, Brenda could have been reciting the Preamble to the Constitution. I had stopped listening after she'd said her first sentence. Scabies. I wasn't exactly sure what they were, but visions of skanky hotel rooms romped in my brain.

"I'm going to kill my sister," I told Brenda.

The lack of emotion in my voice must have startled her because she laughed nervously and assured me that this type of thing is more common than I realized. "Not in my house, it isn't," I said. Brenda adjusted her glasses and left the examination room.

I looked down at Chance. She was the sweetest dog, so cooperative and kind. When things didn't go well for her, she never said a word, just smiled and went on with her day. I felt so bad for her, this little one with the unmentionable ailment. I knew that, somehow, my sister must pay for this embarrassing situation into which I had been thrust.

Glancing to my right, I noticed a small chalkboard hanging on the wall, one used by the vets at the clinic to explain to clients, through diagrams, all things veterinary. This would do just fine. I picked up a piece of chalk, and on the board I wrote the following:

Bobbi Carmitchell's dog has scabies.

As we left the clinic, Chance chuckled. So did I. So did the next client who walked into the exam room, and so did Brenda as she erased my proclamation. I don't remember how Bobbi came to know about my childish prank, but she took it all in stride. We couldn't add this incident to social media because the internet hadn't been invented yet. But I am proud to say that I literally posted something on a wall long before Facebook came into play.

THE SUIT OF CUPS can depict the best that we have to offer— romance, humor, forgiveness—and can also expose the worst of our flaws—stubbornness, jealousy, emotional unavailability. We humans are an odd mix of all of these characteristics, and thank goodness that's the case. The only way we're able to grow is to see the cracks on the surface and repair them from within. If the Queen is emotionally removed, the King's humor will help her to engage. When the Page is fearful, the Knight will calm her. And at the end of the day, with all four coming to the others' rescue, the family emerges as a cohesive entity, one founded on affection and determined to lift each of its members to his highest potential.

Yeats' dire observation that "the center cannot hold," while not referencing families in particular, could serve as a reminder that without laughter, understanding, and love, no group of people can experience the joy of being alive and present with each other. When things start to fall apart, as they always do, the center *will* hold as long as love is at its core.

THE ACE OF SWORDS

Separation Anxiety

WE NOW ENTER THE TERRAIN of the most challenging suits in tarot. Leaving behind the Suits of Wands and Cups, which represent our creative passions and our emotions, we're now faced with the Suit of Swords. These cards embody just what the name implies: conflict, either internal or external. In order to deal successfully with the problem at hand, sharp, intellectual prowess is required.

As with the previous ace cards, the Ace of Swords pictures a hand coming out of the clouds. It is grasping a double-edged sword, pointing upward, upon whose tip rest a crown and some leaves which hang precariously. Even the landscape seems hazardous, a desolate view of mountains under a darkening sky.

When the Ace of Swords is drawn, a problem has presented itself. You know you have the capacity to solve it, but you must proceed with prudence. Your intellect will guide your way; however, you must not leave your heart and spirit behind when making your decisions.

Bill and I reached a decision a few years ago which was a bit challenging but was one that we were glad to accept. Now, when I use the word "we" here, I'm really referring to just myself, as is true with most decisions that Bill and I make. My boyfriend is pliable. If I'm convinced that something is absolutely right for us, he'll agree, short of covering our backyard with playground turf to avoid mowing, or dressing up for Halloween.

We wanted to stay for a couple of nights in Jim Thorpe, a small town in northern Pennsylvania. Bill had run a race there and was convinced that I would love the quaint atmosphere of the area. There was much to do in this idyllic village, he assured me. Ghost tours, shopping, hiking, antique stores, train rides, and the foliage. Ah, the foliage.

"We should go there this fall," he'd told me. "It's only a couple hours away, and the ride there will be great. So much foliage."

I had to admit that this trip did sound delightful, especially since our destination was relatively close to home. Bill agreed to take care of the arrangements and found a bed-and-breakfast in the heart of Jim Thorpe. The only obstacle we could foresee was what to do with the puppies.

Normally, Bobbi would spend the weekend here with them. However, she was unavailable. The other person on my list of dog sitters was a trusted friend known to all my pets in the past as Uncle Phil despite the fact that of course he was not their biological uncle. Phil had cared for my dogs so many times that he had the routine down pat. But I paused before calling him as I recollected how anal I'd been during the weeks leading up to his previous visits. I wasn't sure I was willing, yet again, to put myself through the mental torment that always accompanied my preparations for leaving my dogs.

As you well know, I am at the mercy of unfounded fears. This disability emerges most vigorously when I must place my pets in the hands of someone else, no matter how competent that person may be. To illustrate my point, allow me to share with you the list of instructions I'd once left for Uncle Phil when he stayed with my dogs Emerson and Tess:

Dear Phil,

Thanks for watching the pups! Here's what you need to know:

1. *The dog food is in the 85-pound bag marked "Dog Food." I've neatly printed these words in black magic marker next to the label on the bag which reads "Dog Food." It is directly inside the front door through which you just walked in order to read this note.*

2. *In the fridge is a gallon jug marked "Dogs." The dogs themselves are not to be placed in this jug. It simply contains tap water that I like to keep cold for them.*

3. *Their collars are on the table in the kitchen. The dogs need these to go outside because I have an invisible fence, and they'll roam the fields without them. Please remove Emerson's collar as soon as he enters the house. It is a reminder to him of his enslavement by humans in a totalitarian regime. Tess doesn't care.*

4. *Emerson's pills are on the kitchen counter right next to the table. Please give him one a day, but make sure that you give Tess a biscuit at the same time. Then quickly give Emerson a biscuit because he knows the difference between Rimadyl and treats and will feel left out. It's best to continue this activity until you've given them five biscuits each. Even though Emerson's received six, including the Rimadyl, Tess can't count past four.*

5. *In case of a nuclear attack, the dogs' gas masks are located in the drawer under the counter. Evacuation plans are not necessary as I've installed a fallout shelter underneath the table. Just lift the rug and you'll see the trap door on which the words "Trap Door" are printed neatly in black magic marker.*

Thanks, Phil! I'll be home Sunday by 3:00, but depending on traffic, it might be closer to 3:17, or maybe even 18. But I'll call and let you know.

Annie

Revisiting my obsession with pet care made me realize that it was time to branch out and do what everyone else seems to do: board the dogs. They were nine months old, and I thought it would be a grand idea to introduce them, at such a young age, to the idea of staying in a kennel. I did my homework and found a place nearby that came highly recommended by friends of mine who cared as much for their dogs as we did for ours. It was a tough decision to make, but it was one based on intellect and not emotion, so I convinced myself that it must have been valid. Bill agreed (as always), and we dropped Maggie and Emma off at their new home for the weekend.

Neither of us was happy with the interior. The dogs would be kept in a room with a concrete floor and surrounded by chain-link fencing. We had brought with us their beds and toys, though, so we figured that they'd be content there (as much as they could be, knowing full well that their parents were selfishly leaving them behind for a romp in the hills of Jim Thorpe). Plus, the kennel was nestled in a wooded area, and the owner promised to take the dogs for walks three times a day. We buried whatever trepidations we had and left for our getaway.

The foliage we witnessed as we left Washington Boro was stunning. Five minutes into our trip, however, the skies clouded over and the rain began. And it kept on beginning as we drove two hours into Jim Thorpe. Any foliage we saw during our trek existed strictly in our imaginations, but we still naively looked forward to spending a couple of nights in a beautiful town that offered enchanting events and rustic charm.

The problem, however, was that in order to experience these events and charm, it is important that one arrive at the proper time of the year. Everything we looked forward to had closed for the season. There were no festivals to enjoy, no ghost walks to terrify us, no rides of any kind, be they of the horse-and-carriage variety, or that of hay. Even the shops had closed for the day by the time we'd rolled into town.

The bed-and-breakfast was not what we'd expected, either. We were provided a bed, and breakfast would be served the next morning; for these amenities, we were grateful. But there was no Victorian allure. Instead, our room looked reminiscent of my father's den, with dark paneling, worn shag carpeting, and varnished end tables. After unpacking, we walked out into the storm and found an Italian restaurant where we ate a meal of extraordinary mundanity. When we returned to our room later that evening, I realized that it was time for me to tell Bill the truth.

"This is all my fault," I confessed.

"What is?"

"This trip. I'm a jinx. Every time Mom and I tried to go away, bad shit always happened."

I went on to list the failed excursions I took with my mother. "But we always ended up laughing about them," I assured Bill. "Eventually."

"Honey, don't worry about it. We still have two days here. I'm sure the weather will clear up by tomorrow."

Bill was such an innocent. Despite my attempts to clearly explain to him the spell I had unintentionally cast on our trip, he still retained hope. He refused to see the voodoo doll that was his girlfriend, lying next to him in the double-that-was-supposed-to-be-king-sized bed. We talked for a little bit, and Bill, as is his nature, was asleep in two minutes. I, on the other hand, lay there wide awake, listening to the rain and wind beating against the window.

I missed the puppies. One of them was always snuggled up next to me. And here I was, puppiless, staring at a plaster ceiling and wondering if they were okay. I was convinced that they were confused and lonely. They had never spent a night away from us. What had we been thinking, leaving them there in that hell-hole? What if they had to go to the bathroom? What if they had a nightmare? What if the kennel had been struck by lightning?

If I'd ever needed a sleeping pill, this was the night. I got up and rummaged through my suitcase. I'd packed everything I needed, boots for the hayride, sneakers for the shopping. But no pills for the sleeping. As I crawled back into bed, I coughed loudly in the hopes of awakening Bill so that he could share in my misery. My plan failed. For the next five hours, I sobbed quietly, picturing our little girls in all their wretched surroundings.

I don't know how we realized that morning was upon us. There was no sunlight peeking through our windows, no birds were announcing the day. We awoke to rain more torrential than the day before.

"I hate this," I told Bill. "I want to leave."

"Let's get out of here," he said, and off we went, imagining foliage all the way home.

Of course, when we arrived at the kennel, Maggie and Emma were fine. There was much jumping and kissing and squealing and panting. And the pups were excited to see us, too.

Now, I'm all about making good decisions based on logic and facts. But the Ace of Swords warns us that, no matter how clearly we've planned our direction, no matter how successfully met our goals may have been, hurting others while achieving this success benefits no one in the long run.

"But you didn't 'hurt' your dogs, Anne," Bobbi reminded me when I called to talk about this card. "You already admitted that they were fine when you picked them up."

"I guess you're right. But I couldn't stop crying when I thought about them. It was awful."

"So, really, you ended up hurting yourself, thinking of all the bad things that could have happened, but didn't. That's pretty much how you operate."

"But how would you have felt knowing that Berkley was all alone in a caged-in place during a storm?"

"Well, I'd never leave my dog in a kennel. That's just cruel."

"Bye, Bob."

"Bye, Anne."

Bugs and Slugs

ON THIS CARD, A WOMAN SITS ALONE on a bench by a body of water. She is blindfolded and grips a sword in each hand. Overhead, a twilit sky holds a quarter moon. The sea behind her appears to be receding, as boulders are peeking over the water's surface. This woman has an issue that needs to be addressed, but she is refusing to move ahead. How long has she been sitting there contemplating what to do? The scenery around her could indicate that she may have been there all day.

The evening is upon her now, but her swords are still crossed in front of her chest symbolizing, perhaps, her inability to pick one over the other. Whatever conflict she's facing needs a resolution, but how can she solve her dilemma when she keeps her eyes closed to her options? The Two of Swords indicates that it's time to get busy and to stop ignoring the problem at hand.

One of the biggest decisions I had to make as an adult, and one that I'd ignored for over 20 years, was how to heat and cool my house efficiently. When my home was built in the early 1970s, radiant heat was all the rage because it was considered aesthetically pleasing. No longer would one have to face unsightly baseboard heaters in each room of her house. Instead, heating elements were cleverly hidden in the ceiling, and heated air would drift down to comfortably warm the area.

Now, when I was in high school, I certainly didn't achieve any academic success in my science classes, but even *I* knew that hot air rises. With my current system in place, I may not have had to worry about stubbing my toe on a baseboard heater. However, I did have to set my thermostat to about 80 degrees so that the heat coming down from the ceiling did its job. As a result, the first electric bill I opened after I bought my house in 1987 was a shocker: over $400. Even using a coal stove had proved ineffective.

All of my neighbors faced the same predicament, but they had eventually taken the plunge and had heat pumps installed. Their houses were warm in the winter and cool in the summer, while mine remained frigid and humid during both of those seasons. Switching to a new system was not an affordable option for me, a single homeowner, so I adapted as best I could. The only rooms I heated were those with beds or toilets in them, or ones that had to be kept warm for company, not that I was in any way prepared to greet visitors properly; I was usually dressed in several layers of Kmart flannel shirts, socks, and sweatpants. When the weather became unbearably warm, I simply placed air conditioners in the bedroom and living room windows, and I sweltered in the rest of the house. This was to be my fate, I assumed, until I won the lottery.

When Mom moved in with me, she didn't mind the heat or the cold. Whenever I'd complain about the temperature, she'd simply say, "It's summer. It's supposed to be hot." After all, we'd both grown up without air conditioning, and to her, living with weather was just one of life's requirements. Stink bugs, however, were not.

My mother was waiting at the door for me as I came home from work one sweltering afternoon. Her face was pallid, and I assumed that she was finally surrendering to the second week of 90 degree heat.

"We have a real problem," she told me. "Stink bugs are getting in the house."

I wasn't surprised. These insects had invaded our area that summer and most everyone I knew had witnessed one or two of them crawling on kitchen tables or hiding in shoes. They are vile creatures who tend to flip over on their backs when disturbed and emit a smell similar to that of burnt cilantro when they feel threatened. I just assumed that Mom was unfamiliar with these critters and didn't appreciate their presence.

"That's not a big deal," I said. "I'll just get jar to put them in and take them outside."

"You're going to need more than that. Just take a walk around. And don't forget to look up."

As I made my way through the house, I could understand Mom's concern. Every ceiling in my home was covered with a dense coating of upside-down stink bugs. Some of them moved. Most of them didn't. They were literally hanging out, except for those making their slow trek up the walls to join their comrades. Looking back, I am impressed with my mother's rather benign reaction. She was only mildly worried. I, on the other hand, was simultaneously panicked and grossed out.

My traditional catch-and-release solution was not going to work this time. So I grabbed the vacuum cleaner and with the hose attachment, I began sucking the insects off the ceilings. My disgust grew as I heard the crunch of their bodies and smelled the odors that their murders produced. Mom stood by my side, urging me on and pointing out bugs that I'd missed.

We were flummoxed as to how the infestation had occurred. No doors had been left open. All of the windows had screens. How did these little suckers get in here?

"Look at that," Mom said, and she pointed to my bedroom air conditioner. A flattened bug, no thicker than a piece of paper, was making its way between the AC's accordion panel and the window frame. Once on the sill, the stinkbug expanded to its original size and began its journey up the wall. Upon further inspection, we noticed that the screens in my windows didn't form a perfect seal, nor did the screen doors. Mother and daughter had inadvertently provided free admission to all of these unwanted patrons, and this show was about to close.

"That's it," I said. "I'm getting central air." Within a month, our problem was solved.

Bobbi also had an infestation problem, but hers was more covert. We reminisced about it one night on the phone.

"You had them in your kitchen, didn't you?" I asked.

"Oh, yeah. They were on my clothes tree."

Bobbi's clothes tree was probably the only one I'd ever seen that really lived up to its name. Hanging on it were not just coats, as is the norm, but also about 30 extra pounds of pants, hats, shirts, socks, and gloves. One rainy evening in the early fall, she needed her barn jacket to head out to the North Forty. (Neither one of us actually has a North Forty, but this is what we call our backyards. It makes us feel like pioneers. For the same reason, we refer to driving the three miles into Millersville as "headin' into town." Childhood games like "Daniel Boone" die hard.)

Wearing a short-sleeved shirt, she grabbed her coat, the one that had hung there for months, and inserted one arm into it as she headed out the door. She was met with a most uncomfortable sensation and began to suspect that she was losing circulation in her extremity.

"I knew I was out of shape," she said. "But I didn't think I was this bad. I thought maybe I was having a stroke. Or a heart attack. Or whichever one happens when you lose feeling on your left side."

She whipped off her coat to find, in her calculations, about 3,000 stink bugs crawling on her, another thousand or so clinging to the inside of her coat, and about five hundred taking off in confused flight. It reminded her of the releasing of doves at weddings, except for the odorous brown cloud that filled the air around her. She walked back into her house, retrieved the clothes tree, and dumped all of its contents onto the flower bed surrounding her deck. Then, one at a time, she picked up each article from the ground, turned it inside out, and beat to death with a broom any remaining bugs.

"But this was outside the house. Why didn't you just shake them off and let them fly away?"

"What, like tag them or something, so I could track them? No way. I wanted these guys dead. I ground 'em into the dirt with my foot."

"So did you wash all those clothes?"

"No. I just stuffed them back into the . . . oh, what do you call that . . . Right. The closet."

My sister wasn't good at putting things away, hence, her hesitation while trying to recall the space specifically *built* for putting things away. While I was laughing at her delayed response, she was quick to remind me that lesbians are supposed to come out of closets, not go back into them. No wonder she was momentarily at a loss for words.

"Well, I think we can agree on this much," I told her, getting back to the topic at hand. "Both of us have an aversion to stink bugs. And you know what? I've never heard you express disgust toward any insect until now. You really aren't afraid of wasps or anything. Even worms don't bother you."

"Oh, but slugs do."

A few years back, Bobbi had been booked to perform at the Pacific Northwest Women's Music and Cultural Jamboree. She was staying with some friends of hers for the week, and after the festival ended, she decided to leave Marie and Pam's and explore the area on her own for a while. She'd always wanted to camp at Orcas Island, and Marie assured her that it was a beautiful place to do so. However, she warned Bobbi to make sure that she turned her shoes upside-down before she herself turned in for the night. Banana slugs were rampant in the region, Marie cautioned, and they would crawl into anything, given the chance.

Bobbi listened to Marie, but she did not heed her words. When she awoke after her first night of camping, she promptly shoved her left foot into her steel-toed boot. She immediately felt the sensation of grape jelly combined with liquid grout, and, pulling out her foot, she realized that she had impaled a slug. All four spaces between her toes were filled with the remnants of it.

"I almost threw up," Bobbi told me.

"Oh, dear God, Bobbi. I'm guessing it was dead?"

"I couldn't tell. Parts of it were moving, like the little antennae that comes out of its head. And its mouth was kind of gaping, too."

"Yeah, after spending the night smelling one of your shoes, I guess it was. It was probably saying, 'Mercy. Mercy. Just kill me now.' You actually kind of did it a favor."

"You know, Anne, if my shoes stink, it's probably because I actually do things in them, like hike and camp. As opposed to your shoes, which just sit around in your closet, bored."

"I see that you now remember the name of that space built to hold things."

This type of good-natured joshing between my sister and me has been going on for years, and I could almost hear my mother saying to us, "Now girls. Settle down." So we did.

I hung up the phone and walked out to my front porch where banana slugs nightly crowd around the cat food bowl, excited to partake of their favorite buffet. I wasn't sure if slugs had the capacity of feeling anything close to excitement, really, but I knew that I did. My goal was to capture one in a shoe box and drop it off at Bobbi's place. Then I could imagine Mom saying, "Tch. This is all you have to do in your spare time?" and I dropped the whole idea. After all, the woman on the Two of Swords tells us that when you're faced with a decision, just make it. No one could force me to do that more quickly than my mom.

Letting Go

THIS IS NOT A CARD that would, as my father used to say, "make you want to jump up and down and slap your ass cheeks together." A red heart has been pierced by three swords as it hangs in a sky filled with rain and clouds. It is a card of loss and grief.

So when it appears in a reading, what are you to make of it? The Suit of Swords itself may provide an answer; after all, these are the cards of straight-forward thinking. The Three of Swords suggests that sometimes logic has to come out on top, to take its place in front of emotion, so that you can heal and move on. If you are facing a period of great sadness, give yourself time to feel this emotion, but don't let it overcome you.

The deaths of both of my parents still resonate with me, but I have to temper my feelings of sadness with a practical kind of humor. I'm sure that this coping mechanism comes to me straight from the horses' mouths, as both my mother and father handled their personal losses with dignity, perseverance, and even a bit of levity. Moreover, they dealt with their impending deaths the same way.

Dad was in the hospital recovering from colon surgery when, two days later, he contracted a staph infection, one that would require yet another operation. After that, he would be looking at a lifespan of five years, if he were lucky. At least, the doctor told him, that's what 50 percent of people in his situation could expect.

Dad's reaction was polite, abrupt, and logical. He had no interest in prolonging this matter. He had lived 72 great years, and he was done. I don't know what kind of prior conversation he had with Mom about his decision. I don't know if she tried to convince him to stay the course and to take the treatments that would extend his life. Neither Bobbi nor I were ever privy to our parents' private matters. All the two of us knew was that Dad had decided that enough was enough.

Bobbi remembers that when Mom told us the news, we both looked at each other and said nothing. We didn't have to. The look itself conveyed our despondency.

"I remember thinking, 'What the hell?'" Bobbi told me on the phone. "I didn't even know how to react. Neither did you." We had both felt like children again, doing as we were told and offering no argument. The ship had left port without our knowledge or consent, and Mom and Dad were at its helm.

After our parents had spoken, my sister and I were called to Dad's bedside.

"I guess you heard," he said.

He became emotional. Looking back, I realize that he wasn't crying because he was dying. He was crying because he had to tell his daughters that he had *decided* to die. That, for him, was harder than the actual death part. He was a man of faith. He knew where he was going, straight to heaven, and he couldn't wait to get there.

Over the next few weeks, I tried to be as stoic as I could. One day, I sat down on his bed, and we discussed heaven and the loved ones he'd meet. I held his hand and told him how much I'd miss him when he was gone. Truthfully, I felt a bit selfish; I wanted him to stay here, not go off gallivanting with dead relatives I'd never met.

"Can't you just try some of the treatments?" I asked him. "You never know. The doctors might be wrong."

"Annie, I just want to get this over with. And the sooner, the better."

207

He was not kidding. He wanted minimal care and even asked that his intravenous feeding tube be removed. The hospital couldn't starve a patient to death, of course, despite the fact that Dad thought it was a fine idea.

"Bob," Dr. Gingrich told him. "That's against the law. I can't take that IV out of your arm."

"Well, what about this morphine drip? Can't you just give me a lot of morphine so I can, you know, move this along?"

The doctor laughed. He was a good guy who enjoyed my father's sense of humor.

"I can do that for you, Bob, to help manage your pain. But just be aware that extra morphine isn't going to 'move this thing along,' as you put it. You'll just doze off a lot more."

Dad glanced over at me. "OK with you?" he asked.

"Whatever you want, Dad," I told him.

"I think sleeping will take my mind off things." And he gave his doctor the go-ahead.

Over the next couple of days, then, Dad did sleep a lot. He had many visitors, and once, eight or nine of us ended up by his bedside at the same time. He'd been sleeping, and we were quietly talking among ourselves. He woke with a start and looked around to see his family, former co-workers, and friends from church smiling down at him.

"This is wonderful," he said.

"How you feelin', Bud?" his sister asked.

"I'm . . . wait a minute. Am I still alive?"

She told him that he was.

"Well, shit. I thought this was heaven. Shit."

He sure was in a hurry to get out of here.

A few days later, he died peacefully in his sleep the second that every visitor had left the room. I don't know why the dying do this. Is it to spare those left behind the pain of witnessing the actual death? If that's the case, I have a news flash for the dearly departed: Sometimes, you leave your loved ones wracked with guilt because they couldn't be there with you at the big moment.

I guess the dead don't care, though, because my mom went the same way. Bobbi and I had left the nursing home and had come back to my place. Within five minutes of plunking our butts down on the couch, we got the call.

My mother had found a way to enjoy life even while she was "actively dying," a phrase with which I had been unfamiliar until Mom was actually doing it. Talk about your oxymorons. Actively dying patients aren't active at all, at least physically. Mentally, though, my mom was still keeping it real even as hospice was hovering around her.

Bobbi had introduced the hospice nurses to my mother, explaining who they were and what their job entailed.

"They're here to help you," Bobbi said, "and to make you comfortable."

"Uh-huh." She looked my sister right in the eye. "So when's the death sentence?" she asked. Bobbi told her that nobody knew, and Mom's reply of, "Okay. Whatever," ended that part of the conversation, and she went on to ask Bobbi what was new and exciting in her life.

As Mom's remaining days passed, my sister and I were spending most of our time at the nursing home. Once, Bobbi had stepped out for some tea, and I was seated beside Mom's bed. I asked her if she wanted me to pray with her.

"Well, sure," she said. "I guess that'd be alright."

As an adult, I had never prayed with anyone, except silently in church or when our family did so together before dinner. I don't know what possessed me to make this my first shot at public prayer, where I was the only one speaking, but I knew I wanted to try. If I couldn't bless my own mother, I figured, what kind of a spiritual seeker was I?

We both closed our eyes. "Dear God," I began. I asked him to watch over my mother, to hold her close, and to help all of us in this difficult time. I talked about the power of God, how good he is to everyone, how he can see us through any hardships, and what a beautiful world he'd created for us. On and on and on I went, throwing in stuff that I'd heard in church and things I'd read in my New Age books. I was summoning all the power in the universe right there into that small room in the nursing home. I even mentioned a Bible verse or two, although these dealt primarily with the Nativity. (I was under pressure, and "An angel of the Lord appeared to them, and the glory of the Lord shone 'round about them" was all I could muster.)

I finished with an "Amen" and opened my eyes. Mom's were still closed. She raised her hand and twirled her index finger in a circle. She then made an imaginary end punctuation point in the air by poking her finger in my direction.

"Period," she said. "Just like Victor Borge used to do."

She then opened her eyes and looked at me. I began rambling.

"How you doin', Mom?" I asked. "Do you feel God's presence? Do you feel his love all around you, holding you and keeping you safe?"

She paused and thought for a minute. "Huh," she said. "Not really."

It was then that I knew my dream of becoming a lay pastor was probably not going to be realized.

Not long after I had finished flexing my theological muscles, Bobbi came back into the room. "What have you two girls been up to?" she asked.

"Not much," Mom replied. Her comment further confirmed the demise of my ecclesiastical future. "Annie said a prayer. It was very nice." Her declaration carried the same emotional impact as if she'd been describing a plate of zucchini. Or that pixie cut I was sporting in the 80s. "But, listen. Bobbi. Is my address book still in the drawer there? I don't want anything to happen to that."

This was one of Mom's frequent questions. She exhibited much concern over that address book in the weeks leading up to her death. No one was allowed to touch it. No one was allowed to use it. She'd never asked me to safeguard it; this was a job that only Bobbi could handle. Neither my sister nor I found her insistence alarming. For all of her feistiness, she was having memory issues, so the repetition of this particular demand didn't seem overly abnormal to us. We did wonder, however, whose address she thought she'd need at a time like this. Our curiosity was soon to be satisfied.

When Bobbi and I were gathering Mom's things the day after she died, we opened the drawer in which rested the address book. There, hidden neatly behind it, was one of my cigarettes. That Charlotte. She sure was a sneaky one.

Smoking was something that Mom enjoyed her whole life. When I'd visit her at the home, we'd sit outside on the bench overlooking the Susquehanna River and have a cigarette or two. When I'd take her to Kmart, I barely had buckled my seatbelt before she'd turn to me and say, "Now. I'll have that ciggie, please." Sometimes, of course, I'd say, "Not today," if I didn't think it was in her best interest. But more times than not, I acquiesced. She was 91, for God's sake. If she wanted to smoke, what possible reason could I give her not to?

So now, the address-book mystery had been solved. My mother had covertly stolen a cigarette from my purse, probably when I was loading her in the car for a Kmart jaunt. She'd kept it hidden in the drawer behind her book in case of an emergency. Where she thought she was going to actually smoke it, I have no idea. But the thought that it was there must have comforted her, and it certainly made Bobbi and me laugh.

"You know what you have to do," Bobbi said. "You have to bury this with Mom's ashes."

"Will the funeral home people let us do that?"

"I'm pretty sure they will. I'm good friends with the owner."

That was the plan. But in all of the hubbub on the day of the funeral, I'd left the cigarette at home. Bobbi and I stood in the lobby of the church, frantic. Friends and family were mulling about, waiting for the service to start, and we caught the eye of Bobbi's friend Marie, the owner of the funeral home. She came to our sides right away, probably certain that we were breaking down under all of the emotional strain.

"Can I do something?" Marie asked.

"Yes," I said, and I explained our predicament.

"You both just wait here. I'll be right back."

The lobby was almost empty now. People were filing into the sanctuary and the service was about to begin.

"Shit shit shit," I said to Bobbi. "The organ music's starting. I think we have to get in there."

"Relax," Bobbi said. "We're the bereaved. They're not going to start without us."

Suddenly, Marie reappeared in the lobby and somberly walked toward us, something small and zipped in her hand.

"Here you go," she whispered conspiratorially, and she handed me a tiny baggie of Mom. "You can just stick the cigarette in here when you get home and place the whole thing in some kind of urn. Will that work?"

Bless her. It would. And it did. The urn sits on my bookcase.

The Three of Swords is a tough card. No one likes to think about sorrow and grief. In fact, I try to avoid thinking about them altogether. Some people may say that my avoidance is unhealthy, that I'm shoving unwanted feelings into the recesses of my psyche, and that one day, these will surface in the form of an ulcer or a mental breakdown. I beg to differ.

When Dad and Mom died, I cried. I grieved. I was depressed for quite a while. I still shed tears from time to time when I think about how much I miss my folks. However, I quickly remember the laughter, love, and support they both gave me when they themselves were dying, and suddenly, my world is a lot brighter.

Embracing Insomnia

After the emotional upheaval presented by the Three of Swords, a bit of a breather is needed. Enter the Four of Swords, which encourages us to rest and regroup. A knight in effigy is lying on his tomb in the basement of a church, a stained-glass window to his right. His hands are folded in prayer or meditation, and his calm demeanor implies that he is taking the time he needs to be silent and to recover. The fact that one sword lies beneath him and three others are suspended above him doesn't cause a break in his introspective state. He lies there peacefully, sleeping, perhaps, unaware of the cares of the world. How I do envy him.

In the past few years, insomnia has been a sword in my side. I used to love crawling into bed as soon as night fell, and I would settle into a quiet, solemn slumber that lasted until daybreak. Then menopause and heredity took over, and I knew the pleasures of sleep no more.

I tried, ad nauseum, all of the gimmicks that are supposed to help. When I entered my bedroom at night, I wouldn't watch TV, I wouldn't read, and I wouldn't eat. However, since these methods didn't work as a group of three, I instead tried a combination of them. I'd watch TV, but I wouldn't eat. Or I'd eat while I watched TV, but I wouldn't read. All of this was to no avail. I'd doze off for seven minutes, awaken, and remain alert for an hour. This cycle then repeated itself throughout the night until I was able to sleep soundly, usually around seven in the morning.

My doctor-prescribed sleeping pills for me, and they were delightful until the hallucinations started. I would see the oddest objects before me as I felt myself drift away from consciousness. Trying to explain my visions to anyone was risky. What would Bill think if I told him, for example, that I'd seen a plastic bag filled with five small blocks of cheddar cheese hovering above me? Or that I'd witness myself standing in the middle of the road as 18 motorcycles approached and then formed two lines, nine bikes in each, in order to glide gently around me?

Googling this phenomenon was helpful. I was experiencing hypnagogia, wherein hallucinations can occur as one moves from wakefulness to sleep. Edgar Allen Poe was a fellow sufferer, so I knew I was in good company. Still, these visions were disconcerting, and since they were brought on by sleeping pills, I decided not to refill my prescription. Instead, I now try various approaches that begin lovingly with a blend of New Age thought and Christianity and end in a torrent of guilt, failed plans, and self-doubt. Let me give you an example.

First, I lie awake with the lights off and stare out at the night sky, pondering the stars and the fact that they really aren't there anymore, nor have they been for eons. After some moon gazing, I try to embrace the love of the universe, the same universe that is expanding inexplicably into another dimension, one that I'll never be able to understand no matter how many Deepak Chopra books I read. I attempt to become one with all of this and let the fear of it rock me gently into slumber.

If this doesn't work, which it usually does not, I keep the lights off but close the curtains. Then I take stock of my day. Did I accomplish everything that I wanted to do? Did I look at this day as a gift from God and spend it in blissful creativity? Not really. I ignored my writing and instead opted for watching the first season of *House* for the eighth time. I did nothing with that new cross-stitch design that has been resting on my kitchen table since last month. Then I think about God. What if he had been this unmotivated when creating the world? He would have never made it past the third day. I realize that I didn't achieve as much as I should have, but I take comfort in the fact that even creativity needs some time off.

That comfort doesn't last long, however, and, giving up on Deepak and God, I turn on the lights. I notice my bedroom ceiling, which my sister and I had recently painted. Bobbi had found the paint on sale, and the color was deceptive. Once on, it didn't resemble anything close to ecru. "They should have called it 'Snot,'" Bobbi said, "because that's what it looks like." I check out my furniture, realize that I've had my bedroom suit since I was 16, and resolve to save money to buy some grown-up stuff.

Glancing briefly at my open closet door, I see the same clothes that have been hanging there for years, but I remind myself that my mother had only three dresses to last her throughout the entire Depression. Next, I think about the Depression and pull that comforter of guilt around my body, snuggling in the thought that I have nothing about which to complain. Then I see those shoes of mine from 1998 that sit on my closet floor, mocking me, and I start mentally complaining again.

Bitching doesn't make anyone sleepy, so I begin to count my blessings. I have more than enough money to buy whatever food I want while other people are going without. I review this food that waits for me in the pantry and think of making a snack of hot chocolate and brownies. Then I realize that I'm looking at about 900 calories, but I tell myself that I'll be fine if I don't eat anything tomorrow. Since this sounds like a reasonable plan and since carbs are supposed to help one sleep, I stealthily slip into the kitchen and hope that Bill doesn't notice the buffet that I'm carrying back into my bedroom.

Now that I have sufficiently consumed enough sugar to keep me awake during a golf tournament, I try watching a little television. I tune in to *Perry Mason* and admire his secretary, Della, wondering how in the world the woman always looked so coiffed. I stare at her waistline so long that I've lost track of the case that Perry is trying to crack. I stare at her hair, so stylish for its time, and consider getting a new 'do rather than continuing to rock this Nellie Oleson look of which Bill, I'm convinced, is so fond.

Why is Bill even with me, anyway? How can he stand my hair, my clothes, my lack of self-control where food is concerned? If

I don't get it together soon, he might break up with me. Maybe I should start running.

The thought of not having Bill in my life makes me take two Tylenol PMs and call it a night. I don't care about my liver at this point. It needs to sleep as much as I do.

So what's the answer to chronic insomnia? I haven't a clue. Everyone stays awake for different reasons, except for the man pictured on this card. Like most men, he is able to fall asleep even with three swords suspended above his head. I'd love to see a tarot card with a woman trying to drift off under those conditions. It wouldn't be pretty.

No Contest

THE FIVE OF SWORDS IS A BIT UNSETTLING. We see two men walking away in retreat, defeated and depressed, their weapons surrendered at the feet of the man in the forefront. Not a pleasant looking fellow, he smiles with a smug satisfaction while holding three other swords, most likely those captured from other combatants not pictured. The card's aura suggests that the winner of this battle was able to achieve his goals, but that he'd lost some friends in the process. Seeing this card in a reading may be a clue that you've stepped on others to get what you wanted. The bridges that you've burned make you wonder if getting to the other side of the river was worth the personal losses along the way.

Bobbi and I were stymied when discussing the nature of the Five of Swords. Had we ever exhibited the callousness of the man in the picture? Neither of us thought so. I've never felt the need to hurt my friends in order to come out on top; in fact, I'm so uncompetitive, even Easter egg hunts used to make me extremely anxious.

I recall being lined up in an open meadow with other five-year-olds who were out of the gate the minute one of the adults yelled, "Go!" My formerly kind playmates suddenly threw their manners to the wind as they ran like lunatics freed from the asylum, knocking each other aside in search of hidden treasures. I took my time, feigning ignorance of the goal of the game; I simply strolled about and admired the scenery until all eggs were found by the other children. If my only choices were to go home egg-less or to body slam my friends, I was willing to shame my family by being the only lass in the village to return to her castle without the spoils of war.

I am equally conflicted at auctions. I remember once placing a bid, two dollars, on a weather-beaten rocking chair. The second bid came from a lovely, unassuming Amish woman who stood across from me. The auctioneer was poised between us as the game continued. The other bidders eventually dropped out, and I, face-to-face with my adversary, stopped raising my hand after she placed a bid of $4.75. All eyes were upon me now, waiting for my next move. This process had been so easy when nine or 10 of us had been involved. Now, I wanted to play no part in another person's disappointment.

The auctioneer looked at me. "Nothing?" he asked. "You don't want to go any higher?"

"No," I said, and I smiled a little. "I want her to have it."

She smiled back, and the crowd "Ahhhhh"-ed. Desiring their acknowledgment for a deed well-turned had not been my intent. I just didn't have, nor have I ever had, the chutzpah needed in times like these. Later in the morning, my new friend returned the favor. We were both interested in the same object, this time a birdbath, when she stopped raising her hand and nodded in my direction. The bath was mine, and the crowd applauded. I am much more at ease with this type of give-and-take than I am with the mad scramble of capitalism.

"I don't remember actually being in any Easter egg hunts as a kid," Bobbi told me, "but when I watch them now, I sure don't like them. Basically because of the parents."

"Too pushy?"

"Everybody's too pushy. These things just bring out the worst in people. And you know, there's always that one little kid at the end of the hunt who has no eggs in his basket."

"Or hers," I added.

"Oh. That was you?"

"From what I remember."

"Well, there ya go. That proves my point. Did anyone offer you an egg or two? I mean, here you have these kids, a dozen eggs in their baskets, and not one of them says, 'Hey. Take a few of mine.' The whole thing's nauseating."

"How about auctions?" I asked her.

"Well, that's different. Pretty much every man for himself. But I will tell you that I keep an eye on who's bidding against me, and if I win, I always approach the other guy afterwards and ask if he wants to make a trade."

"See? That's what I'm talking about. So much nicer to do things that way."

"Unless you're talking about sports," Bobbi said. "Then you have to be competitive."

But Bobbi and I never talked about sports because I don't care about them, especially because of one incident that occurred when we played basketball in high school. Wanting to be part of the crowd, I tried out for the team as a sophomore. I made the last cut, and I remember vividly the look on my coach's face when she made her final decision. It was one of mild disgust and self-loathing. I imagined her saying to herself after tryouts, "That was a big mistake. What the hell was I thinking?"

My playing during practice did nothing to assuage her concerns. I could dribble a little, but after four or five bounces, the ball would take on a life of its own and end up rolling down the court behind me. I could never quite master the layup for the same reason that I never mastered country line dancing; there were just too many steps to take in a small amount of time.

And forget about rebounding. I'd fold my body into a kneeling position, my hands covering my head in protection, as all the other players jumped for the ball. (Really, if they wanted it so badly, they could have it. I didn't want to be stingy and rip it from their hands like some bossy kid during an Easter egg hunt.) My inability to sink a basket from the foul line wasn't an issue. Since I was never put into a game, I was never fouled.

But one evening during an especially important game, our starting center, Roberta, broke her glasses. She was helpless without them, and our team was helpless without her. The coach looked at me, the only other center on the team, and told me to get off the bench and hit the court. I ran out to the middle of it, right where that big circle was, and faced my opponent. The ref threw the ball in the air and through some miracle of physics and prayer, I tipped it to one of my team members. I don't remember what she did with it after that, as I was too busy congratulating myself on my fine performance to keep track of the ball's whereabouts. But shortly thereafter, the ball was back in my hands.

I suddenly recalled something from practice called a fast break, and I figured that this was the time to put that drill to the test. I began to dribble down the court so furiously that I was leaving all other players in my wake. The ball miraculously stayed in front of me as I approached the basket. Aware of the shouts of encouragement from my coach and team members, I felt a sudden rush of love for this sport that I'd never experienced before. Through my peripheral vision, I could see my teammates on the bench and the spectators in the bleachers jump to their feet as they wildly cheered me on. What a splendid sight I must have been as my feet and hands came together in an almost poetic symmetry as I performed the perfect layup.

For the other team. Who got the two points. Apparently, my supporters hadn't been supporting me — they were screaming at me to head the other way. But my sense of direction had failed me once again, and I returned to the sidelines, dejected and ashamed, as Roberta was put back into the game without her glasses. Realizing that even a blind girl was a better player than I could ever be, I finished the season on the bench and never gave sports another thought. I was just so much better at other things, like watching television.

"I didn't want you to be my sister after that," Bobbi told me. "That was just a banner day all the way around because I fell off the curb getting into the bus after that game and twisted my ankle. I was off the team for three weeks. Just a great day for the Carmitchell girls."

"But at least you were missed," I said. "You were such a good athlete."

"Well, we all have our gifts. Speaking of which, what are you going to watch on TV tonight?"

"Probably *Law and Order*. Or *House*. Maybe *Frasier*."

"Hey, the WNBA playoffs are on ESPN. You could just watch them."

"And you could just blow it out your ass."

Most of our conversations don't end with such unsportsmanlike conduct on my part. But in this instance, I could see no other way. For the first time in my life, I had scored the perfect passing shot. Victory, at last, was mine.

Escape from Rocky Springs

DEPRESSING, DECEITFUL, AND DESPONDENT. How's that for a group of uplifting descriptors that categorize the Six, Seven, and Eight of Swords? Here's hoping that these cards don't show up often in your readings. If they do, however, remind yourself that life contains moments of both joy and challenge and that this suit can be a real rascal where the latter is concerned. But humor can still find its way into the most dismal of situations, at least if the Carmitchell Sisters and their mom are involved.

On the Six of Swords, a woman and her child are in a rowboat, calm waters to the left of them and still waters to the right. An oarsman guides them to safe haven as they sit huddled together, their heads covered and downcast, indicating a state of depression for both as they leave behind them a difficult situation.

The sadness continues in the next card, where a man is stealing four swords from a group of seven. Tiptoeing away, he's peering over his shoulder, hoping no one sees him. The card suggests that you be cautious of people trying to deceive you.

Next, eight swords surround a woman who stands tied up and blindfolded under a desolate sky, her feet covered in murky, shallow water. Obviously trapped yet uninjured, she is unable to leave her situation. Perhaps the unknown keeps her stuck in this lonely marsh. She seems bound by fear more than by the loose ropes around her, and the card is implying that she could break free if she leaves her past, bad decisions, and even guilt behind her.

In what tomfoolery had the Carmitchell Sisters engaged that could possibly reflect the nuances of these cards? And how did it involve their mother? These are valid questions, and ones that I hope can be answered in my conversation with Bobbi.

Annie: I don't remember this story at all. I'd only heard about it from you and Mom.

Bobbi: Well, yeah. It's pretty clear why.

A: You and she decided to go to Rocky Springs amusement park. Just like the mother and her child on the Six of Swords. That's the Card that reminded me of this story. Just the two of you. And not me.

B: We couldn't go with you. You were passed out on the couch.

A: Because I was heavily sedated.

B: You'd had your wisdom teeth pulled that day, and you couldn't drive home. Dad picked you up. You were drugged, so you just hit the couch.

A: And apparently, you and I were fighting?

B: Yes, we were mad at each other. We weren't really talking.

A: So that's why you didn't ask me along. You were mad at me. You just asked Mom, and the two of you snuck away, just like the guy on the Seven of Swords.

B: Anne, I didn't ask you along because you were totally out of it.

A: Plus you were mad at me.

B: I'm ignoring you now.

A: OK, so you get to Rocky Springs, and what happens first?

B: Well, Mom was really excited that the park was open again. She wanted to see if it had changed a lot since the last time she was there. And that was, like, 30 years before. We walked through the gate and the whole park was surrounded by a chain-link fence, which hadn't been there in the "old days." Mom didn't care for that. It made the place look like a jail. But we walked toward the rides and Mom was reminiscing. The Whip was still there, and the Fun House.

A: Was the park crowded?

B: No. We got there around dusk and the place was pretty empty. But that was a good thing because by the time we got to the carousel house, no one was in line. We talked to the operator, and I told the guy Mom's history with the park. He was ready to shut down for the night, but he thought Mom was a hoot and let her take a spin all by herself.

A: And you didn't ride.

B: Right. I stood inside the calliope house with the operator and asked him all kinds of questions about how the ride worked. He thought this was great, I guess because no one ever bothered with him much. And he and I could talk and look out this little window and watch Mom go around on her favorite horse.

A: And around and around and around and around and around and around.

B: Yep. A three-minute ride turned into about 10, and every time I saw Mom's face go by the window, her smile faded a little. Then you could see her getting a little frantic, then a little pissed. Like, if Mom ever said the "F" word, she would have said it then. Or something like, "Jane! Stop this crazy thing! Jaaaaaaaaaaaaaaaaane!"

A: But she still had a good time?

B: Mom had a great time. But she stayed on the horse for a while after the ride stopped because her head was still spinning.

A: But she wasn't mad or anything.

B: Oh, God, no. Then we walked over to the Fun House. It wasn't open, and no one was around. We thought it was probably time to go home since it was getting dark. So we walked over to the gate where we'd come in. But here's where it started to get weird. The gate we'd entered was now rusty and covered with moss and old weeds.

A: How long had you been there at that point?

B: Probably longer than the time you and Mom were in New Hope. About an hour.

A: But you were at the wrong gate.

B: We were at the wrong gate. But we didn't know that at the time. So we walked back to the carousel, but it was completely shut down and the guy was gone. We just started walking around the park, but it was completely empty. We were the only people there. It was spooky. I said to Mom, "Here's where the rides start moving by themselves." It was one of the few times she'd ever told me to shut up.

A: There you were, trapped in the park. You must have felt pretty hopeless at this point.

B: We did, but then out of nowhere comes this old, bald guy driving a golf cart. And you know who that was.

A: Tom Browning, my old boss.

B: Right. So I introduced us and explained that we were lost. And he just said in this really creepy voice, "Oh, I know your sister, Anne." And that's all he said. Like, he didn't explain how he knew you, he just said that one sentence and stared at us. And then Mom was really creeped out.

A: And what were you thinking?

B: All I could focus on were these khaki overalls that he was wearing. I kept thinking, "After he stabs us to death, he can just ditch the pants because they'll be covered with blood, and then he'll dump our bodies in the Conestoga Creek" because that ran right past the park.

A: So when did you call me?

B: Well, Mom was really wanting to get away from this guy, so she told him that we had to make a phone call. We knew right where the pay phone was because we'd just walked by it at the carousel.

A: Why didn't you just ask Browning how to get out of the park?

B: I don't know, Anne. This was 40 years ago. I think Mom just needed to put some space between us and this insane guy in the golf cart. Oh! And I remember that neither of us had any change, so we had to ask him for some money so that we could make a call. He gave us a dime. Just one. It's like, if we dialed a wrong number, he wouldn't give us another dime. He'd just murder us. I also kept thinking about how I was going to pay him back, you know, for the dime he gave us, not for the "killing us" part.

A: You know that guy was a millionaire, right?

B: Not at the time. So anyway, Mom and I hustled to the pay phone and I called you. Before we'd left the house, Mom had moved the phone into the living room beside the couch in case you needed it.

A: And I answered the phone.

B: You kind of half answered it. I could hear the TV in the background, and you were mumbling something. I kept saying, "Anne! It's me! Don't hang up! We're trapped in the park!"

A: And then I hung up?

B: No, you didn't hang up. You tried to put the phone back on its cradle, but you weren't coordinated enough in your drugged-out state to even do that. I could still hear the TV, but you must have gone back to sleep. I don't think you even knew that you had been talking to anyone.

A: Well, what did you expect me to do at that point, anyway?

B: You were gonna have to come pick us up.

A: But I was drugged.

B: But you could have told Dad.

A: Where was he?

B: Downstairs in his shop. He missed the whole thing.

A: So how did this all end? How did you get out of the park?

B: We walked back to where Tom Browning was and told him we couldn't get a hold of anyone. He just pointed his finger toward the exit, the gate that we should have gone out, and took off in his golf cart. He didn't say another word.

A: Why the hell didn't he just point to that gate in the first place?

B: I have no idea. Again. Forty years ago.

A: But you and Mom had a blast, despite how frightening this was. And how pissed off you were at me.

B: Oh, yeah. It was the best. The fact that we'd had this great adventure, this harrowing experience just ten minutes from home? And watching Mom's face go from elation to nausea when she was on the ride? The best.

227

A: Did you tell me any of this when you got home?

B: Yeah. Right. When we got home, you were passed out on the couch. And there was the phone off the cradle, a dial tone buzzing away. We told you the next day, but you swore that you never got a call.

A: I'm still sticking with that story.

B: I know you are, Anne.

. . . .

Stories of mothers and their daughters sharing memorable moments are not uncommon. However, these occasions usually occur when all three women are in the same place at the same time. Mom, Bobbi, and I found a way to make this happen when one of us was home asleep on the couch and the other two were facing a madman with a sword hidden in his khaki overalls. That's what I call Livin' the Tarot.*

Bobbi's wistful and lovely song about this park, "Rocky Springs Saturday Night," appears on her album County Wide: Song Stories from Lancaster County. *You can hear the song on YouTube, and for more information about Bobbi's music you can contact her through Facebook.*

Wombs and Sinners and Death, O My!

THE NINE AND TEN OF SWORDS paint two more dismal pictures for the readers of tarot. The first is a woman sitting up in bed, sobbing into her hands, sadness and anxiety all around her. In complete despair, she is flanked by nine swords that hang on the wall to her left. She is frightened and filled with anxiety and feels that she is doomed.

The Ten of Swords appears equally horrific: A man lies face down, 10 swords impaled in his back. He is not physically dead, since in tarot, death symbolizes a reawakening, a discarding of past behaviors that no longer serve us. Loss is indicated, but it's a finality of something that needed to come to an end. The calm sea and brightening horizon bring us hope for the future. The cycle is over and it's time to move on.

I have much in common with this poor woman on the Nine of Swords, as my inclination to hear burglars and aliens in the middle of the night has often left me paralyzed in bed, deciding whether to fake sleep or to rush the bedroom door, screeching and charging like a wild animal to scare off my intruder. Of course, the latter of these options never materializes. I usually just lie there, praying and sweating, until the sounds of breaking glass or the hissing, unintelligible voices of extraterrestrials dissipate.

For this reason alone, I would not be a candidate for the job of forest ranger or even that of camp counselor. God knows that the woods are filled with creatures even more threatening than those who could enter my bedroom. In my most frightened state, I still remain a postmenopausal woman with excess belly fat and a lot of rage, and while these descriptors would be enough to scare off any alien, they are no match for a grizzly bear or Sasquatch.

"No, you're not the kind of person to stay calm when you're scared," Bobbi said.

"I don't know how our counselors at band camp did their jobs. The first snap of a twig, and I'm terrified."

"You know, you were that way when we were kids sleeping out in the backyard. Or I should say, those two times that you actually *did* sleep out with me."

I ignored her comment, but it reminded me of one of our favorite babysitters, Vicki. She'd assured me during one of my nights of terror that if aliens were to land on Earth, they wouldn't visit 105 Locust Lane. Bobbi and I would have nothing to offer them, she'd explained. And she was right; our parents hadn't produced any Rhodes scholars. (Remember, we were the kids who ran the wrong way on the basketball court and set the coffee table on fire.)

My sister remembers Vicki, too, and quite fondly. "But do you remember Carol Elliot?" Bobbi asked me. "Now THAT was a girl who should have never been a babysitter. I think she was more afraid of everything than you are."

Ah, yes. Carol had babysat us a few times. I remember her being very nice and quite stylish. She was about sixteen and was the kind of teenager I wanted to be when I grew up, one who dressed in miniskirts and go-go boots and had a beehive hairdo. All in all, based on her fashion sense alone, she was one together gal, in my eyes. She also came from a good family, and I could see why my parents trusted us to her care.

The three of us were watching TV one night when she heard a loud noise. Suddenly, the atmosphere in the living room turned tense as she gasped and began peering down the hallway.

"Did you girls hear that?" she asked nervously.

We hadn't, but the more agitated she became, the more we were convinced that something was amiss.

"Stay here," she told us. She left the room, tiptoed down the hall and into the kitchen with much trepidation, and returned hurriedly with a steak knife. She was perspiring now and was visibly shaken. "Come over here. Sit with me on the couch."

We did as we were told, one on each side of her. Placing the knife on her lap, she wrapped her arms around each of us and told us to be very still. I glanced over at Bobbi for answers, but she, younger than I, had none and looked back helplessly.

Carol held us tightly as her eyes, widening now in fear, kept a close watch on the front door. Apparently, she'd heard another noise, and she started and whimpered a little. She then released her hold on us and dug into her jeans pocket. She pulled out what looked like a necklace. I felt it odd that she would want to accessorize at a time like this, but being only about seven years old, I had not yet made any real fashion decisions. (I assumed I would start doing so once my breasts grew to an appropriate size. Neither event happened, and I'm still waiting.)

"What's that?" Bobbi asked, reaching for the pretty bauble.

Carol pushed her hand away. "Don't touch," she said gravely. "These are rosary beads." Immediately, she wrapped them around her hand and starting praying in a way with which Bobbi and I were unfamiliar. She started talking about someone named Mary and wombs and sinners and death. I had no idea what a *womb* was, but I sure recalled enough from Sunday school to know what sinners were. And the death stuff didn't strike me as very comforting in a moment like this, either.

"And then what happened?" I asked Bobbi. "Nobody was breaking into the house."

"She just kept freaking out. We sat there a long time while she rocked and mumbled stuff and told us to keep praying."

"You're right. I remember the rocking and the praying. That whole thing was so bizarre. But I don't really remember being scared, do you?"

My sister had to think about that question. "I don't think so. I was more scared about what she was doing with those beads and that knife than any burglar breaking into the house."

Did our parents ever know what happened that evening? I'm not sure. Either they suspected that something had gone awry, or Carol declined any further requests to babysit for us. Whatever the case had been, we never saw her again.

When Dad drove her home that night, she must have felt like the man on the the Ten of Swords, her future bright now that she was out of the House of Horrors. It was true that she had lost a babysitting job on Locust Lane, but it was time for her to move on to a more populated, developed neighborhood, one without corn fields in the back that could hide any number of prowlers. And believe me, Bobbi and I were fine with that. A sitter with a necklace in one hand and a sword in another doesn't make for very good company.

Avoiding Corporal Punishment

AS BOBBI AND I WERE GROWING UP, the Carmitchell Clan knew its share of the challenges inherent in the Suit of Swords. Some conflict was inevitable in a family built on German and Scotch-Irish ancestry. A spirited group of four, we had our share of problems throughout the years, but the King and Queen always managed to balance these confrontations with compassion and understanding. Well, maybe not *always*. And maybe not in the exact moment of conflict. But our love for one another always prevailed, smoothing over the sharp edges of anger and heartache.

The Queen of Swords represents a woman who is direct in her communication and is a real problem-solver. My mother, though often reticent to share her true feelings, could at other moments rise to the occasion and nip something in the bud when the bud needed nipping. These times, I recall, were reserved specifically for when Bobbi and I were being bad. (I realize that I am showing my age when I refer to our behavior this way, but I've never been a proponent of the phrase "acting inappropriately" when describing conduct unbecoming a child. No need for descriptors that would spare our self-esteem. We were just bad.)

One evening, Mom was icing cinnamon rolls fresh from the oven and, shortly before that, fresh from a tube. I stood by her side, a little girl amazed that anything so lovely could come out of a circular piece of cardboard, and even more impressed that tucked into that same contraption was a small container of frosting. I dipped my finger into it and gave it a taste. Mom told me to knock it off. After a few seconds, I did it again. She gave me another stern warning. But the sugar was in my system now, and it was affecting my ability to make rational decisions. I dipped again.

Mom stopped her dinner preparations and looked down at me. "Do that one more time," she said, "and see what happens."

I may have been only six, but even at that age, I was inquisitive. I wondered what the Queen had meant by her mysterious proclamation. What *would* happen if I did it again? Was there a prize at the bottom of the container of icing, similar to the one found in a box of Cracker Jacks? I was already exhibiting a characteristic of the Knight of Swords, using my intellect to solve a problem quickly, and I became more and more curious as to the meaning behind what sounded to me like an invitation from my mother.

Bill says that my search for knowledge is one of the things that he loves most about me. Apparently, my mother didn't share that sentiment, for as I stuck my finger into the icing for the fourth time, she smacked my hand with great vigor. The shock on my face didn't properly convey to her the thought process that had led to my final indiscretion, and I didn't have a chance to explain myself before Mom began reprimanding me.

"I told you not to do that. Didn't I tell you not to do that? What did you think was going to happen?"

Well, I sure as hell didn't think it was going to be *that*. But as a six-year-old, how could I explain to my mother that her sense of irony was lost on me, that I couldn't quite grasp her use of figurative language? We laughed about this episode many times over the years, but I suspect that Mom wasn't as convinced of my innocence as I thought she should be. My side of the story always seemed a bit contrived to her.

Bobbi's story, though, has always rung true. One day, when she was about five, she had been raucously galloping around the house pretending to ride a horse, much to the dismay of our father, who had told her several times to behave. King Robert was known for his ability to articulate his desires, and he was fair and just in his judgments if these desires weren't met. The way Dad told the story, he knew better than to spank her. He'd tried that with me the year before.

No one remembers what crime I had committed to warrant such retribution, but a tiny swat to my backside was all it took for me to understand his point. Dad said that I turned and looked up at him, crushed, as if my whole world had fallen apart. No more would corporal punishment be used in his castle, the King decided. He would have to find another way to curb his children's behavior that didn't involve breaking his own heart.

Instead, his approach to Bobbi would be a verbal one. As she ran down the hallway, he surprised her by suddenly side-stepping out of the dining room and standing directly in her path. She had no choice but to stop, breathless, and await his verdict. Our father's voice was raised.

"Goddammit, Bobbi! I told you to stop running in the house!"

Bobbi said nothing.

"Do you hear me? Don't make me spank you."

Like the Page of Swords, my sister was always ready for action. However, she could also foolishly beg for a challenge if enough action weren't presenting itself in the moment.

"But I thought you said you weren't going to do that anymore, Daddy."

What a brave thing to say. Or a stupid one. The situation could have gone either way. But the King was flummoxed. Stymied. It took him a few seconds to garner his intellect, which Bobbi's statement had shredded to pieces.

"You know why I don't want to spank you girls? Because I'm afraid if I start, I'm never going to stop." He held his gaze for a minute or two longer, just for effect, and left the hallway, joining my mother in the kitchen.

"Well," my mom said. "That went over well."

Both of them later admitted to being slightly in awe of Bobbi's boldness in a potentially butt-warming situation. They also admired her ability to pull from the recesses of her young mind damaging evidence that could be used against a rival.

"Maybe she'll be a lawyer when she grows up," Mom suggested.

"I doubt it," Dad said. "Unless the courtroom comes with a horse."

Bobbi has related this story many times over the years, and always in a humorous way. "But listen," she told me on the phone one night. "What he said put the fear of God into me."

"I don't think he knew that at the time," I said.

"No, he didn't. But all I could think about was that Dad could turn into a wild man at any moment. I just kept picturing him as the Tasmanian Devil, the cartoon, all blurry lines and kicking up dust."

"But it didn't stop you from being bad," I reminded her.

"No, but I'm pretty sure I knew my limits after that."

"And yet I'm the one who got spanked. And smacked. You never did. I really took one for the team back then."

"Yeah. And it was probably the only athletic thing you've ever done, Anne."

Bobbi's remark was cutting but true. It was also reflective of the way things worked with the four of us. Swords could be drawn from time to time, and they could even do a little damage. However, the trick to keeping the situation from deteriorating was to rule with a mixture of logic and emotion. Logically, it made sense for Dad to smack my behind. Emotionally, it didn't do him much good. By the same token, Dad's emotions held him back from spanking Bobbi, but her use of logic seemed to be his undoing.

Like all families, the four of us certainly had our share of difficult moments. In the end, though, it's nice to know that when Bobbi and I reminisce, mostly only humor remains, and that our conflicts, no matter how upsetting at the time, have now either disappeared into the humorous, spinning vortex of a Tasmanian Devil or are buried in the sweetness of a box of Cracker Jacks.

PENTACLES

THE ACE OF PENTACLES

The Cycle of Life, Death, and Furniture

WE NOW LEAVE BEHIND US THE INTENSITY of the Suit of Swords as we enter a more uplifting group of cards, the Suit of Pentacles. A hand holding a pentacle, or coin, comes forth from the clouds and is offering all of the abundance that you deserve. Below the hand, a lush garden overflows with greenery and flowers and provides a path that leads to a mountain range in the distance. As with previous Aces, this is a card of fresh starts and inspiration. However, instead of inspiring you to begin a new project or a relationship or to tackle a new challenge, the Ace of Pentacles signals the start of a new phase of prosperity in your life, usually in the form of material possessions or finances.

Since Pentacles deal less with the spiritual world and intellect than the other suits do, gone are the Wands of creativity, the Cups of emotion, the Swords of power. You're now immersed in the reality of the physical realm. For this reason, I've always enjoyed drawing any card from this suit if I'm not in an esoteric kind of mood. I'm all about digging into my psyche to find some hidden meaning to my life, but sometimes I like digging into my pockets and finding a hidden 10-spot. That experience can be as uplifting as seeing Jesus or the Buddha walk in my front door.

I will admit to being fairly attached to my possessions, probably more so than the above-mentioned fellows would like me to be. Jesus tells us to sell all that we own in order to gain eternal life. That's a tall order, and one with which I'm not completely comfortable. To be clear, though, he *was* speaking to a ruler, a very wealthy man, who kept nagging Jesus to be more specific about heaven. Maybe Jesus' answer was a tad hyperbolic to encourage a new line of questions. This must have been the case; otherwise, all of the Christians I know have traded eternity for a dining room set or an iPhone contract.

The closest I came to being possessionless was after my divorce. In the settlement, I got the mortgage and the house, and my ex-husband got the stuff in it, including the living room furniture. I had little money left to redecorate, but I managed to do so with creativity and panache.

I found an adequate gold lame sofa at the Salvation Army and discovered that Mom's card table with a throw draped over it could function quite well as a coffee table. A few folding chairs added nuance, and my sister donated the bentwood rocker that I'd given her for Christmas 10 years before. Mom and Dad brought over a plaid recliner from their basement, and before long, my living room suite reflected my personality at the time: scattered, rough around the edges, worn at the seams, but functional. All in all, it was a good fit.

Over time, I began to recover financially from the divorce and bought a sofa, a loveseat, an overstuffed chair, and an ottoman because those are the mandatory pieces that everyone must have in her home. (I assumed that the law had something to do with people's decor, in the same way that I'd once thought it had something to do with tampons.) The suite boasted a lovely Southwestern design and was fairly expensive, so I figured it would last me for most of my life, just as my parents' sofa had lasted for most of theirs.

However, they didn't have to deal with planned obsolescence or three dogs in their home, and within a few years, I found myself back in the furniture store picking out another pricey suite. This time, I opted for a blue contemporary one with a chaise lounge because I thought it would make me look hip. It didn't, nor did it hold up well as a dog bed for two lab mixes. When I next shopped, I decided to do so wisely and bought just a sofa and a loveseat at a furniture warehouse. I made sure that its fabric matched the color of any dog I might have for the next 20 years, as I vowed that I was finished spending money on living room furniture.

Soon, however, Bill moved in, and with him came a sofa, a loveseat, an overstuffed chair, and an ottoman. (I noted with satisfaction that I had picked a boyfriend who was not only cute but also law-abiding.) I sold my sofa and put the loveseat in the basement. But after three years, Bill's furniture showed signs of wear, and we shopped together for a sofa, a loveseat, an over-stuffed chair (now called "a chair-and-a-half") and an ottoman.

It lasted for three weeks. The fabric began to pill and tear, and the cushions imploded. Stunned that $2,000 bought such a shoddy product, we fought with the company until they acqui-esced and offered us a store credit. We refused, not wanting to patronize them in any way, and demanded a full refund, which we received after a bit more haggling. We now had an empty living room and debated where to shop next. Then began a shift in my thinking.

"Who says," I asked Bill, "that we have to buy new living room furniture?"

"Nobody," he told me. "It's not like it's a law or anything."

I was fairly certain that he didn't notice the epiphanous look on my face, but, just to be sure, I kept rambling.

"I used to live with Salvation Army stuff and I was happy."

"Is that where you want to shop?" he asked. "Because you know me. I pretty much sit on the floor."

He was correct. Much like the Buddha reposing under a tree, Bill, more often than not, sat cross-legged on the carpet, his back propped against any sofa that might be behind him.

239

So what were we worried about? All we really needed was a tree for him and a straight-backed chair for me to sit in while I cross-stitched. This was improbable, of course, but it's just this kind of thinking outside the box that led to the invention of the Pop-Tart and maybe even the iPhone.

Oh, I was inspired. I went all rogue in a Steve Jobs kind of way, looking around the house for furniture we could bring into the living room. Up from the basement came the brown loveseat and a red papasan chair. From the front porch came a cushioned wicker chair that the outside cat had been using. Before long, I was able to look at my decor and proudly proclaim it, and myself, as eclectic and minimalistic. I had a label. I was, at long last, hip.

When I called her, Bobbi shared in my excitement as I told her about my new way of life. She only did so to a certain point, though, because she'd been living that way as long as she could remember.

"Have you ever paid for new furniture?" I asked her. "I don't remember if you did."

"Well, a few things here and there," she replied. "But not many."

Bobbi's house is a cornucopia of pieces hailing from friends, dead relatives, and demolition sites. The blue chair in the corner of her living room belonged to her landlord's mother. It nestles comfortably next to Uncle Tom's oak barrister bookcase. After Tom died, it had been stored for decades in Uncle Digger's basement, and Bobbi is convinced that it is worth more than her entire house. In front of the chair sits Mom's brown ottoman, and beside it is her candle stand table, a three-legged colonial knick-knack that falls over when one sneezes too harshly in its vicinity. Mom's hutch shares the wall beside my ex-boyfriend's bookcase, and next to that rests Bobbi's bed, the one that she made herself and has found totally acceptable to place in her living room. Another small bookcase that Bobbi rescued from a hotel that was being torn down completes the ensemble.

"Oh," Bobbi added. "And those two end tables in there? I made them."

"Out of what?"

"Just scrappy pieces of wood I had lying around. Same stuff I used to make my bed."

"So you basically didn't pay for anything in your living room."

"No. But I did pay for something in my kitchen. That sideboard I have in there? I got that for three bucks at an antique store in York."

Also in Bobbi's kitchen one can see my grandparents' table, which our father had used for his finishing table in his shop. Bobbi had resurrected and restored it after Dad died, and it looks beautiful surrounded by chairs that she'd found at the side of the road or for which she'd bartered at yard sales.

Her bedroom contains no bed, but it does boast a parlor grand piano gifted to her by one of her friends after his mother had passed. Also present is Aunt Cottie's mahogany chest of drawers made in 1846 and passed down to Aunt Lou when Cottie died, then to Mom when Lou died. Our parents' small, cherry kitchen table holds Bobbi's CDs and her computer. Mam Mam's sewing machine cabinet provides a spot for Bobbi's books and albums, and Mom's secretary's desk does what it was intended to do: It houses Bobbi's bills and stationery. A stunning piece, it belonged to our great-great-grandmother, who, of course, is also dead.

"You're lucky that people die," I told Bobbi, "or you'd never have anything in your house."

She agreed that she was fortunate in that aspect but was quick to point out that she had acquired many things over the years without harm having come to anyone.

"You and Mom gave me stuff that you got tired of and were replacing, like a stove and a fridge. And some rugs."

"And still," I said, "they were free. So back to my original question: Did you ever actually pay for anything besides that sideboard?"

She had to think for a bit, but she was pleased to report that pentacles sometimes did leave her pocket. Over the last 30 years, she's purchased the following:

1. A headboard for $80 at an auction
2. A fainting couch for $75 from Craig's List
3. A new futon for $300 from J. C. Penney's
4. A new couch from a furniture store for $400
5. A refrigerator for $25 from Goodwill
6. A box spring and mattress for $10 at a yard sale

Bobbi wanted to make clear that she owns none of these items anymore. The headboard is now at an ex-girlfriend's house; the fainting couch has been broken into pieces which Bobbi reused to build the bed for her screened-in porch; the futon is in a friend's barn; the new couch is at a co-worker's home; and the refrigerator, mattress, and box spring are all in the landfill. It is important to realize, my sister said, that most items she'd purchased may have outlived their usefulness in her home, but not in the homes of others.

I now understood the cycle of furniture and appliances that have come and gone at my sister's place. It makes me wish I'd followed suit, as I could have saved a lot of money and helped a lot of people in the process. I did some quick math (*addition*, to be specific, which is really the only kind of math I do) and realized that, over the same time period, I'd spent close to ten grand on my living room sets alone.

The Ace of Pentacles may also indicate that one may be too caught up in the material world. I used to be guilty of that, but no more. I have come to embrace Bobbi's methodology of home decor, at least for one room in my house. But I draw the line at buying a mattress and a box spring for 10 bucks at a yard sale. I can just hear my mother saying, "Think about the people who slept on that thing. Think about where they've been."

"Did Mom know where you bought that bed?" I asked.

"Oh, she knew. She knew because every time we'd pass the farm where I bought it, she'd say with a bit of disgust, 'That's where you got that *mattress* that was leaning against the tree.'"

"Wasn't she grossed out that you had that *mattress* in your house?"

"Probably, but she knew she couldn't say anything because it was on the bed she slept on when she stayed overnight. And she loved staying overnight here. So her hands were tied on that one."

"And weren't you worried about bedbugs or anything?"

"Oh, God no. That thing had been outside for so long, anything on it was dead."

"Well, you did have the new brown couch at the time. And she liked that."

"Yes, because it replaced the old green one that had a nest of dead mice inside one of the cushions."

"Bobbi," I said. "That's disgusting."

"So was the smell," she replied. "The smell is what made me get a new couch."

"And Mom was proud."

"Oh, she was so proud, she probably told her bridge club. I think she was excited that maybe I was turning into you."

I, for one, hope that never happens. Where would all of that used furniture find a home?

Give Credit Where Credit Is Due

THE TWO OF PENTACLES IS A HAPPY CARD. A young man dances while juggling two coins that are bound together with the infinity sign, a figure eight. His cone-shaped hat provides more levity to the situation, showing that this fellow marches to the beat of his own drummer both in a fashion sense and in a rhythmic one. He doesn't seem to mind that the two ships behind him are being tossed on a stormy sea; he just keeps moving from foot to foot, balancing his coins and enjoying the fluidity of their movement.

The Two of Pentacles encourages you to do the same: Be flexible with and open to the infinite possibilities available to us in the material world. Keep your sense of humor when navigating through tough times and don't give a lot of credence to negativity. The material world can provide a myriad of joyful experiences if we keep our wits and our sense of humor about us.

Wits and humor. These have always been two indispensable components of my personality as I've navigated through my finances over the years. A single homeowner with an older house, I was never able to save a lot of money and therefore relied on part-time jobs to supplement my income. I also relied on the kindness of credit cards. Oh, they were wonderful friends to me, these thin pieces of plastic. *You need a few new windows?* they'd whisper. *Swipe away. How about a sump pump? It's all yours. And just so you know that we're serious about our love for you, we'll charge you no interest for the first year.*

The idea of 12 months without interest was as calming to me as slipping some Tryptophan into my hot chocolate, and the plans I made for cutting back on luxuries and paying off my balance in a year increased my serotonin levels to mythic heights. I swore to eat only boxed macaroni-and-cheese three times a week. I would shop at thrift stores and keep my thermostat set at 62 degrees in the winter. I would live as frugally as Daniel Boone must have, growing my own crops and making my own soap. And at the end of the year, I would owe nothing except gratitude for no interest payments. I was starting a new chapter in the Book of Anne, and I was excited.

Of course, as anyone with a credit card relationship knows, the road to debt-free living is paved with those high interest rates that kick in when you *don't* keep your promises about prudent eating, shopping, and heating. Before I knew it, I was ending my love affair with Credit Card A and had moved on to one with Credit Card B. After a year, I dumped Credit Card B and found myself in bed with Credit Card C. I had become a credit card whore.

Meanwhile, my friends were beginning to pay off their houses while I was refinancing mine for the third time. This dependency on borrowing money used to be a great source of shame for me until I discussed my concerns with Bill.

"I feel like such a loser," I told him. "All this credit card debt at my age, all the home equity loans over the years."

"But did you ever declare bankruptcy?" he asked. "Are you ever late with your payments? Do you have a bad credit score?"

I answered no to all of his inquiries.

"The way you've handled your money has worked for you," he said. "Using cards and bank loans has helped you manage your cash flow and allowed you to keep your house."

I had been so sure that he would have chided me over the exorbitant amount of interest I'd paid over the years, but he didn't. The closest he came to any type of admonishment was when he asked me, "You never paid 23 percent or anything like that, right?"

"Of course I didn't."

Of course I did, but I saw no reason to curb the flow of Bill's kind words. They were making me feel much lighter than I'd felt in a long time. I'd kept my head above water, my wits were intact, and suddenly, my sense of humor about my monetary predicament returned. I saw myself as the juggler on the card and realized that, like so many other folks, I'd be in debt until I died. And after that, who was going to care?

When I visited my bank one day, I relayed this financial plan of mine to the tellers, three young men who would never deposit my money without engaging me in some kind of conversation. This branch was a new one in Millersville, and its employees were extremely diverse. For this reason, when the bank opened, a lot of its customers left. They weren't too fond of an establishment, apparently, that employed black, Hispanic, and Asian folks.

The guys enjoyed my theory about staying in debt as long as I lived. More often than not, however, our conversations usually revolved around the subject of race and politics. It was refreshing and eye-opening to be able to converse with people whose experiences were so different from mine. Before long, I found myself stopping by the bank just to chat and become enlightened.

One January morning, as I entered the bank, I was surprised to see only Morgan and Bob.

"Where's Mike?"

"Mike who?" Morgan asked.

"You know. Mike. The manager."

"Who are you talking about?"

"Mike. The guy who sits back there in that little room."

"That's where Ted sits," Bob said.

"Who's Ted?" I asked.

"The guy who sits back there in that little room."

"I don't know Ted," I told them. "I know Mike. The manager. You know. The guy from Peru?"

"Nobody from Peru works here," Morgan said.

"Yes, he does. Remember I brought you all a plate of Christmas cookies, and he took the extras home for his kids? I just wondered if I could get my plate back."

"You mean Ted," Bob corrected me. "You gave Ted the cookies."

"Then who's Mike?" I was completely bewildered. The two men stared at each other until realization crossed Bob's face.

"Oh, you're talking about Mark. He used to be the manager. But he left, like, over six months ago."

"But . . . wait. Was he from Peru?"

"He was from Colombia."

"So is Ted from Peru?" I asked.

"Ted's Asian. And he's been here for six months."

"Holy shit," I said. "I thought they were the same guy."

All three of us froze, and the awkward cloud that enveloped us dissipated only when I said, "Wow. I am the whitest person I know right now."

Lucky for me that the tellers at my bank had a sense of humor and that they understood my financial planning for the future. Borrowing money from Credit Card A to pay off Credit Card B wouldn't be prudent for everyone. But it got the approval of Morgan and Ted and Mark (or whoever's from Peru), and has kept me in good stead with my bank *and* with the Two of Pentacles.

Walton's Chickens

THE THREE OF PENTACLES REMINDS US that functioning together as a group is the best way to get things done. Inside a cathedral, a young mason explains his work thus far to two people holding blueprints. He seems to be demonstrating how he's making his plans come to life, and his friends are there to help him.

When I taught school, I was fortunate to be surrounded by other teachers who could share in the implementation of my goals. One person in particular whose opinions I valued was John, a social studies teacher whose methods were unorthodox and delightful. When the two of us wanted to develop a unit of study, we'd meet at a local bar over a couple of drinks and decide on a course of action. Our ideas would have the same fluidity as the beer flowing out of its tap, and in a couple of hours, our plans would come together and were usually successful.

That word "usually" is always a devilish one, isn't it? It implies that something wicked this way comes, something dark and unexpected that two middle school teachers, especially after a bit of alcohol, wouldn't have predicted. Such was the case with John's unit about ancient Egypt.

The seventh graders in his class that year were fascinated with the process of mummification. They wanted to try it. John thought that this idea had some potential, so he did a little research and discovered that chickens could be mummified pretty easily. (This thought of using poultry came as a relief to me, as I had been concerned that John, with his tendency toward using unconventional teaching methods, might have stopped by the morgue to do some investigating.)

Knowing that I didn't eat meat and was concerned with animal welfare, John checked with me first to make sure that this project wasn't going to upset me. It didn't. I was never a militant vegetarian and since the birds were already going to be someone's dinner, I didn't have a problem with my colleague's idea. Much better, I reasoned, to be buried with honors than dipped in breadcrumbs and deep fried.

John was also concerned with his choice of burial plots. He thought that the environmental center would be a good choice, and since I was instrumental in getting that small tract of land up and running, would I be offended if some mummified fowl were laid to rest there? I couldn't think of a reason why this would be a bad thing. After all, the kids in my Environmental Club had planted butterfly bushes and flowers and were tending to their upkeep on a weekly basis. The thought that our area would now be put to good use as a memorial garden seemed morbidly pleasing to the kids and to me.

John explained the process to his students and they did the work at home. Each bought his own roasting chicken, along with the salt, oils, and strips of muslin needed for the procedure. After the work was done, the birds were placed in small cardboard pyramids that the kids had built, and in keeping with the Egyptian tradition, trinkets, including items such as marbles and pennies, were placed beside the departed to ease their transition into the afterlife. The following fall, the birds would be exhumed and studied to see if the mummification had been successful.

Unfortunately, over the summer, the district did a little digging of its own. Unaware of the sacrilege it was committing, the maintenance crew laid some beautiful, curved sidewalks that wound through the environmental center. In addition, other small areas were paved over to support benches and tables whose legs were cemented firmly in place. All of this provided a lovely spot in which students could enjoy some downtime, but it also inadvertently crushed the hopes of John's budding archaeologists. The digging up of birds through slabs of concrete was not going to happen.

To this day, then, the tombs of a few dozen mummified souls rest peacefully under the grounds of Cocalico Middle School. Working together as a group, John and his students successfully yet unknowingly provided invaluable information for future civilizations who, when excavating the landscape of Denver, Pennsylvania, would uncover the pyramids. The only conclusion possible would be that, in this region, a race of chickens once flourished who worshipped roasters and took great care to preserve their remains. And who would argue with that hypothesis? Considering the shape of our world right now, this theory would make as much sense as any other. More than that, it might actually serve as a more favorable alternative for all concerned.

Keeping the Filth at Bay

THIS IS ONE NEGATIVE TAROT CARD. The man pictured here is an uncompromising force, one with which very few of us would want to reckon. He's a scowling, tight-fisted fellow whose money keeps him in one place. He holds on tightly to a pentacle, has two others resting under his feet, and keeps another balanced atop the crown on his head. Money is his god, and the hold it has on him prevents him from experiencing more meaningful parts of life.

Of course, money isn't something we can ignore. I'm always looking for ways to curb my spending habits in the hopes of becoming wealthy, like hanging the laundry outside or using the same tea bag three times. I'd like to think that I was saving our household some dough by practicing these small acts of financial sorcery. Did Bill even notice? I waited until he turned from the computer screen to look at the dogs.

"Hey, honey, I have a question for you."

"What's up?" he asked.

"Can you list some ways that I help to increase our capital around here?" I was trying to sound like Warren Buffett to keep Bill's attention rapt.

"You mean the little things you do to make us filthy rich?" he asked me. "You could start with your hair."

So he did notice. And he remembered my telling him once that I don't wash my hair often in order to save money on shampoo. I suspect he knows by now that this was a lie. I just hate washing my hair. The lathering and rinsing part is kind of fun, but the subsequent combing after the towel removal sends rivulets of water over my now-dry body. The wet hair clings to my head, framing my face in such a way that I resemble the woman in one of Picasso's paintings, *Girl in Front of Mirror*. (Go ahead and Google that image. It's what I think I look like naked even when my hair isn't wet.)

I then need to apply some kind of styling product after towel-drying my locks, thus making them rather wet again and defeating the entire reason for the towel-drying ritual in the first place. Blow-drying is next, and I spend as much time on that as I would writing a research paper. Then it's time for the curling iron and hairspray or some kind of serum to keep the whole 'do in place. If I were independently wealthy, I'd visit my hairdresser daily and have her take care of all of this. Since that's not an option, my hair is filthy several days a week, not necessarily from dirt, mind you, but from product build-up. Ironically, though, these are also the days when I look my best. Bill agrees with this assessment, to a certain extent.

"You know," I told him, "usually when you compliment my hair, I laugh and tell you that it's really dirty."

"Right."

"So do you ever, on your own, actually notice when my hair is dirty?"

"No, not until you point it out, really. But I can always tell when you've washed it."

"Exactly," I said. "Because it doesn't hold its style due to lack of excessive product."

"No, that's not it. I notice it when we're outside. If the wind is blowing and your hair moves, it's clean. If it doesn't budge, it's dirty. Or if you brush your bangs off of your forehead and they just kind of stick up like a big mohawk. Or if I ask you when you washed it last, and you ask me what day it is."

"I get it."

"Oh, and when you shake your head, your hair stays totally in place. Kind of like the hair on a sculpture."

This quiet man with whom I live certainly is a lot more observant than I thought. And his level of patience was now reaching new heights, considering we'd just spent over three minutes discussing hair care and he was still willing to go on.

"So you think my hair looks pretty good, though, most of the time?"

"Honey, I think your hair looks great most of the time. Or you can substitute any other superlative for 'great' if that makes you feel better."

"And you'd agree that by not washing it a lot, I'm saving us money."

"TONS of money," he said. "In fact, we could probably go out to eat five nights a week with the money you're saving on shampoo."

I knew then that we were finished talking.

When I called Bobbi that night to ask about her ways of pinching pennies, we immediately talked about mayonnaise sandwiches. In her late teens, remember, she was working at Skyland Lodge and was living in the dorms there. When the resort closed for the season, the employees either went home or found temporary work and housing elsewhere. Instead of coming back to Pennsylvania, though, she chose to house sit for a friend of hers who lived off the mountain. My sister enjoyed staying at his rustic place in Rappahannock County, where she lived off of her savings for about two months.

Toward the end of her stay, however, her funds and her food supply began to dwindle.

"I remember that I had exactly $2.86 left in my checking account, and I was sitting in front of the kerosene heater waiting for the flame to die out," she told me. "I was bundled up in a blanket, rocking back and forth, trying to stay warm, and eating a mayonnaise sandwich."

"And I remember you saying it wasn't bad."

"You know, it really was amazing. It was solid food. Real mayonnaise, not Miracle Whip. And when you stop to think about it, the mayonnaise and the bread are the best part of any sandwich."

"Did Mom know?" (You may notice that this question is a recurring one. I ask it after discussing most of Bobbi's adventures as a young lass.)

"Oh, she was mortified. She kept asking why I didn't come home."

"And why didn't you?"

"I have no idea. Probably because I was 18."

I don't think that Bobbi or I has any fear of the Four of Pentacles. Between my credit card obsession and her Bohemian lifestyle, we never have to worry about hoarding money. It comes in. It goes out. And somehow, we're still here. Lack of shampoo and lunchmeat can ne'er deter us, and if hoarding money makes one resemble the fellow on this card, who's miserly and miserable, I think that we're both content to stay just the way we are, a couple of filthy-haired, mayonnaise-eating, happy-go-lucky gals.

Dabbling in Druidism

IF THE FOUR OF PENTACLES IS A NEGATIVE CARD, then this one is downright depressing. Two homeless people are walking in the snow, a crippled man limping with a crutch and a barefooted woman pulling her worn, hooded cape tightly around her body. As the couple passes a church, warm light radiates through its stained glass window. This sanctuary could provide them with a safe place to spend the night, but they are ignoring its welcoming aura. The Five of Pentacles is indicative of hard times, so having it show up in a reading could imply that you are experiencing a lack of money or even a lack of spiritual connection.

I have always believed in God, but there have been times when I've felt detached from him. (Or her. Feel free to substitute any pronoun you see fit.) Not surprisingly, these are the times when I wasn't making any kind of an effort to hold up my end of the bargain. And like it or not, Whoever Is Out There does require a little bit of give-and-take from us. In order for any type of bond to form between God and us, we need to provide communication, whether in the form of prayer, meditation, or just plain bitching about our own behavior. In fact, most of my prayers usually start out with the last of these styles. Here's an example:

> Dear God. Seriously. I cannot believe that, once again, I didn't spend enough time doing what was important. I just sat on my ever-widening butt in front of the TV and watched the last season of House for the tenth time. I could have been spending those hours in quiet meditation, or taking a walk, or hanging out with the puppies. But no. I had to sit there and shove candy in my mouth and wonder why I didn't go into the medical field so I could have worn scrubs to work every day. I seriously do not know how you can put up with me sometimes.

Prayer was so much easier as a young one when, with my parents' direction, I asked God's blessings on Pudgy and Bobbi (in that order) and that was about it, except for the part about his taking my soul if I died during the night. Then when I was a bit older and started going to Sunday school, the minister told us that when we talk to God, we should be sure to say, "Forgive me, help me, and thank you" somewhere in the conversation. Even as a child, I loved a good framework, and using this equation made my prayers very easy:

Dear God: Forgive me for fighting with Bobbi. Help me not to fight with Bobbi. Thank you for Pudgy.

And then I'd call it a night.

As I grew older, though, I began to question the nature of God himself and how it applied to me. And as an avid reader, I began to explore all of the possibilities. Before I knew it, I was knee-deep in Buddhism, Taoism, pantheism, gnosticism, and Celtic Christianity. When I closed my eyes at night to pray, I didn't know whether to ask God to help me end my attachments, balance my yin, expand my sense of wonder, understand secrets lost to time, or revel in creation. In short, I was becoming a theological mess. I even started reading Richard Dawkins' books on atheism, and they were making sense to me.

And then Mom died. And then I retired. And then I almost died. When I came home from the hospital, I lay in bed recovering for weeks, trying to pray or meditate or worship the ficus tree next to my dresser. Nothing was helping me ease my disconnect with God. I called the prayer team at church and asked them to send someone to Miller Road to talk me off the spiritual ledge.

The church understood completely and sent Sandy, one of its lay ministers, to help me. I remember telling her that I couldn't go to church anymore because I was too emotional, that I couldn't make it through a service without crying. To make matters worse, I didn't know why I was crying.

Sandy listened to my woes for about an hour. The first thing she said when I finished babbling was, "Do you think that you're the only person who cries in church? Look around the next time you're there. Everyone loses it from time to time." The more we talked, the more I realized that I had to stop taking myself so seriously. It had never occurred to me that emotions can run high for everyone when worship is involved. Also, I wasn't the only woman who had temporarily drifted away from God.

So I went back to church and I cried a lot. I cried for my mom, my retirement, my "I almost died" experience. This trifecta of life-changing events wasn't going to dissolve on its own, and attending church was helping melt away *some* of my remaining fears (like the idea that the surgeon really didn't remove all of my appendix and that infected pieces of it were still inside of me). However, even though I was feeling a little better spiritually, I still didn't feel complete.

Then I met Alicia one day after the 11:00 service. A retired minister, she was now working as a spiritual director and asked if I'd be interested in coming to see her once a month. I was intrigued. The idea of discussing my spiritual path, deepening my relationship with God, and figuring out "What's next?" in my retired life sounded very appealing. Plus, theologians are my rock stars. Tell me that you're ordained and I will bombard you with questions that begin with the two trees in the Garden of Eden and end with the New Jerusalem. Nothing is more fascinating to me than hanging out with someone who has a degree in All Things Biblical, and I could hold that person captive for days with my inquiries.

During our first session, I'd asked Alicia if she was familiar with a book I had recently read, *The Wisdom Jesus*, by Cynthia Bourgeault, which presents Jesus as an enlightened being who can help us transform our consciousness. I had been fascinated with the book's premise and was willing to reread the book and discuss it with someone who really knew her stuff. Alicia was game, and for the next couple of months, we shared ideas on each chapter after we'd read it individually.

However, I have a habit of perusing an author's footnotes, endnotes, and bibliographies when something she mentions strikes my fancy, and this fancy of mine had been struck many times as I read Bourgeault's work. I needed to dig deeper into the topics she'd examined, so I'd check out her chapter notes, order a book that she'd referenced, and read it immediately. Needless to say, each new piece of information I was consuming was like a tiny stick of dynamite that was planted in my brain, and by the time I visited Alicia a few sessions later, my mind was completely blown.

She asked how I was doing, how I'd enjoyed chapter four of the book, how my week had been. I opened my mouth to form words, but instead, I uttered a guttural cry of helplessness. After about two minutes, my syntax was restored, and I was able to tell her (between sobs) about the extra books I'd read in the the past few months whose topics covered a wide scope of spiritual and religious thoughts. I'd explored the ideas of Christian mysticism. I'd researched the Council of Nicaea and was shocked by the seemingly random way that certain sacred texts were deemed worthy of inclusion in the Bible while others were not. I studied prayers by Thomas Merton, J. Philip Newell, and John Wesley. I even went to my old buddy Depok and read his views about the future of God. Then I'd topped off my ecumenical sundae with a book written by a priest who, even though still a Christian, put forth the notion that the historical Jesus really didn't exist at all.

"So, that was how my week has been," I told her as I stared down at the wet, crumpled tissue I held in my hands. "I have no idea what to believe anymore. I doubt that I'm even a Christian in the conventional sense of the word." I paused and looked up at her. "I'm probably more of a Druid. But a Druid who reads the Dead Sea Scrolls. And who's working on raising her awareness to a higher level of consciousness. With a koan. Maybe. Or not. How was your week?"

Alicia stared back at me like she'd just witnessed the Apocalypse (but a totally Presbyterian one, with four committee members riding to an Elders meeting rather than four creatures on horseback, carrying scrolls and whatnot). "You realize," she said, "that the amount of books you've covered is more than you'd be asked to read in one semester of seminary. You do know that, don't you?"

I did not know that.

"You need to put them all away. Save them for later. Right now, let's concentrate only on the one that we've been discussing."

Oh, that Alicia was so wise. She realized that I was doing the same thing with Christianity that I'd done with all of those other spiritual paths. Such is my habit. I go in too deep for my own good and get drowned in the process. The trick, at least for me, is to explore one spiritual idea at a time. I test its merits. Then I compare it to and blend it with others, but I do so only after its foundation is solid and its tenets have resonated with me. Otherwise, I'll end up like the woman on the Five of Pentacles, seeking God but walking right past him in an effort to understand him as completely as I can and from as many angles as possible.

No one expects us to do this, least of all God. And certainly not my sister. I was really excited to explore this card with her, and I left her a voicemail telling her just that. "Call me when you can," I said. "This discussion is going to be fun."

She phoned me the next day.

"So what's up with this card?" she asked me.

"Oh, it's a good one. I have lots of questions for you. Let me start by asking you this: Do you have a framework that you use when you pray?"

She didn't say anything for a while. I could tell that she was deep in thought, turning the idea around in her head so that when she gave me her answer, it would be one founded on earnest contemplation. I was trying to be patient. Heaven knows that this was an intense topic. But I couldn't wait any longer, and after a few seconds of silence, I said, "Are you still there?"

"Oh, yeah, sorry. I have this piece of Frito lodged between my back teeth, and I was trying to suck it out with my tongue. What was the question again?"

"Do you have a framework for prayer?"

"No."

"No?"

"No."

Well, this conversation was going nowhere fast.

"Like, you have no framework, or you don't even pray?"

"Well, that all depends on what you mean by pray," Bobbi said. "I'd say the closest I come to that is when I wake up in the morning and say that I'm grateful."

"But whom to you say that to?" I asked.

"Huh. I don't know. But I know that no one's up there keeping score on a big tote board."

"But it you're talking to someone, someone has to hear it."

"I don't think anyone's hearing it. I think it's a way for me to check in with myself."

"Do you believe in God?"

"I thought you said this card was going to be fun."

"It *is* fun."

"If you say so." Bobbi took a deep breath and then exhaled. "Here's the thing. I don't look at God as one being. I think it's more of a collective thing with all of us. We do good things, think good thoughts and it benefits everyone. It's all positive energy we're transferring."

"Right. There's a school of thought that says God is evolving as we evolve, that we're all God, actually, responsible for what we say and do."

"That makes more sense to me than talking to one being."

"But I don't like that."

"I didn't think you would, Anne."

"I need order, someone at the top who knows what he's doing. I don't trust the human race to be in charge. Too many assholes."

"That's why we have the responsibility to the collective to be positive and do good things. To balance out the asshole-y part of humanity."

My sister and I then talked about a few other things, like how I hug my pillow when I pray, kind of like we used to hug our dolls when we were little. Bobbi didn't have a doll, of course, but she did have Linus, a stuffed lion with a really soft tail. We don't know what happened to Linus. We think that Poopsie, our dog, might have gotten ahold of him. That made me a little sad, and I found myself whispering a silent prayer that God would watch over Linus' remains, wherever they may be. I didn't tell Bobbi that. She would have called Bill on her other phone and expressed her concern.

"So what are you up to the rest of the night?" I asked her.

"I don't know. I think I'll watch *First Contact*."

"A movie?"

"A *Star Trek* movie. The Borg are in that one. They're bad guys, but they're a collective and they can share consciousness with each other. All this talk about God reminded me of the Borg. God could be the Borg, but in a good way. "

"That kinda freaks me out. It reminds me of *The Matrix*, where everything's just an illusion and God is one big computer program."

"Yeah, that could be, too," she said.

I didn't need to hear that. I was hoping that she'd scoff at the idea and put my mind at ease a bit. Our entire conversation had me going down that path again where Jesus, Buddha, and Laozi were meeting at a coffee shop, but this time they were sitting right in front of a computerized tote board and Richard Dawkins was their server. When I said my prayers that night, I prayed to a kind man in the sky with a white beard and a long robe. It was the only way I was going to get anything done.

Was Bobbi Actually Born?

AN OBVIOUSLY WELL-TO-DO GENTLEMAN stands in front of two beggars kneeling before him. He drops coins from his right hand to one of the men, and in his left hand he holds the scales of justice, allowing us to assume that he will give an equal amount of money to the other man. The antithesis of the fellow featured in the Four of Pentacles who guarded his riches selfishly, the philanthropist here is sharing what he has with others. The Six of Pentacles is a positive card, indicating balance and sharing in all relationships, whether they are of a business or personal nature. Pull this card, and you may expect a bonus at work. Or perhaps you're being given a pat on the back for being a good parent to your children, loving and caring for all of them in a balanced, supportive way.

Mom and Dad raised Bobbi and me with an equal amount of affection so that neither my sister nor I ever felt that one of us was the favorite. Dad, being the more demonstrative, used to say regularly, "You girls have no idea how much I love you." Mom, on the other hand, might simply nod in agreement at Dad's assertion. But their intentions were clear and well-received by

both of us. The idea that our parents showed more affection to one of their daughters is unreasonable, unless someone uses our baby books as a barometer for fondness and attention. Then, the concept of inequality holds some degree of truth.

My baby book begins with the announcement of my birth and is followed by details of my christening, complete with the date, the relatives for whom I was named (my mother's sisters, Anna Mae and Louise), and family members in attendance. The tome goes on to outline my first 10 days on Earth, describing any of my respiratory, circulatory, and genito-urinary disturbances, noting that I enjoyed drinking something called "Lactum" and that I vomited only infrequently.

My footprint record in all of its faded glory is taped to the next page, and notes, cards, and letters of congratulations are taped to the following four. Lists of gifts brought to my first birthday party follow, and the minutiae of my feeding habits for the next two years are well-documented: Dad even writes that I switched from Lactum to Gerber's Mixed Cereal. My fondness for some foods and not others is recorded on a chart on page 17, and my physical and mental development is chronicled, detailing important events such as my ability to roll on my back or lift my head.

I cooed in my seventh week. I said "Da-Da" in my seventh month and "Mommy" in my twelfth. The trivial details of my first birthday party are provided, as are those relating to my self-help: I could use a spoon at 13 months and a fork at three-and-a-half years, the same age at which I could also put on my shoes and brush my teeth. (My ability to "play simple catch with a ball" is, unsurprisingly, not noted.)

I had birthday parties at two, three, and four years old with multiple guests, and I got good grades in kindergarten. I had chicken pox, measles, roseola, and a tonsillectomy. I was sent to Sunday school, where, Mom writes, I "spoke favorably of [my] lessons."

Now, if my baby book reads like the collected works of William Shakespeare, Bobbi's reads like a condensed version of *Fun with Dick and Jane.*

"The only thing in my book is a picture of my feet and my high school graduation announcement," Bobbi told me when I called her.

"You always say that. But there has to be more in there, right?"

"Nothing. First page, feet. Last page, graduation."

"The record of your growth? Of your vaccinations?"

"Nope."

"What about gifts when you were born?

"Again, Anne. Nothing."

Well, now I felt bad. Mom recorded in my book 36 gifts that her friends and family gave her and Dad when I arrived, and each gift was followed with a brief description of its color (if relevant), its texture (if appropriate), and its origin of purchase (if necessary to understand the gift's importance). If we had to rely on lists like these as the only historical records of our births, Bobbi, apparently, had never been born.

But as a validation of our existence, we at least we have our birth stories. Mine was one I never tired of hearing. When Mom went into labor, Dad loaded her in the front seat of their 1940 Dodge, while my Aunt Marg and Uncle Digger, who lived three doors down, climbed in the back. It had not been necessary for Dad to call my aunt and uncle to tell them a hospital trip was imminent; they'd kept a close watch on our house as Mom's "time" grew closer. The minute they saw my parents head out the door at 10:00 that night, they grabbed their coats and hurried down the sidewalk. Much as my mother wanted her delivery to be a private one between her and her husband, it was not meant to be. This was Dad's family, and as you recall, they did everything together.

When they arrived at the hospital, Mom was wheeled into the delivery area. Marg, Digger, and Dad settled into the waiting room with the other expectant families. In just an hour or so, an attendant entered the room with a big smile and announced, "It's a boy!" as he pushed a gurney on which rested my mother, exhausted from her experience. Dad, overcome with emotion, jumped up from his chair, ran over to Mom, and kissed her. A sudden tap on his shoulder interrupted his ecstasy, as a man standing beside him said, "Hey, buddy. That's my wife."

What happened next is a matter of opinion. My aunt's version of the story is that Dad was so angry about his lapse in judgment that he stormed over to his chair, picked up his hat, and slammed it to the floor, all the while taking the Lord's name in vain, repeatedly and quite fervently. My father denies this. It was true that he *had* worn a hat to the hospital that night. But he did *not* use said hat as a prop in his sister's dramatic retelling of the story. He simply grumbled a bit, walked back to the chair, and sat back down. He then held his hat in his hands as he continued to grouse, staring at the floor.

I feel that the truth lies somewhere in between the two recountings: As much as I wanted to believe my dad, his favorite curse words more often than not did invoke the Trinity, so my aunt's version definitely had a stream of legitimacy running through it.

"See? I don't even have a story like that," Bobbi said. "Every year on my birthday, I'd call Mom and ask, 'Anything? You've had some time now. Is there any part about my birth that you can remember?' And she'd laugh and always say the same thing: 'Now, Bobbi, how would I know? Back then, they just gave you gas when the contractions started. You woke up. You had a baby. Done.'"

I'd clearly hit a nerve here, and I was reminded that when the Six of Pentacles is drawn, it's sometimes a sign that a relationship, even between sisters, may be unbalanced. The card is also asking you to be careful that you're not the one constantly acquiescing during times of conflict. Instead, stand up for yourself, even if it's to throw down your hat in aggravation, rather than hide your true feelings to avoid an argument.

This time, though, I decided to stop talking. I had no other choice. What I *did* have was the better baby book and the only birth story. It was wise to just step away and admit that, yes, our parents were a lot more consistent recording the events of my young life than they were recording those of Bobbi's. When my sister I and next reminisce, I'll stick with stories about all those times we got in trouble in high school. The scales will then be tipped inordinately in Bobbi's favor, and there will be justice for all.

Lies, Sitting Bull, and the Continental Drift Theory

LOOK AT THE LUSH GARDEN ON THIS CARD. Apparently, money does grow on trees—or, in this case, on some type of flowering shrub—and the gardener couldn't be more satisfied. He takes a break from his work and leans on his hoe, admiring the blossoms of pentacles and taking stock of how beautifully his garden has matured. He's pleased with his success and deserves a pat on the back for his labors.

As teachers of eighth-grade English and reading, my colleagues and I were very impressed with both of our curricula, especially the latter. We required that our students read four books per marking period and report on them through a combination of written responses and oral conferences. Three periods a week of uninterrupted reading were allowed, and we were lucky to have administrators who understood the importance of this method of instruction. I believe that, due to the way we designed our course of study, our students read more than the average teen. Like the man pictured on the Seven of Pentacles, we couldn't have been more proud of our flourishing garden of young scholars.

Most of my kids loved their "free" periods, especially those students who enjoyed reading. And those who didn't? Well, they relished the opportunity to snooze stealthily, their novels propped open in front of them, until they got caught. However, I was usually too busy conducting oral conferences to really patrol my classroom and seek out the sleepers. I was instead focused on the student in front of my desk who was discussing her latest book with me.

The idea of an excited young person delving into the intricacies of a self-selected novel with her instructor seems like heaven, does it not? And it was, for the most part. Avid readers of all ages can't wait to share their theories of theme and characterization with other like-minded individuals.

The sleepers mentioned earlier, however, had a much more difficult task, as they'd never really read the book on which they were reporting. Their main objective wasn't to share the delights of literary analysis but to convince me that they actually did the work. The fun part about conducting these individual conferences was that I never knew which student was going to show up, the reader or the prevaricator.

For example, the conversation I would have with a student trained in the art of balderdash might go something like this, where the child begins with a level of excitement that implies that she'd not only read the book, but that it had bestowed upon her a life-changing impression of how she views the human condition:

So what book are we going to talk about today, Maria?

> *I read* The Old Man and the Sea. *It was really, really good. One of the best I've ever read.*

Great! Tell me what you liked about it.

> *I couldn't put it down. When I got to that part about the sea, I was up all night. Just so awesome. I mean, wow. Just wow. It really left its mark on me.*

Why don't we discuss the climax?

> *That was really cool, wasn't it? What a high point in the story. I loved the way that the characters and plot just melded together with all of that action. And what that poor old man went through! I feel like this was one of the most challenging conflicts in all of literature. It must have been really tough on the old man.*

What specifically was tough on him?

> *Well, you know. The whole sea thing.*

How did he handle "the whole sea thing"?

The only way he knew how. He never, never gave up.

How does the book end?

Well, he caught enough fish to feed his family.

His family?

Yes. His little boy.

He didn't have a family.

Oh. But I saw that there was a boy in this book.

There was. But it wasn't his son.

At this point, the conversation would die a slow, uncomfortable death, the student finally admitting defeat when even she realized that "man" and "sea" were the only two words critical to the plot that were peppering her end of the discussion.

Some perjurers, however, are more coy, and to save face and their grade, they keep their responses to a minimum and their emotions in check:

So what book did you read, Jared?

I read The Mouse and The Old Man.

I'm not sure what you mean. Did you read *Of Mice and Men* or *The Old Man and the Sea*?

Yes.

Which one?

The first one.

Tell me about the main characters.

There was Lenny.

And who else?

A guy named George.

Tell me about Curly's wife.

> *She was married to Curly.*

Tell me about the puppy that Lenny killed.

> *It died.*

What was the best part of the book?

> *The beginning.*

Was that the only part you read?

> *No.*

Tell me about the ending.

> *I didn't really understand that part.*

Did you read that part?

> *Yes.*

Then tell me what you didn't understand about it.

> *All of it. And parts of the middle, too.*

Bear in mind that these kinds of conversations took place before the internet was specifically created (in my mind, anyway) to provide students with plot summaries of every book ever written. With no plagiaristic pathways to follow, the non-reader characterized here had nothing to fall back on but his emotionless expression and lack of forthcoming details. He invoked his fifth amendment right until the bitter end, when I would call the time of death on our conference and send him back to his seat with a failing grade.

Not all students, of course, behaved this way. Most of them enjoyed reading, were anxious to share their books with me, and answered my questions confidently and correctly. From start to finish, the entire discussion took about 10 minutes. However, much more time had to be allotted if, walking toward my desk, was the child who read three books a week on her own and who took her studies very, very seriously. As she would sit down in front of me, I knew that my mind had to be sharp enough to follow her detailed account of the book and that my eyes had to be carefully focused on her mouth so that when she took a break between sentences, I could interrupt her with a question that I'd hope would move things along:

> *Here are my book, reading journal, grade sheet, note-*
> *book, and pen. May I place these items on your desk*
> *before we begin our discussion?*

Of course, Tracey. Tell me about *A Day No Pigs Would Die.*

> *The story takes place in the 1920s. Rob is a young*
> *boy from Learning, a small town in Vermont, and he*
> *lives with his father, mother, and aunt on a farm. One*
> *day, a boy at school makes fun of Rob because he*
> *is a Shaker and he dresses differently than the other*
> *kids at school. Rob becomes so mad that he runs*
> *away from the school yard that day, and who can*
> *blame him? Those boys are mocking his religion. This*
> *was probably really hard on his self-esteem. I know*
> *how I feel when people make fun of me for being a*
> *born-again existentialist. Everyone has a right to her*
> *own religious beliefs. The Constitution guarantees it.*
> *So Rob has a lot of thinking to do, and as he's run-*
> *ning and pondering the way to true enlightenment*
> *through the crafting of simplistic furniture design—*

He sees a cow.

> *I'm getting to that part, Ms. Carmitchell. He sees a*
> *cow in distress. She is trying to give birth, but her calf*
> *is not coming out. What is he to do? How can Rob*
> *help? He just ran away from the bullies at school, and*
> *he was determined not to run away from anything*

else. He decides that he can help birth this calf, so he takes off his pants, ties one leg around the calf's neck and the other around a tree. Then he gives the cow swats on the behind until she pulls away enough so that her baby is born. And it's born right on top of the Rob! The description of that scene is unforgettable. The author uses . . .

Now, at this point, I am aware that we have only covered the first three pages of the novel, and my mind starts to wander. I think about what errands I'm going to do on the way home from school and what songs I need to learn for band practice this week. In fact, I even mentally run over the words to those songs so that I won't need the lyrics in front of me. I then think about what I'm going to make for dinner that night, and when I last washed my hair. Could I push it one more day, perhaps wear a ponytail to work tomorrow?

Suddenly, I realize that the student in front of me has stopped talking. I glance at the clock. 20 minutes have passed. I search my brain for the last sentence that she spoke: *"Rob realizes that he's the man of the household."* I go from there:

Yes. Yes. That's right. He is. Now, tell me about Pinky's death.

I already did, Ms. Carmitchell.

Yes, I realize that. But can you explain it to me on more of a metaphysical level, and how you think it applies to Rob's religion?

This girl is so bright that she is able to answer my question, one which, as you may have guessed, has no relevance to the novel whatsoever, and, moreover, is baldardashic in nature. (I'd had so many oral conferences at that point with children who'd never read a book that I felt like I'd learned from the masters.) But my inquiry does give me a little time to wake up a bit, award her an A+ for a job well done, and send her back to her seat.

"I love how some of the kids would just outright lie when they came to talk to you about their books," Bobbi said that night on the phone.

"Yeah. Sometimes, I just wanted to say, 'I can hardly see you due to the smoke from those flaming pants you're wearing. Finish the book and reschedule another conference.'"

"But you couldn't say that."

"Sadly, no. But it sure would have saved a lot of time."

"I don't think I'd have been that brave, to lie right to a teacher's face like that."

"You did it much more easily on paper, right?"

"Oh, sure. *Black Like Me*. My famous book report when I was in ninth grade."

"You didn't actually read that book."

"I didn't read any book in high school."

That was a brave admission on my sister's part. I guess she figured that the statute of limitations had passed by this time and that her diploma was secure.

"Did you get a good grade?"

"Oh, my teacher told me I did a good job. But the paper was late, so I didn't get any credit."

"But you must have read something in school," I said. "You wouldn't have graduated if you didn't."

"Well, let me think." Bobbi paused. Then she said, "There was that report I did in fourth grade on Sitting Bull. We were studying the Indians of North America. I loved that unit. And I traced a picture of Sitting Bull from a book. Oh, and I read stuff about tomahawks. I thought those things were so cool. I gave the tomahawk a page all by itself. Just a tomahawk in the middle of the page. Nothing else around it. I traced that one, too. I remember thinking that no one would know, that everyone would think it was my original drawing."

"But what about the writing itself?"

"I just lifted those ideas from a book."

"But that was okay," I assured her. "That's how anyone writes a report. You literally report on other people's ideas."

"Well, if that's the case, then I also wrote one on the continental drift theory. That was in high school. I called it *The Theory and Validation of the Continental Drift.*"

"I remember that one! And I remember telling you that you never wrote it."

"Again, Anne. For the last time. I wrote that fucking report."

I was sorry I'd said anything. I tried to apologize. "It's just that you never really did any work in high school, so I assumed you'd plagiarized this report, too."

"Well, I didn't. And, yes, I don't remember anything to do with classwork when I was in high school. But you know, you can ask me what musical we did my senior year. Or what song I directed when I was student director of the band. Sports stuff. Those kinds of things I remember."

So the academic part of school didn't ring a bell with my sister. But scoring a goal in field hockey did.

"The *Black Like Me* book that you never read. How did you report on that?"

"I have no idea. I think one of my friends must have given me hers and I just rewrote it."

"I'm still trying to figure out how you didn't get caught cheating on that report."

"How should I remember? I keep trying to bury the idea that I pilfered someone else's work, but you keep bringing it up. Hey, do you want a lamp?"

"What's it look like?"

"It's really cool. It's a desk lamp, kind of Tiffany-looking, but not the real thing."

Since most of the lamps in my house were bought when I got married in 1983, I jumped at the offer. I knew that I wasn't going to get any more information about her lack of wisdom in copyright infringement, so I figured it was time to end the call.

"Well, thanks for the interview, Bob. I feel like I have enough to work with."

"And I got rid of a lamp," she said.

I could see that Bobbi was closing our discussion on a high note, hoping that, when I'd look back on our phone call, I would remember only her willingness to part with fake Tiffany, and not her habit of writing fake dissertations. I decided not to chide her anymore about ninth-grade English. Not everyone's gardens are well-tended in high school, but does it really matter? After all, Bobbi is a successful singer/songwriter, so her garden eventually did yield a bumper crop. Even if it were due to the large amounts of fertilizer that she'd used.

Grading the Carmitchell Sisters

THE MAN ON THIS CARD IS A TRUE ARTISAN. He has already completed making seven pentacles and is now focused on the eighth. The fact that his previous work is on display, with all pentacles neatly aligned, proves that he is an expert in his field. Years of practice have molded him into a successful artist, one whose work is no doubt in high demand. However, the expression on his face is a bit reflective. Could he somehow enhance his finished product to make it even more appealing? The Eight of Pentacles is asking you to do the same: evaluate your work and see if it could be improved in some way.

The profession of teaching is one that invites constant evaluation. New ways of reaching young people are always being developed, and some of these ideas can be a boon for the education system. Others, however, have all the staying power of an Snapchat message and would better be left on the shelf. Such was the case when students had to start preparing for standardized tests issued by the Pennsylvania Department of Education.

Grammar, writing, and literature had always been vital parts of my curriculum, but because I was apparently leaving children behind, I was now required to add another component to my program, a class where I taught my students how to take the state test. It was essential that they practice for this exam with the same tenacity and rigor used by an Olympic athlete or a honey badger in order to succeed in his respective fields.

My kids were issued workbooks that included small "prompts" to which one had to respond in writing. These multi-paragraphed pieces were written by a group of educators employed by the Department of Education. Although they had not been in a classroom since the Eisenhower administration, they were supposedly experts in the field of Communication Arts. Examples of such riveting pieces of quasi-literature included *How to Build a Better Bird Feeder, Selecting the Proper Vegetables for Healthful Salads,* and *Riva Makes a Dress for Prom.*

To make matters worse, I had to start grading these student responses and all classroom essays using a rubric, a chart that listed across its top what the state considered to be the five areas of good writing. Under each area were four blocks in vertical columns. Beside each of these blocks were numbers descending from 4 to 1, and the expectations that needed to be met in order to achieve that number were detailed inside of the block itself.

"That's confusing," Bobbi told me one night on the phone. "So there are five areas, and to get a perfect paper, you have to score a 4 in all of them, right?"

"Right."

"That sounds a lot like math. I can see why you didn't like using them."

She had no idea. Some of the expectations of rubrics generated by the Department of Education had the density and complexity of a list of characters in a Russian novel and would have made Tolstoy run for cover.

What was fun, however, was when Bobbi and I delved into the idea that many parts of our own lives could be measured by a rubric, if the components were relevant and were written by us. What would a scoring guide look like, for example, in order to evaluate the Carmitchell Sisters acoustic act? Perhaps it would resemble the following.

CARMITCHELL SISTERS PERFORMANCE RUBRIC

Job Preparedness	
4	You are aware of the exact location and start time of the gig. All gear is neatly organized in one vehicle.
3	You know the approximate location and start time of the gig. You have an address, so your GPS can help you find exactly where you need to go. Some of your gear is in Anne's car, some of it in Bobbi's.

2	You don't have an address for the gig, but you remember the booker saying that the job was in Lancaster and then mentioned something about Central Market. You think that the gig starts no sooner than nine o'clock and no later than ten. Most of the gear is in both cars except for the mic stands that are on Bobbi's porch and the mixing board that is under Anne's bed.
1	You have no address for the gig and no recollection of ever having booked it. But you do have a phone number that you can call once you leave the driveway. The start time is irrelevant at this point, since the job may not even exist at all. Gear is scattered among both cars, Anne's bedroom, Bobbi's porch, and in the basement of the keyboard player in Anne's other band.

Set Lists

4	Two copies of three sets lists are printed in bold type and tucked neatly into the cord bag. Songs have been appropriately selected to fit the nuance of the evening and the sensibility of the audience.
3	Two copies of three set lists are neatly written in longhand on legal paper and placed in Anne's purse. Any song deemed inappropriate will be skipped during the performance.
2	One master list of all songs performed in 1992 and written in magic marker on a faded piece of orange construction paper had been found inside the pocket of Bobbi's old barn jacket and was thrown on top of the gear bag in the back of the Anne's car. Newer songs are scribbled in the margins and include those outing Bobbi and describing Anne's Pap test. The appropriateness of said songs for gigs (such as a country club banquet) was decided, unfortunately, after they'd been performed.
1	No set list was prepared. Songs are jotted on the backs of grocery store receipts and old insurance cards found in the glove box of Bobbi's car. Complete reliance on audience to call out requests resulted in dead air and no need for an encore.

Organization of Gear	
4	Every mic, speaker, and instrument cord is wrapped, secured with cord clips, and placed neatly in the Yamaha cord bag.
3	Wires are neatly wrapped, but the Yamaha cord bag that was left at the last gig has been replaced with Anne's Coach suitcase. Uncertain if this is an actual designer bag and not a knock-off, no one feels comfortable picking it up, so no help was provided loading or unloading gear.
2	Only mic wires are wrapped, and those are wrapped around the instrument and speaker wires. The Coach suitcase still causes problems.
1	No wires are wrapped and all have been shoved inside plastic grocery bags.
Lyrics	
4	Both Anne and Bobbi know all the words to all of the songs.
3	Both Anne and Bobbi know some of the words to all of the songs.
2	Bobbi forgets the most important words to a wedding song ("Our love in Christ will be alright") and sings words that may have made the marriage itself invalid ("Our love in Christ will not be fine").
1	Anne has an audience member hold lyric sheets during the performance.
Style	
4	Comedic timing is impeccable.
3	Some jokes are funny.
2	Most jokes are not.
1	"Cut the schtick and just play the song."

The more Bobbi and I talked, the more excited I became to use this document in order to make our performances more appealing. I would assign each of us a task: Bobbi would reorganize the cord bag and I would make copies of the rubric and distribute them to audience members willing to give us a score in the appropriate categories. Then we could study the results and use them to improve our act. Better organization would surely bring us more work, and maybe even Oprah—dare I hope?—would hire us for her next fundraiser. I enthusiastically began planning this new life of mine, which would materialize easily because Bobbi wrapped a few mic wires and I made copies of a simple scoring guide.

My passion was reaching fanatical proportions until I realized that all of this was dependent on whether or not these rubrics would eventually end up on Bobbi's porch or stuffed into one of her old barn jackets. Also, did my sister even *remember* how to wrap a mic cord? Furthermore, it occurred to me that if Oprah actually did hire us, Bobbi would have to wear pants and I'd have to get on a plane.

That fellow on the Eight of Pentacles might be striving to reach new heights, but not this gal. Choosing to stay on the ground with a messy cord bag and jokes that don't work sounded like a fine idea to me, and the idea of rubrics, sadly, went the way of missing lyrics and set lists.

Buddha Bill, Superstar

I WANT TO BE THE WOMAN featured on the Nine of Pentacles. She is wearing an attractive, flowing dress that cascades beautifully around her ankles and has a waistline that surely must hide a multitude of sins. She wears a hat with confidence, something I have never been able to do, and her hair frames her face, something that my hair has never been able to do. The vineyard through which she strolls is in full bloom, and her dream house sits in the background. Most importantly, she is alone, a strong, independent gal who is comfortable in the life that she has created for herself and by herself.

Luckily, I'm able to keep my independence in my relationship with Bill. We have varied interests and are free to pursue them without fear that one of us will feel neglected by the other. This is especially true in the area of entertainment, specifically that of watching television. Having two TVs in the house is a necessity since Bill is drawn toward science fiction and action movies, while I enjoy just about everything else.

One could say that we have an open marriage of sorts in that Bill is quite comfortable knowing that I have several boyfriends with whom I spend as much time as possible. He is not threatened by my relationships with Hugh Laurie, Raymond Burr, or Gary Cooper. In fact, he encourages them. What better way, he feels, to enjoy *The Matrix* and *Pulp Fiction* without my constant questions concerning character or plot development? Much better for me to retreat to my bedroom where I can admire the sarcasm, intelligence, and quiet demeanor of my handsome leading men.

However, there are times when the show that I want to watch is best viewed in the living room. I don't know why, since the TV in there is the same size as the TV in my bedroom. Perhaps it's because I don't want to lie down to watch my show, that I have some need to be sitting on the loveseat so that I can feel more actively engaged in the presentation. Whatever the reason, Bill understands, like he always does, and finds something else to do. But this doesn't prevent him from walking into my viewing area from time to time and making unfavorable comments. I find this habit irritating. He knows this, which prompts him to continue.

Therefore, I often feel the need to make a list of guidelines that must be strictly followed if our relationship is to last. When a live production of *Jesus Christ, Superstar!* aired one Easter night, it was necessary that I chronicle my demands and tape them to the refrigerator well in advance so that Bill could familiarize himself with my terms:

"Jesus Christ, Superstar!" is being shown live two Sundays from today. Bill, you will be subject to rules similar to those I posted prior to the "Downton Abbey" finale. They are as follows:

1. *I will be singing along with every word to every song. Some of these songs are not in my range. I do not care. You are not to mock my singing. You are free to sing along or leave the living room.*

2. *There will be no questioning of the historical accuracy of this musical. I realize that you are a recovering Catholic, but those nuns who taught you didn't know everything.*

3. *Based on the preview I saw of this event, period costuming may not be a thing. I would assume that this is happening to make the message more relevant to a younger audience.*

I realize that Jesus probably did not wear jeans. There is no need for you to point this out to me.

4. *I will begin crying quietly at the start of "Gethsemane," and by the end of the song I will be in full-blown sob mode, my face contorted and my eyes mere slits of their former selves. Your eyes, however dry they will surely be, are to remain focused on the television and will not roll upwards.*

5. *If you join me in the living room and insist on keeping your tablet with you and opened to Facebook, there will be no interrupting of my viewing pleasure in an attempt to make me pause the show and watch a video of a skateboarder crashing into a lamp post.*

6. *If you see a glimmer in my eye that suggests I find Jesus very attractive, ignore it. It's not my fault that every single man who portrays Christ in any movie or stage production is hot. I am able to separate his appeal from his message. Do not make any kind of implication that you will come to bed that evening dressed in sandals and a robe.*

7. *If, after all of this, you choose to bring your fabulous, agnostic self into the living room, remember the most important of the Beatitudes: Blessed are the meek who shut their pieholes.*

Yours in Christ and in uninterrupted viewing,

Annie

I assume that the woman on the Nine of Pentacles would applaud my independence in this instance, but there are times when I do need Bill. This admission runs contrary to my personality. I've always felt that it's better to do things myself, just in case my partner decides to run off and join the circus. *Then* who's going to haul the 40-pound bags of solar salt downstairs to the water softener? And who would help with our pet birds?

We have three parakeets who need to visit the vet for pedicures and physical exams from time to time. Moving them from their flight cage to a smaller one creates a great deal of stress. As I try to capture them with a net inside their cage, they get so upset that I can actually see their little hearts beating in their chests. This in turn makes *me* so distraught that I often pause for an hour or two, going outside to smoke cigarettes until I relax.

Then I try again, but one of the birds invariably escapes and flies around the living room, banging into a window and ending up on the floor. Then the dogs start to investigate, and the carnage that I envision would fit well into one of Bill's favorite movies. I run circles around the room with the net at ground level and whimper for the bird's well-being ("Oh, no. Oh, no. Dear God. Shitshitshitshit . . . ") while simultaneously yelling for the dogs to stay away ("GetbackgetbackgetbackIsaidgetback!"), all of which, of course, promotes a calm, nurturing environment for my feathered and canine children.

Enter Buddha Bill, the master of all things Zen. He is able to corral all three birds with very little difficulty. His method is two-fold: He visualizes the birds already in the smaller cage. And then he tells me to get the hell out of the room. This works for both of us. I'm not surprised at his ability to perform this task, as the Tao Te Ching states that if one carries in him the attributes of the Tao, birds of prey will not strike him. Nor will they attempt to flee in terror through a closed window.

I thanked Bill for making our recent bird-transference painless for me and for Yon, Farra, and William. But because I can't just hand over a serving of praise to someone without dishing up some for myself, I felt the need to remind him that my prayers helped, as well, and that I was grateful that he allowed me to bless him before he began his journey.

"You blessed me?"

"Yes."

"When?"

"We were standing in the hallway before you forced me out of the house, remember? And I prayed that the bird angels would surround you with white light. Then I asked God to make sure that everyone would be OK."

"We were in the hallway?"

"Yes. You were looking right at me as I closed my eyes, verbally summoned the angels, and held up my hands to the heavens."

"You did that?"

I did. But I didn't feel the need to belabor the issue any longer. After all, the Tao also says that wise people don't need to prove their point, and my boyfriend wasn't the only one who could be all Buddha-like; I could throw around my cosmic consciousness with the best of 'em. I just hope that Bill is content to stay a Zen master and not become a ringmaster; how would the parakeets ever be transported?

Well, maybe I could take care of that myself, since the woman on the Nine of Pentacles has a falcon resting comfortably on her outstretched hand. In the meantime, though, I'm perfectly willing to let go and let Bill, to surrender my independence when it makes sense to do so. He will surrender his, also, if for no other reason than that explained in the Tao. It says that he who follows the Great Way knows when to shut his mouth, especially when his girlfriend is watching TV.

That Laozi and Jesus. They sure knew a lot about relationships.

Where It All Began

The Ten of Pentacles and the court of Pentacles are cheerful cards of success and attainment for an entire family. They assure you that you've lead an accomplished life and are fortunate enough to be able to share it with those you love. Everyone on the Ten of Pentacles, from the grandfather to the children, is elegantly dressed; even the dogs are well-groomed. The young parents beam with contentment, and pentacles cover the area surrounding them. The four royals of Pentacles also represent folks who are financially secure and spiritually content and, may I add, even more impeccably attired than the family who comes before them.

I think that my parents would have been pleased to see the lives that Bobbi and I have built. There aren't a lot of pentacles floating around us, but we both feel that we've carried on the Carmitchell tradition of treasuring the non-monetary joys of life. We'd never consider ourselves royalty, of course, as we don't have enough dough to qualify. However, if indiscretions could elevate a family to a state of nobility, I'd say that the four of us might be in the running. In addition to a few skeletons in our closet, there is one whopper of a scandal. It's so big, in fact, that it almost prevented Bobbi and me from even being here.

The four of us were visiting my grandmother at her home on East Orange Street. I was 17 and took my spot on her hassock as she sat on the overstuffed chair in front of me. I picked up the family Bible, the one that she'd read cover-to-cover 13 times, and opened it to one of the first pages, that of the family tree. I started investigating my blood line. They were all there, all seven of my father's siblings, with their birth dates written beautifully next to their names. Then something caught my eye.

"Mam Mam," I said, looking up at her. "It says here that you and Pap were married in June of 1900. But Uncle Charlie was born in October of that year. Did someone write down the wrong dates or something?"

As soon as I'd made my inquiry, I understood that there *had* been no mistake in the recording of dates. I blushed, and regret began to creep into my consciousness. I was asking for some pretty personal information of the woman who could flick a child's earlobe better than anyone. I was sitting right at her knee, and even though she was 90 years old at the time, she had lived alone for the last 30 and she hadn't lost her feist or her reach.

To my relief, a smile crept across her wrinkled face as her eyes narrowed a bit behind her glasses. She began to chuckle and then nodded in my direction. "You ask too many questions for a girl your age," she said.

Dad had overheard the conversation and he was taken aback. Did he react this way because he'd been unaware of the information that I'd exposed? Or was he worried that the Cat of Family Secrets was now slowly crawling out of its bag? I decided to leave that discussion for the car ride home. My mom, however, took the lead.

"Did you know?" she asked Dad.

"No idea," Dad replied, his eyes on the road.

"Huh. Isn't that sumthin'," Mom said.

The conversation ended there, unless it was one of those whispered kinds that parents have in front of their children, but Bobbi and I heard nothing as we sat in the back seat, listening

intently. I'm certain, however, that our parents talked about it later between themselves, my mother smiling smugly behind my father's back while being supportive to his front. She had heard so many stories about her God-fearing, perfect in-laws that she must have been a bit satisfied to discover this crack in the Sistine Chapel that was their marriage. Surprisingly, Mam Mam and Pap hadn't guarded their celibacy before tying the knot, and Mom, I'm sure, was happy to discover that the knot had been a little frayed.

Years later, after Mam Mam had passed away, Dad would joke about the whole thing at family reunions. "That Annie," he would say. "When she asked Cos that question, I almost dropped my front teeth." *Cos* was the nickname bestowed upon my grandmother by her grown children. I'm not completely sure what it meant. It had something to do with the fact that Mam Mam could be a little scrappy and spunky at times. I guess Dad just never realized the amount of spunk she actually had, that saucy little tart.

But the story doesn't end there. After Dad died, my cousin Chuck, the unofficial family historian, provided the addendum. Yes, Mam Mam was indeed pregnant before wedlock. But so was my grandfather's other girlfriend. He had to choose which woman to marry and he chose, for reasons unknown to anyone, my grandmother.

"Which means," Bobbi told me one night on the phone, "that you and I have aunts and uncles and cousins running around all over the place."

"Isn't that weird? For all we know, the cashier at John Herr's could be related to us."

"And you're sure, you're positive, that Bill's family came from Philadelphia?"

"I'm sure."

"'Cause the two of you kind of look alike."

"I'm sure."

"And where did they come from before that?"

"From Italy, Bobbi. His grandparents were first generation, right off the boat, from Italy."

"But some of them could have moved to the Coal Regions."

I was regretting that subscription to Ancestry.com I'd given her for Christmas. "All that matters," I told her, "was that Pap picked Mam Mam. If he hadn't, we wouldn't even be here arguing over whether or not I'm having sex with my cousin."

And that's not the only incident that could have prevented my sister and me from making our entrance into the world. Mom almost put the kibosh on that too, since she wasn't quite sure about Dad when she first met him.

She lived a few doors down, if you'll remember, from Aunt Marg and Uncle Digger. Every time Dad would visit his sister, she would talk about the pretty widow who was right up the road. Dad told Marg he was quite aware of the widow right up the road. He made a point to wave from the car whenever he saw her out in the yard, but the wave she'd returned to him always looked like one that took a lot of effort. "She seemed like a cold fish," Dad would later say. But he promised Marg that he would stop by for a proper visit, once he had a chance. Knowing my father's popularity with the ladies, I can assume his response was probably code for "When my dance card isn't full." But one hot day, he nonchalantly meandered up the sidewalk to 732 South Plum Street so that he could see for himself what the fuss was all about.

And there was Bubbles, in shorts and a halter top, using a push mower to cut the small front yard of her row home. Dad stopped at the house and smiled at her, while she, acknowledging his existence with a slight nod, continued mowing. He stood there for about three minutes, he'd told us, until Mom finally stopped and asked what he wanted.

"I can finish mowing that grass for you," he said.

"You could," she said. "But I don't want you to. I can do it myself," and off she went for another turn around the yard.

Like the King of Pentacles, my father was a very attractive man who wasn't used to being pushed aside. So he stood there, he said, "with my thumb up my ass," not quite sure what he should do next. But Mom did. When she and the mower circled back to where he stood, she told him that she was almost finished. If he wanted to wait until she was done, he could come join her on the porch for a cold beer. He waited, smart man that he was, showing tenacity and persistence. A true leader, Dad knew that perseverance was necessary to reach his goal of making this woman his queen.

As for Mom, her story about meeting Dad was the same as his. She found him quite handsome and charming, but she didn't like the implication that she was incapable of cutting her own lawn. Her husband had been killed in the war. She was working full time. She was running the house by herself and taking care of her mother who was blind and had lost a leg to diabetes. And here comes this guy who thinks that she needs help walking behind a push mower.

"He was just being nice," Mom told me once, "and I liked him. But I wanted him to know that I could take care of myself."

She certainly could. And her work ethic was passed on to Bobbi and me as we went through our teenage years. Our parents expected us to get jobs to keep my sister in guitar strings and me in hair products. We approached our work as young Pages and energetic Knights would, with exuberance and hope, and took part-time employment that ranged from landscaping and driving catering trucks to waitressing and pumping gas. (I'll leave it up to you to decide which Carmitchell sister took which job.)

If money were all that was required to make a loving court, the Carmitchell dynasty would have been overthrown a long time ago. But the Suit of Pentacles isn't just about money. It's about manifesting prosperity in any form, about success taking shape in the physical realm. The four of us created a family that prospered and overcame obstacles with practical jokes, story-telling, and a lot of love. Family has always been our savings plan into which we invested patience and understanding; it has been our fail-safe in times of heartache and struggle. I don't think any of us would have traded that for all the pentacles in the tarot.

KNIGHT & PAGE

PENTACLES

JOURNEY'S END

TWO YEARS AGO, I RECEIVED a friend request on Facebook from a lovely woman in Missouri. Since I had no idea who she was, my suspicions were aroused. Like everyone else, I had become fairly adept at spotting fake friend requests, and I was positive that this gal who resembled Emmylou Harris was really a guy working on an oil tanker in the middle of the Baltic Sea, or a lonely goatherd standing high on a hill somewhere in Montana. I deleted the request promptly.

A day later, I noticed something on Facebook I'd never seen before, this thing called Message Requests. Intrigued, I opened it, and there was a message from Laura Erickson Carter, the goatherd.

"This guy does not give up," I thought, but I went ahead and read his letter since I was bored watching videos of unlikely animals bonding over a box of cornflakes. (Okay. That's a lie. I never tire of that.)

Much to my surprise, Laura was exactly who she claimed to be, a good friend of mine from 35 years ago who sang at my wedding. I called her immediately, and the more we talked, the more bewildered we became about the history and even the origin of our friendship.

"Do you remember how we met each other?" I asked her. Neither of us had a clue. "And why did we lose touch? We were pretty tight back then."

"Maybe we were just self-absorbed," Laura ventured. And we were. I got married, she moved out of state, and life went on without either of us giving the other a second thought. We had a lot of ground to cover in this conversation.

She told me that she owned a publishing studio. I told her I was writing a book. She wanted to see some of my work, so I obliged. And before you could say, "What just happened here?" this book was published by one of my best friends whom I'd ignored for over three decades.

I'd never firmly envisioned the finished copy when I started. I had a vague idea of maybe mimeographing the pages, stapling them together, and giving them to a few friends for Christmas. In my more creative moments, I'd imagine foregoing the stapling part, and instead, with the help of a three-hole punch, would put the pages in one of those report covers I had left over from my days of teaching middle school.

But the universe had something else in mind for me. It works in mysterious ways, and in this case, the way was Facebook.

"Can you believe it?" I asked Laura on the phone the other night. "If it weren't for social media, this book would have never been published."

"Yes, pretty amazing," she agreed. "And speaking of actually being published, have you written the last chapter yet?"

Of course I hadn't. I wasn't ready for this experience to end, so I was dragging my feet. As long as I was still writing, I could continue the fun I was having in my late-night conversations with Bobbi and Laura. Still, I knew that I had to wrap up this project. I needed direction. So naturally, I pulled a tarot card.

And there it was, the Two of Cups, the card that tells of new partnerships, new relationships filled with mutual respect. It is indicative of a commitment between two people who share a common goal and work together to achieve it with a sense of honor and admiration for each other.

My goodness. There really is something to this tarot card stuff, don't you think?

So I raise my two cups, one to my sister whose laughter and storytelling were enhanced by the cards that we discussed; who always took my calls and answered my questions honestly; and who never minded being the Fool on the cliff or the Bee on The Bank.

And to Laura, my dear friend, who often knew what I was thinking before I said it; whose suggestions and direction kept me balanced; and who talked me off the Tower when I wanted to stop writing.

Ladies, this has been quite a journey. Here's to both of you.

ABOUT THE AUTHOR

 Annie Carmitchell is a retired eighth-grade English teacher, spiritual enthusiast, and insomniac. She sings with her sister Bobbi in an acoustic duo and stands behind a set of congas used primarily as a prop. Though *Conversations With My Sister: A Fool's Journey Through the Tarot* is her first full-length book, she is the author of numerous song parodies, hundreds of lists, and countless amusing Facebook statuses.

You can hear Annie and Bobbi performing live on *Two Live Wires* by the Carmitchell Sisters, Locust Lane Music. Annie, Bobbi, and Charlotte Carmitchell can all be heard on the *Winter Tales Collection*, also on Locust Lane Music, produced by Bobbi Carmitchell and featuring women artists of Central Pennsylvania. Contact Bobbi through Facebook if you're interested in purchasing either CD.

Annie lives in Washington Boro, Pennsylvania, with her partner Bill, their dogs Maggie and Emma, and their parakeets, the ULBs.

You can follow Annie on Facebook.

PHOTO BY JANE FETNER, THE PHOTOGRAPHY WHISPERER

CPSIA information can be obtained
at www.ICGtesting.com
Printed in the USA
LVHW092240220419
615089LV00008B/926/P

9 781732 982628